THE COMPLETE IDIOT'S GUIDE® TO

Raising Girls

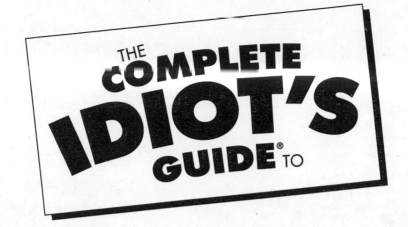

Raising Girls

*by Dr. Gary J. Weisenberger, Kathy Sherwin,
and Deborah S. Romaine*

ALPHA

A member of Penguin Group (USA) Inc.

For Jane and Caroline, the two girls I'm proud to be raising. —Kathy
To my wife, Kimberly, who has been a blessing to me both as a wife and mother of our four wonderful children. —Gary
To Cassidy, who's taught me what it means to be a mother. —Deb

ALPHA BOOKS

Published by the Penguin Group

Penguin Group (USA) Inc., 375 Hudson Street, New York, New York 10014, USA

Penguin Group (Canada), 90 Eglinton Avenue East, Suite 700, Toronto, Ontario M4P 2Y3, Canada (a division of Pearson Penguin Canada Inc.)

Penguin Books Ltd., 80 Strand, London WC2R 0RL, England

Penguin Ireland, 25 St. Stephen's Green, Dublin 2, Ireland (a division of Penguin Books Ltd.)

Penguin Group (Australia), 250 Camberwell Road, Camberwell, Victoria 3124, Australia (a division of Pearson Australia Group Pty. Ltd.)

Penguin Books India Pvt. Ltd., 11 Community Centre, Panchsheel Park, New Delhi—110 017, India

Penguin Group (NZ), 67 Apollo Drive, Rosedale, North Shore, Auckland 1311, New Zealand (a division of Pearson New Zealand Ltd.)

Penguin Books (South Africa) (Pty.) Ltd., 24 Sturdee Avenue, Rosebank, Johannesburg 2196, South Africa

Penguin Books Ltd., Registered Offices: 80 Strand, London WC2R 0RL, England

International Standard Book Number: 978-159257-881-8
Library of Congress Catalog Card Number: 2008939797

11   10   09   8   7   6   5   4   3   2   1

Interpretation of the printing code: The rightmost number of the first series of numbers is the year of the book's printing; the rightmost number of the second series of numbers is the number of the book's printing. For example, a printing code of 09-1 shows that the first printing occurred in 2009.

Printed in the United States of America

Note: This publication contains the opinions and ideas of its authors. It is intended to provide helpful and informative material on the subject matter covered. It is sold with the understanding that the authors, book producer, and publisher are not engaged in rendering professional services in the book. If the reader requires personal assistance or advice, a competent professional should be consulted.

The authors, book producer, and publisher specifically disclaim any responsibility for any liability, loss, or risk, personal or otherwise, which is incurred as a consequence, directly or indirectly, of the use and application of any of the contents of this book.

Most Alpha books are available at special quantity discounts for bulk purchases for sales promotions, premiums, fund-raising, or educational use. Special books, or book excerpts, can also be created to fit specific needs.

For details, write: Special Markets, Alpha Books, 375 Hudson Street, New York, NY 10014.

Publisher: *Marie Butler-Knight*
Editorial Director: *Mike Sanders*
Senior Managing Editor: *Billy Fields*
Executive Editor: *Randy Ladenheim-Gil*
Book Producer: *Lee Ann Chearney/*
Amaranth IlluminAre
Development Editor: *Lynn Northrup*
Senior Production Editor: *Megan Douglass*

Copy Editor: *Jan Zoya*
Cartoonist: *Steve Barr*
Cover Designer: *Becky Harmon*
Book Designer: *Trina Wurst*
Indexer: *Celia McCoy*
Layout: *Ayanna Lacey*
Proofreader: *Mary Hunt*

Contents at a Glance

Contents

Introduction

You've got a daughter! No matter where you are on the parenting path, you've got questions: Can she play with trucks? (Sure.) Can she play with dolls? (Yep.) She sent me a text-message that said, "yyssw." (yeah, yeah, sure, sure, whatever.) She wants to go to a girl/boy mixed sleepover. (Is she 3 or 13? You've got to draw a line somewhere.) But enough for now; we don't want to give away the whole book on the first page!

Every parent who picks up this book enters the experience of raising a daughter at a different place on the arc of girlhood. Wherever it is that *your* daughter happens to be on that arc—from toddler to grade school to middle school or high school—we'll take a look in this book at the joys and challenges you'll find *today* in parenting *your* particular girl. As well, we'll follow you with your girl on her journey through to young adulthood. You might even have two, three, or more daughters at multiple points along the arc of girlhood!

These are exciting and challenging times to be raising a girl, times unlike any other generation of parents before you has faced. It takes quick wits, keen humor, and those parental eyes in the back of your head to even keep up with your daughter, let alone get ahead of her. You need a guide to help you find the shortcuts, pitfalls, and signposts. (You're reading it.)

And finally, we'd like to say that we're excited to bring you a diverse and uniquely experienced writing team for this book! Mostly we speak as a unified voice. But every now and again we may have differing perspectives. Then, the text will identify which of us has something specific to say and which hat we're wearing (Gary as pediatrician or Gary as dad, for example) in saying it.

How to Use This Book

We've organized the chapters of this book into four sections, each of which explores a different stage of your daughter's development and experiences.

Part 1, "My Girl," looks at what it means to be a girl, from the obvious to the subtle. What factors shape who she is, and which of them can—or should—you influence? Chapters also investigate the special bond between dads and daughters, what it means to let your girl evolve and emerge on her own terms, and the unique circumstances of this generation.

Part 2, "Girl Power," celebrates your daughter's curiosity, creativity, and sense of adventure as she expands her experiences to extend beyond home and the circle of her family. Chapters look at learning and school; the roles of teachers and mentors, and other adults; body image, health, and food issues; cliques, bullies, and teasing; and competition. And oh, yeah, boys.

Part 3, "For the First Time," explores the middle years—a time of firsts that are launching your daughter toward womanhood. From first period to first date, these are years of new experiences. Chapters take a girl's-eye view of this transformational time, looking at how your daughter finds her personal balance between the often-conflicting messages she sees around her and the sense of herself she's already developed.

Part 4, "You Go, Girl!" She's ready to test her wings. Are you ready to let her fly … and how far? Your girl is a strong and confident woman now, capable and eager to make her own decisions (as though this is something new!). She's out in the world more than she's home in the nest. Chapters look at how your role as parent begins to shift and how you can best support your daughter as she embarks on the journey that is her life.

The Resources appendix lists books and websites that provide further information about all aspects of parenting.

Extras

There's no shortage of things to say about the raising of girls. Sometimes what we've got to say doesn't quite fit in the flow of the main content. So when something extra pops up, you'll see it in a special box:

Girl Pearls

These boxes feature quotes that offer wisdom and insight about raising girls.

In Her Shoes

These boxes present advice, practical tips, and miscellaneous information related to the topic.

def•i•ni•tion

These boxes define words and terms that may be unfamiliar to you, or that we're using in a specific way in this book.

LOL

These boxes share humorous anecdotes and interesting tidbits.

Oh, Puh-leeze!

These boxes present cautions about risks and potential hazards.

Acknowledgments

I would like to thank Deb Romaine and Gary Weisenberger for being wonderful collaborators, Lee Ann Chearney for a great opportunity, and my family for all their support—with special thanks to my husband, Bruce. —Kathy

There are many components of what helps us develop our personal and professional skills. I have both learned and have been taught on the many aspects of parenting by my four children. My daughters, Carrie and Becky, and my sons, Nate and Andy, have been major influences on my skills in pediatrics and as a father. We all have learned together. I have been blessed by them and am proud of their development as fine daughters and sons. Over years in my pediatric practice the daily interaction with all my mothers, fathers, and grandparents has been instructive and helpful in ongoing discussions on raising children. I thank them for those opportunities and times. Finally, all the children I care for, both now and in the past, have taught me so much with regard to life in general. Thank you. —Gary

I thank Kathy and Gary for their insights, humor, and willingness to indulge lengthy telephone conference calls; Lee Ann Chearney for her amazing vision and tenacity to make this book both timely and timeless; and my daughter and her friends for sharing their opinions, thoughts, and experiences about being girls growing up today. —Deb

Trademarks

Part **1**

My Girl

What makes a girl … a girl? We'll explore the nature and nurture of girlness, investigating physiological, developmental, and environmental influences. We'll take a look at what dads need to know about the special concerns, challenges, and joys of being father to a girl. Most of all, we'll champion the notion that you can let your girl be a girl … *on her own terms.*

1

It's a Girl!

In This Chapter

- What daughters learn by watching and imitating their moms (and dads, too)
- Mothers and daughters: in your image
- Dads and daughters: love me tender
- When expectations clash with reality

What an amazing time to be raising a girl! Just about anything she wants to do or be, *she can*. "You can't do that, you're a *girl*!" sounds confusingly outdated to her—if she ever hears it at all (maybe if she watches old shows on TV). Most remarkably, it doesn't even occur to her that there would be any reason she couldn't. If there's a slogan for the girls of today, it might simply be "Girls rule!"

As unique as the opportunities for this generation of girls, are the challenges of raising them. Today's girls are growing up in a world of ever-diminishing boundaries. Your girl hears, sees, and experiences *so much* every day, it's enough to make your head spin! It's all you can do to keep up, yet here you are, taking the lead on this wondrous journey that is your daughter's life.

When we become parents ourselves, our own parents start looking a whole lot smarter than they did when we were growing up. But the ones who hold the answers for our girls now are the moms and dads reading this book. Yes, you! Together, we'll negotiate new signposts that will take our girls to a future we can't yet see but we can help shape, as surely as we shape and nurture our daughters with our choices every day.

Parent Patterns

Your expectations about parenting a daughter may be rooted in your own relationships with your mother and father—a lesson from Psychology 101, right? Often for better and sometimes to our dismay, we tend to think we'll become our parents when we become parents ourselves—maybe you have the same kind of bedtime ritual with your daughter that your parents had with you when you were little. Most of the time, only small shifts take place from one generation of parents to the next; change is a slow and sometimes unsteady process ... except, maybe ... now!

For as much as you might feel your own generation marked a quantum leap forward, you may be feeling that the world your girl is growing up in is a radically transforming landscape. You'd be right; and how exciting to be parenting in a time when the old rulebook is tossed. With your girl, you'll help shape new patterns of being and doing. This requires common sense, courage, trust, and an appetite for adventure.

 LOL

How different are things today? Consider this. A mom we know told her daughter that as a grade school student in 1967 (the oh-so-famous Summer of Love), she'd been sent to the principal's office for wearing pants under her dress to school on a snowy winter day. She wore the pants not to make a fashion statement or flaunt school rules—she wore them because her own mother insisted she be warm! "What do you mean, you couldn't wear *pants*?" The story became the topic of the week among the daughter's friends, who couldn't quite believe there used to be rules forcing girls to wear dresses to school. Talk about changing the rules so much that you put your daughter in a whole new game!

You bring unique perspectives, ideas, and experiences to your views of parenting and raising children. You probably look back on your childhood as a blend of things you hope you can do as well as your parents, and also things you hope you never do when it comes to your children. But unlike your own parents, you have the advantage of a wealth of knowledge that wasn't so readily available when you were growing up. The Internet puts, literally, a world of information at your fingertips, with scores of credentialed, accredited parenting and health websites (see the Resources), as well as a world of connection through message boards, blogs, and social-networking forums. Playdate friendships and other social interactions expose us to different ideas and parenting styles, too.

You Do the Best You Can

Your parents weren't perfect, and neither are you. But that's okay! You turned out all right, didn't you? You'll do the best you can by your daughter, and she'll turn out just fine, too. Of course you want to give your little girl the very best of everything. But what matters most is that you give her the very best of *yourself*—your love, guidance, support, and presence.

Parenting is hard work, no question about it. And raising a daughter has unique challenges. Opportunities, expectations, and even risks are very different for girls growing up today than for girls growing up even 10 years ago. Often, it's having a daughter who first thrusts you into this brave, and sometimes intimidating, new world.

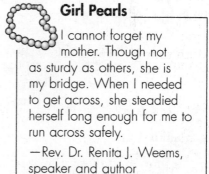

Girl Pearls

I cannot forget my mother. Though not as sturdy as others, she is my bridge. When I needed to get across, she steadied herself long enough for me to run across safely.

—Rev. Dr. Renita J. Weems, speaker and author

How you feel about your own childhood has a lot to do with how you feel and behave when you step into the role of parent. If you believe your parents did a good job meeting the needs of their children (especially you), you may strive to structure your own parenting approach to be similar. If your childhood was difficult, you might turn your insights into ways of doing things differently with your daughter.

Parenting is a balancing act. When there are two parents in the family, each parent brings different experiences, expectations, and skills to the table. How you integrate them in ways that complement, rather than oppose, requires considerable thought and effort. While child development experts agree that differences in parenting styles can be beneficial for all kids, girls and boys, parents must also work with each other to present consistent messages and values. When there is a single parent, the balance is more about parent and child. Other influences—such as from grandparents, adult siblings, caregivers, and friends—often come into play even more strongly.

Today's parents of young daughters are the first generation to come of age at a time when nearly as many families had both parents working outside the home as had stay-at-home moms. You might've grown up with a variety of caregivers—other family members, perhaps, or a nanny or babysitter—who came into your home. Maybe you went to a daycare center. A broader base of influences shaped your development, exposing you to perspectives beyond those of your parents. All the people who helped take care of you left their impressions with you. And you carry these impressions, some consciously and some without awareness, in your bank of parent-stuff.

Outside Influences

Community, in an astonishingly broad context, plays a great role in shaping your daughter's perceptions of her world. It truly does take a village to raise a child, as the African proverb says. That community may include family, school, friends, church, organizations like Girl Scouts and Big Sisters—and your daughter's peers and their extended communities.

The community that influences your daughter is virtual as well. Television and the Internet can bring literally the world right into your daughter's daily environment, at home and at school. While yours may have been the first generation to grow up with television as the standard rather than the exception, electronic media *define* your daughter's generation. TV is almost old-fashioned, what with computers, iPods, and even cell phones that can download television shows (and movies) that your daughter then can watch at her leisure and convenience.

It's a wonderful thing to know that your daughter has so many role models and mentors beyond you. It takes a bit of the pressure off when your daughter recognizes, early in her life, that you do the best you can and that most of the time, you do pretty good by her. It helps you to see, too, that you're doing okay as a parent and mentor yourself. As much as you might worry about the downside of such broad exposure as TV and computers make possible, the upside is that your daughter develops a framework for just how good she's got it! And your daughter's a smart girl. She's got a good head on her shoulders; she knows what's real and what's not.

The Mother-Daughter Bond

As a new mom, were you thrilled beyond words to bring home a daughter? Kathy was! Kathy came from a family of girls and found herself overjoyed to be in familiar territory. "This," she thought (and even said to her friends and sisters), "is something I know how to do." Growing up with sisters, however, is not a prerequisite for providing special insights into the raising of a girl, so don't feel left out if you were an only child, or a sister among, yuck, *brothers!*

It's natural for a mom to feel an instinctive bond with her new daughter. Looking into those curious eyes, you can't help but ponder what seems to reflect your own self. Your thoughts race ahead, duplicating your fondest memories of growing up as well as creating for your daughter experiences you didn't have. Raising a daughter becomes a way for a mom to reconnect with her childhood and her own mother as much as it is a path into the future.

My Daughter, Myself

As much as moms see themselves in their daughters, daughters see themselves in their mothers. Kids—both boys and girls—are great observers, and they love to imitate what they observe. In the context of child development, the *imitation theory* holds that kids

def•i•ni•tion

The **imitation theory** is the concept that children learn, in large part, by observing and repeating the actions of others.

begin learning key skills and behaviors by watching and copying what others do.

You can test this theory yourself through games you can play with your daughter as her awareness of herself and her surroundings emerges. For many parents, the first and most delightful act of imitation is your daughter's first smile. And the more you smile at her, the more she smiles at you. Parents sometimes fail to recognize the close scrutiny their young daughters bestow upon them, which can have embarrassing consequences. We're sure you can fill in your own anecdotes to illustrate this point!

Welcome to the Sisterhood

Many moms tend almost reflexively to expect their daughters will be pretty much like them. When your girl is still in her bassinette, you might stand and watch her sleep while you think about all the adventures that lie ahead for you to share. Most daughters do have at least some things in common with their mothers, if only because mom is who they imitate.

Moms are often surprised when their daughters have vastly different interests from theirs. It's harder to find common ground, sometimes. By the time she's two years old, your fantasy princess might be so unlike you that you wonder whether you brought home the right baby! Maybe you're athletic and outdoorsy, and your little darling hates to get dirty. Maybe you like nothing more than to curl up with a book, but you dare not let your imp out of sight because she'll take something apart to see how it works or put a rescued frog in the bathtub.

"Go with the flow" often is much easier said than done!

Military Moms

"Your mother wears combat boots!" was once the most slanderous insult one kid could hurl at another. Today it's likely to be true—and a compliment. Dads have always gone off on military assignments. But this generation of girls is the first for whom the same is true of moms.

Military parents might be away from their daughters for a year or longer. Any separation is a long time, from your daughter's perspective.

It's challenging enough to help her pick out a new pair of shoes when you're standing right beside her in the store. It's certainly no easier when you're on the other side of the world. You've got to be creative to stay connected with your daughter's daily life when a dozen time zones separate you.

Stepping Into Parenting

If you're a stepparent, you already know you face special challenges. Some are frustrating, some are rewarding. You may feel as if you inhabit an odd middle ground. If her birth mother is also part of her life, your stepdaughter may not know quite how to balance her feelings and interests between the two of you. She might want to be like you in certain ways, but then feel guilty or that she's betraying her birth parents. It takes a lot of sensitivity and patience to help her find the balance she needs.

Dads and Daughters

If the eyes are the windows to the soul, there are no curtains between you and your new daughter as you gaze into each other's eyes for the first time. All the emotions you have within you (and some you didn't know you had) are all of a sudden right out there, swaddling your baby girl like the blankets wrapped so snugly around her. This little girl's got a hold on your heart she's never gonna let go!

Dads often don't know quite what to do with their feelings and emotions when it comes to their daughters, Gary says—an observation that comes from the raising of his own daughters as well as his perspective as a pediatrician. So dads tend to defer to the mom, especially right at first.

Sometimes this is because they don't know what to do or even what questions to ask, though often more because they believe that no matter what they think, mom knows best when it comes to girls. And during those first few months, mom is certainly center stage when it comes to taking care of baby. But dads can and should look for ways to share in the raising of their daughters from day one. Chapter 3 takes a close and focused look at dads and daughters.

Girl Pearls _____

With my first daughter, I remember waking up and thinking, "My god, I get to be her mum again today. Wow. It's amazing." They just take my breath away. All I do is serve themselves back to themselves. My job is just to provide a secure environment where they can just be themselves. It's the cycle that keeps going forward. You give to them, so they can give to their kids. You have to be delighted by that.

—Thandie Newton, English actress

It's a New Game

Wherever you are along this adventurous journey of raising a daughter, your girl is no doubt putting your preconceptions to the test. What other assumptions are heading for a clash with reality? Here's a short self-quiz to shine the spotlight on some of your expectations. Choose the answer that best fits; there are no wrong answers.

1. When your daughter is five years old, she decides she's only going to wear boys' clothes. You …

    a. Buy her the clothes she wants to wear, with a "girly" item of your choosing every now and then.

    b. Let her choose clothes of a similar style in the girls' section.

    c. Insist that she wear what you choose.

2. When she's seven, your daughter announces she's no longer going to eat meat because she thinks she's fat even though her weight is healthy. You …

    a. Continue to put whatever you've fixed for meals, including meat, on her plate and insist she eat it.

    b. Ask your pediatrician what foods you can substitute to make sure your daughter gets enough protein and other nutrients.

    c. Sit down with your daughter to talk about why she feels she's fat.

3. Your 10-year-old daughter has a nightmare and wants you to stay with her in her bedroom until she falls back asleep. You ...

   a. Pull out an extra blanket and pillow.

   b. Explain to her that her nightmare was not real, talk with her about what happened in the nightmare and why it scared her, and offer to let her sleep with the light on.

   c. Invite her to sleep in your bed because it's bigger and more comfortable, and you need to get a good night's sleep, too.

4. At age three, your daughter's verbal skills are comparable to a six-year-old's. Yet one afternoon you get a call at work from her day-care provider who says your daughter just gave a boy a black eye. You ...

   a. Offer to apologize to the boy's parents.

   b. Take the rest of the day off to go pick up your daughter so she can de-stress at home.

   c. Pick up your daughter at the regular time, and ask her on the drive home what happened and why she chose the behaviors she did.

5. You've filled your nine-years-old daughter's bedroom with books and toys you feel are creatively and intellectually stimulating. An old friend from college comes by when she's in town on business and brings your daughter a Barbie-goes-to-the-beach play set. You ...

   a. Take it away before your daughter can open the package, and tell your friend these are not the kinds of toys you want your daughter to have because they perpetuate stereotypes—"At least bring my girl the *doctor* Barbie set ...."

   b. Allow your daughter to accept the gift, but plan to sneak into her room after she falls asleep and take it away.

   c. Allow your daughter to accept the gift and observe how she plays with it.

6. When your daughter enters middle school, she decides she wants to play football. Because there is no girls' football team, she asks you to request the school allow her to play on the boys' team. You …

   a. Head right off to the school; no athletic activity should be off-limits to girls.

   b. Suggest that your daughter instead try out for the cheerleading squad (which, by the way, is co-ed these days).

   c. Sit down with your daughter to find out what appeals to her about football, and to share your perspective that you wouldn't be keen on her playing if she were a boy, either.

7. Your 15-year-old daughter comes home from school one Friday afternoon and announces that she's going on a date later that night. You …

   a. Tell her, no way, José, the rule is no dating until you're 16.

   b. Ask her who the date is, where they're planning to go, how they're going to get there, and who else will be going. You let her go if it's clearly a group activity.

   c. Tell her she can't go out with anyone, boy or girl, until you meet the person.

Did some of these questions give you pause? Or did you have your answers at the ready? Here are some thoughts about the possible choices.

1. At age five, there's no difference in size or quality of clothing. Your preferences are really about appearances and appropriateness. Forcing your daughter to wear what you choose (c), or even to make alternative choices within your parameters (b), are likely to at best create confusion about why it matters, and have the potential for a full-fledged confrontation at an age when your little princess is not yet capable of reason. Let her wear what she wants to wear (a), and maybe she'll add flair to her style with the items that you choose.

2. Body image is a significant concern among increasingly younger girls. It's crucial to find out why your daughter might think she's fat (e). A meatless diet may not provide the protein your daughter's growing body needs. If she insists on not eating meat, discuss healthy alternatives with your pediatrician to make sure she at least gets the right balance of nutrients. And keep talking with her.

3. By age 10, most kids are able to accept reassurance that their nightmares were only nightmares, and once they calm down are able to return to sleep. If your daughter is highly agitated and hasn't calmed down with talking (b), pull out that extra pillow and blanket (a). Most child development experts feel it's not a good idea for kids to sleep in bed with their parents (c).

4. It's hard to know what might cause a three-year-old to hit another child. It's important to talk with your daughter to first find out what happened that led her to do so. If this is a one-time situation, (c) is the most appropriate choice.

5. Toy choices are difficult because they reflect values, though not all adults perceive them that way. Often, the most effective way to reinforce your values is to observe how your daughter plays with the doll (c). It's a good way for you to see just what your daughter's making of the lessons you're trying to teach. And she might lose interest pretty fast, especially if she's not used to having such toys.

6. Gary, like many childcare experts, feels it's usually okay for girls to compete against boys in sports as long as the physical match-ups are fairly comparable. However, you don't want your 80-pound child—girl or boy—out there being slammed by other players who could weigh twice as much. The risk for injury is too high. It's best to find out why football appeals to your daughter (c); maybe another sport might be more appropriate and still be suited to your daughter's curiosity. Pushing her instead into cheerleading pushes your daughter into a stereotype because you're encouraging her to play on the sidelines instead of getting into the game. Fitness is critical for growing girls and there's always a good game she can play. There's more about girls and sports in Chapter 7.

7. Bet you thought you'd get to ignore this one for a while yet, huh? It's important to be discussing matters like dating, at least in general ways, long before the question comes up. Many parents do establish age rules; if you do, you should stick by them (a). Other parents want to know more about the circumstances and are willing to consider each situation (b) and (c), rather than make a blanket rule.

Dreams and Goals

We all want our daughters to achieve success in their lives. What dreams and goals do you have for your little girl? You might blog about them or record them in a mother-daughter scrapbook so you can pull them out every now and again as your daughter grows up. Your goals can help especially to shape your early interactions with your daughter, though it's important to remain flexible enough to change them as your daughter's personality and interests emerge.

Girls today have more opportunities and choices than ever in history—and that's true whether or not they look at you blankly when you say the name Gloria Steinem. The role of parents has shifted from advocating for their daughters' right to participate (mostly) to one of guiding their daughters in making choices that match their abilities and interests. How cool is that!

The Least You Need to Know

♦ Television and popular culture influence parenting in evolving and compelling ways.

♦ Girls model what they observe their mothers doing.

♦ Dads are often unsure how to show their feelings and share their daughters' interests.

♦ The expectations you have at the start of your life journey with your daughter are very likely to begin changing the moment you bring her home.

♦ Everything is possible for your girl!

2

Gender by Nature, or Nurture ...

In This Chapter

- Taking a look at what makes a girl a girl
- A short self-quiz for insights into your perceptions and biases
- As simple —or not—as X and Y
- Nature's influence: what genetics bring to the picture
- Nurture's influence: what family, social, and cultural attitudes and beliefs bring to the picture
- Beyond pigments: colors and gender associations

"Oh, don't worry, dear! His hair will grow in before he starts school. What's his name?"

Nothing turns your parental pride and confidence inside out faster than a stranger on the street who stops to admire your darling. Sure, the best way to describe her hair is fuzzy. Yeah, she's on the ground on her knees, her short toddler fingers holding onto a worm that's trying desperately to escape into the grass. But how could anyone mistake her for a *boy*?

I Am Woman (Well, Not Yet, but I'm Working on It)

In the beginning, babies are just babies. If you dress a bunch of six-month-old infants all in the same color—say, green—and line them all up together, it's nearly impossible to tell the girls from the boys. Both grow and develop—physically, intellectually, and emotionally—at about the same rate. You really won't be able to tell, setting aside matters like names, hairstyles, and clothing, which of the bunch are boys and which are girls until *puberty*.

But we want to be able to tell, and we want others to be able to tell, that this little sweetie is a girl. So much so that we'll guess when we don't know for sure. Dainty, fussy, wants always to be held? Must be a girl. Strapping, inquisitive explorer? Gotta be a boy. Headful of curls? Surely a girl. Less fuzz under that hat than a tennis ball? Definitely a boy. *Gender* is such an important component of who we are as individuals and how we fit into society that we strive to establish a sense of it very early in life.

def•i•ni•tion

Puberty is the medical term for the onset of male or female physical characteristics marking the transition from childhood to adulthood and the capability for reproduction. In the United States, girls typically reach puberty between 9 and 13 years of age. **Gender** is an individual's perception and expression of being male or female in the context of behavior and social roles.

The perceptions we form about gender define our expectations and interpretations of behavior. Child psychologist John C. Condry, Ph.D., conducted a landmark study in 1976 in which he asked adult volunteers (a mix of men and women) to characterize a nine-month-old infant's reaction to the startling pop-up of a toy jack-in-the-box. Participants who believed the baby was a boy identified the reaction as anger. Those told the baby was a girl identified the same reaction as fear.

That's My Girl!

You're reading a book not about parenting in general but about raising a girl. Being the parent of a daughter has special meaning for you. What do you believe are the forces that shape your daughter as she moves from infancy to adulthood? Here is a short self-quiz to see what you're thinking. Choose the answer that best fits—there are no right or wrong answers!

1. To make sure well-meaning strangers knew my baby was a girl, when she was a newborn, I ...

    a. Taped a bow to her head.

    b. Dressed her in ruffles and pastels.

    c. Always said, "This is my daughter _____" and gave her name.

    d. Let them guess.

2. When I first started thinking about names, I made a list of ...

    a. Three names for a girl and three names for a boy.

    b. Traditional girl's names.

    c. Names I'd be happy with for either a girl or a boy.

    d. Names for a girl that were not specifically girl's names but were not traditionally boy's names, either.

3. I decorated my daughter's bedroom in ...

    a. Pinks.

    b. Lavender and purple.

    c. Blue.

    d. Green.

4. The first toy I bought for my daughter was …

   a. A stuffed animal or doll.

   b. A character from a favorite book or movie.

   c. A rattle.

   d. An educational item designed to stimulate her vision and coordination.

5. The first gift for my daughter from someone outside my immediate family was …

   a. A blanket or diaper bag.

   b. A stuffed animal or doll.

   c. A pink or lavender outfit of clothing.

   d. A savings bond to start her college fund.

6. When I daydream about my daughter as an adult, I see …

   a. Grandkids.

   b. A doctor, lawyer, or corporate officer.

   c. An artist, writer, or dancer.

   d. A carpenter, welder, or plumber.

7. One driving desire I have for my daughter as she's growing up is for her to …

   a. Believe she can do anything she sets her mind to.

   b. Excel in academics.

   c. Excel in sports.

   d. Learn a second language and to play a musical instrument.

Did you struggle to choose a single answer for some or even all of these questions, or any answer at all? That's okay—raising a girl is a complicated undertaking. Here are some thoughts about what you might draw from your responses:

1. If you chose (a) or (b), it was (and maybe still is) very important for others to know your baby was a girl. The choice of (c) suggests you perceived your daughter, even as an infant, as a distinct individual. If you chose (d), either it really didn't matter to you if strangers knew this was your daughter or you have a bit of a twist to your sense of humor.

2. If (a) or (c) was your answer, you either didn't know you were expecting a girl or it didn't matter to you whether your new addition would be a boy or a girl. A (b) response suggests you knew you were having, or really wanted, a girl. If you chose (d), you might be more comfortable with the idea more than the reality of gender neutrality.

3. A choice of (a) or (b), your soft side is showing. A choice of (c), bold! The most neutral choice is (d).

4. A rattle, answer (c), is both traditional and gender-neutral. A choice of (d), an educational item, might speak to the hopes and dreams you hold for your daughter when she grows up, and perhaps a sense for the competitive environment her generation faces (more on this in Chapter 5). Answers (a) and (b) are pretty general; these might reflect either a sense of nostalgia or an openness to the unique characteristics and personality your daughter brings with her into the world.

5. A gift of a blanket or a diaper bag (a) is quite practical. A stuffed animal or doll (b) is rather sentimental and gentle, with a hint of gender bias. A pink or lavender outfit (c) is definitely girlish. And a savings bond for her college fund (d) is admirably forward-thinking!

6. Grandkids! This choice, (a), is both traditional and more focused on you than on your daughter. You might've had some difficulty choosing among (b), (c), or (d); they are limited and come nowhere near to covering the spectrum of opportunities open to your daughter. Answer (b) might suggest you want your daughter to meet or exceed your own achievements. Answer (c) desires for your daughter to pursue her creative side, perhaps in ways that were not available to you. And answer (d) is strongly nontraditional but secure.

7. You might well've wanted to answer "all of the above" here—and if so, good for you! These are all worthy desires. A choice of (b), (c), or (d) suggests you have a clear vision of specific opportunities that perhaps were not available to you when you were growing up, or that reflect values you hold about your daughter's place in the world at large.

X Marks the Spot

The biology that separates girls and boys is surprisingly little: a little squiggle, there in the twenty-third pair of *chromosomes*. Girls have the squiggle, giving them a matched chromosomal pair we call XX because that's how the chromosome set looks in the *karyotype*. Boys don't, giving them an unmatched pair we call XY.

The male *gamete* determines *sex*, so dads, it's your contribution that's responsible for the presence or absence of the defining squiggle. Mom's ovum (egg) brings only an X chromosome to the reproductive effort; dad's sperm adds either the second X or the Y and that determines if you have a son (with the Y) or a daughter (with the X).

def•i•ni•tion

Chromosomes are molecular strings of DNA, genes, and other proteins that contain a cell's genetic information. Humans have 23 paired chromosomes, one pair of which determines gender. A **karyotype** is a photomicrograph presentation of chromosomes. A gamete is a reproductive cell (female ovum or male sperm) that carries one half the normal number of chromosomes. Sex is the biological determination of being male or female.

The double-X chromosome pair that biologically defines your daughter as female carries all the genetic instructions that direct her body to develop the appropriate physical characteristics. But does this chromosomal structure also dictate your daughter's behavior? Ah … sit back and fasten your seatbelt. This is one of science's most hotly debated questions.

DNA or TBD?

So what does determine whether your daughter prefers denim and dirt or ruffles and dolls? Is it in her genes, or does it remain to be determined through family and social influences? Despite a significant volume of research, there is no clear answer. Most experts believe gender roles are a blend of genetics and environment—nature and nurture.

Nature: Girls Will Be Girls

The "nature" end of the spectrum argues that certain characteristics are inborn—and, in the extreme, unchangeable. Now, most of us don't have any trouble with this concept when it applies to, say, blue eyes. The challenge comes when we start to look at behavior. Do little girls play lovingly and gently with dolls because that XX chromosome carries some genetic code instructing them to do so?

In 2005, researchers at Texas A&M University conducted a simple experiment. They offered a range of human toys to a colony of vervet monkeys, evenly divided into 44 females and 44 males. The purpose of the experiment was to see what, if any, gender preference there was among the monkeys for the toys that caught their interest—keeping in mind that the monkeys, until the time of the experiment, had not been exposed to human toys of any kind.

The results surprised even the researchers. Male monkeys showed a clear preference for trucks and balls; female monkeys took control of the dolls and cooking utensils. Both males and females spent equal time investigating and playing with items the researchers considered gender neutral, such as picture books and stuffed animals.

Our daughters and sons are not monkeys, of course. Many factors influence their choices and decisions, with toys and with all other kind of behaviors. (Remember the imitation theory we discussed in Chapter 1.) But research like this experiment suggests that what defines our daughters as *girls* may be more closely linked to what makes them *female* than we've recognized.

Nurture: Girls Learn to Be Girls

From nursery rhymes to television commercials, traditional society presents girls as soft, somewhat delicate, and sometimes a bit on the helpless side. Not what you see when you're rushing to rescue the puppy your little darling has by the tail? It's hard to figure, sometimes, just where such a *stereotype* comes from. Eee-gads … could it be that somewhere along the line we might actually *teach* our daughters to be (or at least act) soft, delicate, and helpless? Indeed we do, say many sociologists and psychologists—some messages we send with intent, and others inadvertently.

def•i•ni•tion

A **stereotype** is a simplistic and rigid generalization, broadly believed or perpetuated, that has limited, if any, connection with reality.

Some experts believe environment—the influences of family, community, and culture—is primarily responsible for how girls (and boys) perceive themselves and their roles in society. Within such a framework, your girl plays with dolls and wears dresses because external influences teach her that this is what girls do—and if she wants to be a girl, this is what *she* must do.

Sometimes these influences are overt, such as school dress codes that mandate girls to wear skirts or dresses. More often these influences are subtle, like magazines that feature images of girls and women wearing skirts or dresses. Relatives and friends may shower a new baby girl with toys like dolls, stuffed animals, and pink rattles.

We all know that kids imitate what they see the adults around them doing (sometimes much to our dismay). When your toddler daughter puts out a bowl, spoon, and drinking cup for her teddy bear to join her at lunch, she sets this place at the table in the same way you set hers. She observes and copies what you do. We often try to manipulate this to teach behavioral and social skills. And it's the key reason that "do what I say, not what I do" fails.

It's important, too, say child development experts, for parents to recognize the significant role of influences outside the family. Some studies suggest that your daughter's friends and classmates—her peers—shape her behaviors and perceptions of herself even more than you do. Chapter 11 delves into this topic in-depth.

Girls Rule, Boys Drool

In the early toddler years, girls and boys don't much notice that they're different. They play together, nap together, snack together, and sometimes tussle with each other—not because they're boys or girls, but because they're kids doing what kids do. Step into a kindergarten classroom, though, and there's a new story line.

Parents and teachers often observe the tendency for girls to use language for better and for worse in their interactions with each other. Especially in middle school and high school, girls can be notoriously mean in what they say about each other. On the flipside, girls are more interested in talking it out to resolve problems. Boys, by observation, take a more physical approach and are more likely to slug each other, then shake hands and go play baseball together.

Fable or fact? Some research suggests that girls begin to break away from boys in several developmental areas by the time they enter school. Recent studies of brain function support the long-held perception that boys and girls process information differently. Boys' brains appear more active when handling spatial information, while girls' brains are busier when processing language and abstract concepts. Such apparently objective observations lean toward inherent differences between girls and boys.

But the power of social influence is intense and begins early. Do behaviors and beliefs influence brain function or is it the other way around? Probably both.

Let Her Wear Pink!

Or blue, or green, or orange, or red, or whatever color she likes! Though we tend to associate certain colors with girls and others with boys, color choices have many dimensions. Take pink, for example—what many people perceive as the classic "girl" color. In countries such as Thailand and Japan, pink is a masculine color viewed as a kinder, gentler variation of the power-color red. Even in the United States, pink was the preferred color for boys to wear until the late 1940s, when blue began to take over.

A pair of scientists, Anya Hurlbert and Yazhu Ling, conducted a study in 2006 to explore whether the stereotype of pink as a girl color and blue as a boy color had substance beyond the marketing of such. They found that while blue actually was a clear favorite across gender lines, men fancied the green end of the blue spectrum and women favored the reddish blues. In this study, these preferences held across cultures, leading the researchers to speculate about a gender predisposition toward color.

LOL

If your daughter tells you she loves pink, she might be talking about the American pop singer rather than the color. Known to her parents as Alecia Beth Moore, the Grammy-award winning artist goes by the performance name Pink— typically stylized as P!nk.

Perhaps, the scientists suggested, women prefer reddish shades because they once had to find the ripe berries … or notice flushed skin as a sign of illness—although the phrase "in the pink" refers to someone who is healthy and vibrant. Other researchers disagree with these suggestions, however, asserting that the evidence is overwhelming that color preference is a cultural or learned phenomenon: girls who like pink simply like pink.

The Yin and the Yang of Color

There's more to pink—and other colors—than meets the eye. In Eastern traditions, colors have feminine (*yin*) and masculine (*yang*) qualities. Yin colors are calming, introspective, and healing. Blue, purple, green, and black are yin colors. Yang colors are invigorating, outgoing, and stimulating. Red, yellow, orange, and white are yang colors.

def•i•ni•tion

In Eastern traditions, **yin** and **yang** are the underlying forces of energy in the universe that exist in balance. Yin is female, passive, dark, and cool. Yang is male, active, light, and warm.

Does your princess do everything with flash and flair? Pink—a blend of yang colors red and white—lets her showcase her yang energy. If everything's coming up lavender—a blend of yin color purple and yang color white—for your little girl, she's showing balance. Blue might appeal more to the daughter who retreats and contemplates.

Color Me Blue ... No, Make It Orange

Colors have strong associations with mood and emotion in Western traditions as well. Psychologists have found blues and greens to have calming effects on people who feel agitated, for example, while orange tends to cause agitation. Orange, then, is probably not the best choice for your newborn's nursery walls. However, orange or bright yellow might serve its purpose in a fast-food restaurant, encouraging people to eat and go. Orange is also a good color, used in limited ways, for stimulating focus and organization—good, perhaps, in the room where your daughter does her homework.

Similar to the Eastern yin-yang concept, the Western tradition views colors as cool or warm. Cool colors, which invoke a sense of tranquility, are the blues and greens. Warm colors, which stimulate, are the reds and yellows. Your daughter might intuitively choose colors that reflect her personality. She might also like colors that seem the opposite of her personality—colors that help her draw into her expression of herself qualities that don't come so naturally to her.

More Alike Than Different

A lot of the time we seem more focused on searching for the differences between girls and boys, as though finding them will help us to better understand our daughters. An increasing number of social scientists are pushing to instead focus on the similarities. Only in such an approach, they believe, will we be able to break through gender-role barriers.

The Least You Need to Know

◆ Equally strong evidence supports the influences of genetics and environment in shaping your daughter's perceptions of herself and her behaviors.

◆ Most child development experts believe a blend of nature and nurture contributes to gender.

◆ Some of our conventions about what's "girl" are not quite what they appear to be.

◆ The differences between girls and boys in early childhood are far less significant than the similarities.

Chapter **3**

Daddy's Girl

In This Chapter

- ◆ The dad instinct: to protect and provide
- ◆ You're changing her diaper, not choosing her college (yet)
- ◆ It's a different world for dads today
- ◆ Mom, move over (please)

Dad, you're the most important man in your daughter's life. You're the first man she lays eyes on, and from that moment forward you're the standard by which she judges all other men. What Gary sees, both as a father and as a pediatrician, is that a dad's influence on a daughter is lifelong—which is why it's so important for dads to be active in their daughters' daily lives.

But don't let this freak you out! You're not walking her down the aisle just yet. Growing up is a minute-by-minute, day-by-day process. Soon enough you can worry about a big wedding, if she'll even *want* one. For right now, though, there are other details that demand your attention. And they're details you can handle and even enjoy … we promise.

Keeper of the Castle

What could be more perfect than this tiny creature who snuggles against your chest? She melts your heart at the same time she activates all those protective instincts. Even as an infant, your daughter trusts in your absolute ability to keep her safe—and you want nothing more than to fulfill that trust.

Whether by culture or genetics, dads are programmed to be the providers and protectors. Traditionally, dads were the ones to go to work to earn the money that supports the family (though this tradition is evolving as more dads stay at home while mom earns the paycheck); truly, today having two working parents is probably the most common scenario. Still, it's safe to say that dads do the things that focus on protecting the family unit: dads test the strength of baby car-safety seats, lock the home's front door before going to bed each night, and check out the boys who are texting their daughters incessantly.

Remember the imitation theory we mentioned in Chapter 1? It kicks in for dads, too. Today's dads tend to follow the model of their dads ... who followed the model of *their* dads. Much of our society continues to encourage boys, from an early age, to think about their roles to support and provide for their families.

But our social fabric and our parenting models are changing. When Gary started his practice in pediatrics 25 years ago, it was the mothers and grandmothers who brought the kids to the doctor. In the past, he helped raise families in which he never met the dads. Now, those kids are grown and bringing *their* children to Gary ... and he knows the dads of this second generation nearly as well as he knows the moms.

Big-Picture Panic

Dads tend to be big-picture people, always planning and thinking ahead. Even as the doctor hands over the surgical scissors so that you can cut your newborn daughter's umbilical cord, you might be thinking, "Oh, man, I'm gonna have to teach her how to ride a bike, how to invest and save, and how to parallel park!" Relax and cut the cord already. Even breathing is new to her right now. She knows she has fingers but doesn't have a clue how to use them, even as she wraps them around one of yours. Want to know what it means to live in the moment? Gaze into those eyes!

Girl Pearls _____

Women's childhood relationships with their fathers are important to them all of their lives. Regardless of age or status, women who seem clearest about their goals and most satisfied with their lives and personal and family relationships usually remember that their fathers enjoyed them and were actively interested in their development.
—Stella Chess, M.D. (1914–2007), American psychiatrist

Gary tells new parents: newborns are really pretty easy. They eat, sleep, pee, and poop. That's all. So start there. What matters most is that you engage in your daughter's daily life from day one—literally. To be there every step of the way, you've got to jump in without worrying about whether you'll stumble. (Of course you will—that's part of parenting.)

As your daughter grows and develops, you'll have the basics comfortably mastered and you can move on as she does. When, at six weeks, she flashes a drooly, gummy smile at you, smile back. At six months when she lies on her blanket on the floor and starts to roll from back to tummy and tummy to back, get down on the floor and roll with her. She'll laugh, study how you move, grab your nose, and laugh some more.

You might feel a bit silly at first, getting down on the floor to roll around with a baby. But it's fun! And in the process, your daughter's learning to trust herself, other people (you), and her environment. Soon enough, she'll be onto grander adventures, like sitting up by herself … and dating. Okay, there'll be a substantial gap there. But see how it all fits into that bigger picture?

What Do I Know About Diapers and Dolls?

Dads, like moms, start dreaming about the possibilities of parenting pretty early in the "I'm going to be a dad" scenario. From the confirmation that there is, indeed, a new life on the way, dads envision fishing trips and Little League, buying that first car and stumbling through "the talk." It's not that dads prefer sons, necessarily—it's that a dad knows what it's like to be a son. (Just like moms know what it's like to be a daughter.)

When you first find out that your newest family member is a girl, you might feel that you've got to shift gears and realign your expectations. This is true to some extent, but not as much as some guys, especially first-time dads, might think. Boy or girl, a baby is a baby. You'll learn what you need to know. And when the time comes, you'll teach your daughter to cast, catch, and parallel-park, too.

Dolls? That's easy. Just follow your daughter's lead. She'll show you how to play!

Following your daughter's lead is a good strategy from the very start. This table gives an overview of what you can expect from your daughter as she grows and develops through infancy, and offers some ideas about how you can interact with your daughter to encourage her and build your relationship with her. Remember, for babies life is all about fun and love. There's nothing your little girl likes better than to laugh and have your full, devoted attention!

Milestones in Your Daughter's Early Development

Age	Your Daughter Is Learning to …	What Dads Can Do
Birth to 6 months	Control her head	Move when you talk to her so her head follows the sound of your voice to look at you
	Smile	Smile at her
		Make sounds
		Coo, gurgle, and talk to her
	Grasp and wave toys and other items	Offer toys for her to hold and play with.
	Roll and sit	Get on the floor and play with her in ways that encourage these skills

Age	Your Daughter Is Learning to …	What Dads Can Do
6 to 12 months	Bounce up and down if you hold her in a standing position	Hold her so she can do this
	Sit by herself	Give her a favorite toy while she is sitting
	Babble and laugh	Talk and sing to her, treat her babbling as though it's conversation you understand
	Open her mouth when she sees you have a spoonful of food	Play "here comes the spoon!" games when you feed her; let her try to feed you
	Move toys from one hand to the other; drop and pick up toys	Hold toys out for her to take with one hand and then the other; pick up toys she drops and offer them back to her
	Imitate facial expressions and movements others make	Exaggerate your movements; make faces at her and laugh when she makes faces at you
	Crawl on her hands and knees	Get down on the floor and crawl with her; pretend to race and let her "win"
12 to 18 months	Use furniture and other objects to pull herself into a standing position	Encourage and praise her efforts
	Make sounds that are close to words; speak a simple word or two	Talk to her and treat her vocalizations as though you're having a conversation with her

continues

Milestones in Your Daughter's Early Development   (continued)

Age	Your Daughter Is Learning to ...	What Dads Can Do
	Engage in routine activities like getting into the high chair at meal times and getting dressed/undressed	Wait for her to participate instead of doing things for her
	Connect "daddy" with you	Use her name when you greet her; refer to yourself as daddy (or whatever you want her to call you) when you talk to her

She Won't Break ... Really

Dads are often afraid they'll be too rough with their daughters, in everything from changing diapers to loading into the stroller to playing. Babies, whether boys or girls, are surprisingly sturdy. Of course they require care in handling—they're not indestructible. But your infant daughter's not going to come apart when you try to put her tiny arm in the sleeve of her tiny sweater.

Dads do things differently than moms, and for the most part that's a good thing. Different is simply another way of doing something. And when you think about it, even some of the things you might do "wrong" are more likely to end up fodder for the stories you'll tell when her first boyfriend comes to dinner—like putting her shoes on the opposite feet or giving her a bath with dish soap—than actions that cause any harm. It is hard, we sympathize, when shoes are made for fashion more than walking, to know which is left and which is right!

In Her Shoes

Dad, talk to your baby daughter! She loves the sound of your voice. Talking to her as though she understands what you're saying strengthens the bond between the two of you. And it'll make it a lot easier to talk with her when she's a teenager.

When it comes to play, take your cues from your daughter. At first, play is all about discovery—finding toes, making noise with a rattle, dropping toys so dad will pick them up. As your little girl grows up she'll develop her own ideas about play, but when she's a baby just about anything she does can be a game—no rules, no planning. Only fun!

Working the Learning Curve

No one knows parenting from the get-go. We all have our ideas and experiences that we bring to the arena, but the first child is pretty much an experiment for everyone. Parenting is something you learn along the way—often just in time, sometimes not quite fast enough. This is true for moms as well as for dads.

Where it differs for moms is that they get a lot of support as they venture for the first time into this unknown territory. Their moms, sisters, girlfriends who are already moms, colleagues at work, and even the nurses in the labor and delivery center eagerly offer suggestions and advice about everything from breastfeeding to diaper choices. It's easy for dads to feel left out of this sorority. But we've come a long way since fathers paced outside the delivery room with a pocketful of cigars, waiting for the doctor to announce, "It's a girl!"

Dad, you do have to work to put yourself in the game. You've got to say you want an active role and then step up to take it. If you're feeling disconnected, that's okay. You'll get over it. And it's natural to feel like you should defer to mom. This whole baby thing is really not part of your world in the same way its part of hers. So you've got to figure it out pretty fast, and sometimes without a lot of help. (Check out the Resources for some books and websites for dads.) But you want this, so you'll do what it takes to make it happen. And your daughter will thank you all of her life—except, maybe, when she's 17.

Red Dad, Blue Dad, One Dad, Two Dad(s)

Once upon a time, long ago and far away—well, the 1950s—the typical all-American family featured the dad, the mom, and the kids. Dad got up every morning and went to work. Mom stayed home to take care of the house and the kids. Mom had dinner on the table when dad got home from work; the kids washed up and took their seats without anyone asking them. Dad led the conversation, which gave each child the chance to talk about his or her day. After the meal, the kids cleared the table, mom did the dishes, and dad retreated to his recliner to read the newspaper. At least, that's how a new-fangled technology, television, presented it.

Not so many families live such a model today (or did even back then, in reality). There are so many configurations of families, it's hard to characterize them. In some, it's easier than ever for dads to be active in their daughters' lives. In others, it seems nearly impossible. But, to put a new spin on a tired cliché—where there's imagination and determination, there's a way.

Busy Dad

Maybe you're a dad whose work schedule is well defined and the rest of your time belongs to you. You're able to coach soccer, build playhouses and doll furniture, and lie head to head with your daughter on the lawn looking for animal shapes in the clouds. Or maybe you work a 60- to 80-hour week and most days the only member of your family you see is yourself in the mirror when you shave.

Sometimes the demands of a profession are all-consuming, and your life starts to feel like every time you turn around, that girl of yours is more grown up. Before you know it, it'll be your *granddaughter* toddling around the kitchen with a gooey graham cracker in her hand!

In Her Shoes

If your daughter is an early riser, have "coffee" with her in the morning before you head for the office. Her cup may hold juice instead, or milk with a splash of coffee for effect. But the few minutes you share through this ritual will be a lifetime of memories for both of you.

This is where getting involved from the day she's born makes it easier for you to stay connected with your daughter as she grows up. She, too, has a life of her own. It's not that you need to be with her every minute of every day. The both of you would go nuts! But you can make it a point to see her and talk with her every day—that's what she wants and needs. As we said earlier in this chapter, sometimes you really have to work at staying involved with your daughter's daily life. You may have to get quite creative to find ways that work for your circumstances.

Stay-at-Home Dad

Staying home with the kids has been great comedy in books and movies for decades. But the premise of dad as primary parent, staying at home while mom headed off to work, began to emerge in real life in the 1980s. Then, changes in the economy coupled with gains taking place for women in the workplace meant women could sometimes earn more than their husbands, or could at least work when their husbands couldn't find jobs. Also dawning in the social consciousness was the realization that "equal opportunity" didn't just mean moms could choose to maintain careers while raising their kids. It also meant dads who wanted to take more of a front-seat role in parenting could choose to do so. Tradition took a radical shift as both moms and dads started reconfiguring their roles.

Today, dads might forgo business lunches for PB&J with the crusts cut off. The stay-at-home dad is no longer just a Hollywood foil but a genuine fixture in the contemporary family. It's a role that gives dad all the time he wants (and then some) as parent. His daughter comes to him when she needs lunch money, a ride to the library, and a shoulder to cry on. Working moms might feel left out of their daughters' lives, so stay-at-home dads sometimes need to make sure they leave room for mother-daughter time.

 LOL

Though today it's not such instant amusement to see dads pushing strollers to the playground or holding backpacks at the school-bus stop, dads remain the clear minority among stay-at-home parents. The U.S. Census Bureau reports nearly 160,000 stay-at-home dads in 2006 compared to 5.6 million stay-at-home moms.

Single-Parent Dad

Dad as a single parent means—like mom as a single parent—there's no one else to step in. You're it. Single parenting, whether you're dad or mom, is no easy challenge. A single-parent dad typically must juggle work and family responsibilities. Before your daughter starts school, this may mean arranging for daycare (or in-home childcare) and preschool.

Changes in attitudes coupled with federal and state laws make it much easier for dads to take off time from work to tend to family matters, especially when your little one gets sick or has a doctor or dentist appointment. It's important to be available to your daughter any time she needs you. And for your school-age daughter, may we offer sage words of advice? *Learn how to text-message.*

Divorced Dad

Nearly half of American couples divorce. Shared custody may mean anything from alternating weekends to half the time with one parent and half the time with the other parent. It's tough to be a part-time parent, particularly when the other parent has remarried. The households invariably have different rules and routines.

Dads are important in their daughters' lives, even if they don't live with their daughters. Marital issues are between the adults (although kids tend to know more about them than the adults recognize). If you and your daughter's mom are divorced and your daughter lives with her mom, your daughter needs to know you still love her and are there for her—and she needs regular, consistent reassurance of both.

If you are the noncustodial parent with limited visitation, use your visits with your daughter to focus on her. You don't need to make every visit a vacation, but choose activities for the two of you. Walk in the park or on the beach, wash the car, sit on the couch and eat popcorn while you watch a movie. Leave plenty of room in your schedule for just hanging out. Remember, your visits with your daughter are about her and you, not her mom (your ex). Resist the probing questions about what might be happening at her mom's.

Kids like routine, so try to establish a consistent environment for your daughter. If your daughter has her own room for when she comes to stay with you, keep that room as *hers*. Let her decorate it as she likes, and keep her things there. Establish a pattern of participation in household activities. If you have pets, let your daughter help care for them when she's there. Do the cooking and cleaning up together.

Try to stay involved in your daughter's daily life, to the extent this is possible within any conditions of your custody agreement. Make sure your daughter can reach you whenever she wants to talk to you. Give her a call, send her an e-mail or text-message her just to see how things are going, or to tell her you love her and are looking forward to her next visit. Ask her how school's going, and arrange to participate in parent-teacher conferences. Such efforts take very little time but go a long way toward keeping the two of you connected.

Stepdad

Raising a stepdaughter is a special challenge worthy of its own book, and we include several titles on this topic in the Resources. Child development experts agree that the most important factor is that you honor your daughter's birth father and her relationship with him. If you don't like the guy, keep quiet about it. When she shouts at you in anger, "You're not my father!," agree with her. You're *not* her birth father. But tell her you love her very much—and leave it at that. It's not a competition, even if it feels that way at times, and you might need to turn off that part of your nature.

The onus is on you to develop and nurture a relationship with your stepdaughter. She may not always be receptive, but have no doubt she's paying close attention to your overtures, attitude, and reactions. She wants you to love her. She's just may not be not sure that you have reason to, especially if you've come into her life when she's older.

Military Dad

Dads serving in the military may find themselves away from home for a year or longer at a time. This is an eternity in the life of a child. It may seem to you that everything freezes when you deploy, and in your mind stays in some sort of suspended animation while you're gone. Even with daily videos, pictures, and phone conversations, in your head your little girl stays as she was when you kissed her good-bye.

Military dads have two distinct issues—the being away and the returning. You might not even be able to stay in regular communication while you're away, depending on your assignment. When you're gone for months to a year or longer, home life settles into a routine that works around your absence. When you return, it takes time for everyone to readjust. Chapter 1 talks about these issues for moms and for families overall.

Love You, Mom, But You've Got to Let Go

Sometimes the greatest obstacle to dad becoming involved in daily daughter care is mom. Moms get downright territorial when it comes to their kids, and sometimes perceive even dads to be intruders on this turf. Moms, too, often operate from within the expectation that they're the ones who should bandage banged-up knees, sew on buttons, and get up in the middle of the night to chase away bad dreams.

Dads can do these kinds of things, and may be eager to give them a go but find that mom's already there. Moms sometimes have to break away from the cultural norms so dads can step in. This is not always easy because our society puts the onus on moms when it comes to taking care of the kids—especially daughters. Mom may feel guilty and inadequate when her daughter rushes past to go to dad for help or attention. It's important for you and mom to set guidelines or boundaries with each other.

Oh, Puh-leeze!

When dad steps in, it's important for mom to step out—all the way out, even if that means leaving the room or the house—so dad can handle things in his own way. This develops confidence for both dad and daughter. When mom hovers, corrects, and criticizes, or even only watches, both dad and daughter feel uncertain and uncomfortable.

Girls learn as much from observing how things work between mom and dad as they do from their own relationship with dad. Your daughter will truly believe her dad is (and men in general are) competent in the role of primary parent when she sees that her mom believes he is.

Father Figures

Not all families fit the traditional model of mom, dad, and child. More than a third of infants born in the United States today are to unmarried women, many of whom will raise their kids alone. Single dads, single-parent adoptions and same-sex partnerships are other family structures.

If your daughter's growing up in a home without a father, other men who are important in her life—grandfathers, uncles, friends—can provide positive experiences that help your daughter establish a framework within herself for how she relates to men. Girls pay close attention to the interactions that take place around them, and learn from their observations as well as their own experiences.

The Least You Need to Know

◆ Dads and other father figures are crucial to their daughters' sense of themselves and their relationships with men throughout their lives.

◆ When you start being an involved dad from day one, it's easy to keep pace with your daughter's changing needs as she grows up.

◆ Girls love to play, and love when their dads play with them.

◆ Moms need to give dads space to interact with their daughters in their own ways.

Chapter 4

Girls Just Wanna Have Fun

In This Chapter

- Play is great practice and learning
- A toy is what your daughter makes of it (mostly)
- Girls and dolls
- The digital playground
- Your daughter's favorite playmate is you

Today she's playing house with her dolls; tomorrow she's doing kickflips at the skate park. She paints her toenails a different shade of green every week, because green's her favorite color, and hooks her own worms when she goes fishing. She takes ballet lessons on Tuesdays and Thursdays, and Taekwondo classes on Mondays and Wednesdays. She melts over puppies with their eyes barely open but shares her room with an iguana named Lizzie (after Elizabeth Bennett of *Pride and Prejudice* fame, that is, not short for lizard).

Is she tomboy or princess? Most likely a bit of each! Your girl is a girl on her own terms, no one else's. She wants to make her own choices, and she wants you to support the choices she makes. There are all kinds of notions about what girls should and shouldn't do. But today's girls don't much think about their lives in such of a way. Do you?

In the Beginning: Everything's a Toy

Watch a toddler with a beautifully wrapped gift. Within three seconds, the bow's in her mouth and drool drips onto the wrapping paper. Rip a corner of the paper and you've got her undivided attention. She pokes a finger at the now-soggy paper and it tears a bit more. She burbles a laugh, waves her hands, and rips the paper again. She's happy just playing with the package—never mind what's inside!

Everything a baby gets her hands on is a toy. She bangs, shakes, and tastes. Through such play, she investigates and learns about the world around her. From a development perspective, these experiences help her improve her coordination, balance, *spatial orientation*, and *motor skills*.

def•i•ni•tion

Spatial orientation is the relationship of one's body within its physical environment. **Motor skills** are learned abilities to move with intent. Gross (or large) motor skills generally relate to movements such as crawling and walking. Fine motor skills are necessary for picking up and holding small objects and performing actions like coloring and assembling building blocks.

Babies like bright colors and shapes they can hold in their tiny hands. They like things that rattle, clatter, and jangle. And, of course, everything goes in their mouths. We adults sometimes find this last one a bit disturbing (and sometimes dangerous) because we do mean *everything*. But this, too, is a kind of play that teaches your baby vital skills. Child development experts caution that rather than trying to stop babies from putting things in their mouths, parents instead make sure what goes into baby's mouth is safe and clean. And if every now and then it really is something she can eat, all the better!

Girl Toys, Boy Toys

Baby doll or truck? Building set or play kitchen? The debate over *gender bias* in toys rages on all fronts, from toy design to packaging and marketing. Parents of daughters often strive to offer their young girls "boy" toys—trucks, Duplo and Lego building sets, play tools, and the like—in addition to "girl" toys—dolls, play kitchen sets, and such—in an effort to establish *gender balance*.

Some girls dive right in, playing with their "boy" toys no differently than boys. Other girls adapt the "boy" toys to their "girl" play, taking a baby doll for a ride in the truck or building a Duplo or Lego house for her favorite stuffed animal to live in. And other girls may give the "boy" toys a cursory examination and then return to their "girl" toys.

def•i•ni•tion

Gender bias is an expectation of behavior or a preference that is based on whether one is male or female. **Gender balance** is an equitable sharing of expectations, preferences, and opportunities without regard for whether one is male or female.

There's not a lot of difference in how girl babies and boy babies play in the first year, no matter what toys they have. By about age two or three, though, kids are paying attention to what other kids are doing. They're also developing a sense of who they are. Girls notice how, and with what, other girls play. By toddlerhood, too, toy manufacturers and retailers begin classifying toys as "boy" or "girl." Never mind that the list for either might be 95 percent the same as the other, or that the only difference between versions of toys that show up on both lists might be color. By late childhood (age eight and up), the overlap shrinks.

Gender bias and gender balance are thorny matters, not so straightforward as we might like. But the bottom line is that *however* your daughter plays with her toys is okay! (As long as she's not hurting herself, someone else, or her surroundings.) At a basic level, kids just want to play. Each child has a unique approach to what that means. Watch a group of kids playing together with the same kinds of toys, and you'll see as many different activities going on as there are youngsters at play. To provide greater emotional, physical, and mental stimulation, make sure your daughter has a wide variety of toys. She'll play with the ones that catch her interest—which changes more often than her diapers.

Rock-a-Bye Baby Doll

Dolls sometimes get a bad rap as gender-biased toys for girls. But there's absolutely nothing wrong with kids—girls or boys—playing with baby dolls. Kids have played with dolls for thousands of years. Among some of the earliest archeological finds are the remnants of roughly shaped dolls fashioned from natural materials.

By the time she's about six months of age, your baby recognizes the baby in the mirror. She likes this other baby-self, who laughs when she laughs and waves when she waves. So when your baby sees a baby doll, she laughs and waves: she sees a variation of herself.

At first, she hugs her baby doll because it's a natural way to further explore this new toy. (She probably puts the doll's hands and feet in her mouth, too, for further examination.) When she reaches about a year old, your baby begins to imitate what she sees you doing when she plays. Now she hugs her baby doll because that's what you do when you hold her. She may play at feeding her baby, or taking off its clothes.

As your daughter gets older, her baby doll play becomes more imitative and involved. Not only does she feed her baby doll, but she may put it in her high chair with a bib (or use her doll furniture, if she has some). Walks with baby doll expand from being dragged along by an arm or a handful of hair to getting dressed in the appropriate clothing and wheeling around in a stroller. Your girl may talk to her baby dolls as though they're real, and even answer back. She becomes totally engrossed in this play, and can stay at it for several hours by the time she's four or five years old. Baby dolls for older kids may be realistic right down to their ability to mimic bodily functions—crying, burping, swallowing baby doll foods, and even peeing and pooping.

This kind of play is important for all kids, whether they're girls or boys. They're learning about themselves and how they fit into their families and their personal environments. At this level of development, your baby is simply exploring her world. Is she laying the foundation for her later roles in life? No doubt. But are you buttonholing her by letting her play with the quintessential girl toy, a baby doll? No way!

And get in there to play *with* her! Be creative and have fun yourself. Dads sometimes want to turn teddy bears and baby dolls into airplanes, zooming them through the air to the accompaniment of assorted noises. This is great! Your girl will laugh at her silly dad, and it's decidedly nonbiased play.

Oh, Puh-leeze!

Check the packaging on toys you buy (or receive as gifts) for your baby to make sure they're age-appropriate. Products intended for children under the age of three years should not contain small parts that could come off and become choking hazards.

Role-Playing Dolls

From the moment she first showed up on store shelves in 1959 dressed in a black-and-white striped bathing suit, Barbie not only turned heads but turned inside-out the way girls could play with dolls. She was the first doll girls could pretend to be. And she was an instant hit. Today, of course, nearly every girl has Barbies, Bratz, American Girls, or similar dolls. Some girls strictly imitate what they see in their lives. Other girls let their imaginations carry them into a make-believe world where they *become* the dolls.

This kind of play lets girls safely explore their perceptions about the adult world, and can become amazingly sophisticated. They try on different roles and experiences. They may play alone and take on the roles of several dolls, or two or three girls might get together to play. It's fun to watch your daughter play with her dolls in this way. You can gain a lot of insights into how she perceives and interprets her observations and experiences. Your daughter might invite you to join in the play, too, although she's probably going to impose a structure around how you do this. No more of that silliness from when she was a baby—this play is serious stuff.

Your daughter might also enjoy playing with action figures of her favorite cartoon or movie characters, ranging from Dora the Explorer to Star Wars and Battlestar Galactica. Variations of these doll-like toys come in versions for all age groups, from the everything-goes-in-the-mouth set to the collector. Though critics often scorn action figures for their flagrant commercialism, girls, especially, tend to play with them in ways that reach well beyond the cartoon or movie that spawned them.

In Her Shoes

The first American woman to become an astronaut was Sally Ride, who spent six days aboard the space shuttle *Challenger* in 1983. She flew a second mission a year later, spending eight days in space. Now retired, Sally Ride works through her company, Sally Ride Science, to motivate and encourage girls to enter careers in science, math, and technology.

Trains, Trucks, and Building Blocks

Toys that move fascinate kids of all ages. When she's pushing a toy truck around on the floor, your daughter learns that she can cause things to happen. She's also learning about the function of shapes: round shapes behave differently than squares or triangles or rectangles. Toy trucks and cars can carry other toys and even things like spoons and partially eaten graham crackers.

Toy train sets—the basic ones, not the scale model ones—often come with "cargo." They run on tracks, requiring a higher level of coordination and spatial orientation. Your daughter (with your help, at first) can put the train cars and tracks together in varying configurations. And who doesn't love to play with building sets? From the basic blocks to Lincoln Logs to Duplos and Legos (and other brands), such toys invite creativity.

Toys like trucks and building sets are often marketed to appeal more to boys. Those that specifically target girls might be pink or purple, have rounded shapes, or feature flowers. Hhmm. Well, if these features appeal to your daughter, there's nothing wrong with that. The play value is the same. But beyond marketing, these toys are simply objects that let your girl explore the world on a scale she can manipulate.

Girl Play: the Toddler Years

Toy	What She Learns Through Her Play
Stuffed animals	Affection and attachment; security
Baby dolls	Behaviors through imitation; how to dress and undress; basic "human" interaction through pretending
Soft blocks and stackables	Shapes; colors; ability to create new configurations by stacking and arranging
Cars, trucks, trains	Coordination; advancing concept of shapes; beginning to understand movement
Play sets	Integrating motor skills and imagination; beginning to understand interactions between people (play figures) and their environment
Books	Reading aloud to her exposes her to a broader base of language; soft books she can handle herself let her explore textures and images (including the appearance of letters and words)
Fingerpaints and play clay	Textures; dimensional creations; colors

Educational Toys

On a certain level, all toys offer educational opportunities—even sticks and rocks your girl picks up when she's playing outdoors. But toys marketed as educational typically target specific developmental skills. Such skills might be physical, like putting shapes into matching spaces or hammering pegs into holes. They might be games of color recognition, or for preschoolers, letters and numbers. Jigsaw puzzles with soft, large pieces help kids develop hand-to-eye coordination and spatial judgment—and often learn colors and shapes as well. The best educational toys are multi-dimensional: they encourage your girl to integrate a number of skills.

Most educational toys have little, if any, gender bias. The toys target the general attractions kids respond to, like bright colors and unusual shapes. They often feature animals and other neutral characters. Play sets may include basic figures that have faces but few other characteristics to distinguish them either as male or female or as a particular occupation, so kids are free to give them whatever roles they choose in their play.

In Her Shoes

What about all those videos and television programs that target toddlers? Most child development experts discourage them. Your girl needs real-life engagement. There's nothing a video can give her that you can't. And watching the screen can set the stage for long-term habits that are not the healthiest. The experts say the longest your toddler should be physically inactive is about an hour, unless she's sleeping.

Play Imitates Life

Many play sets attempt to provide toy versions of real life, most commonly household activities. Kid-size toy kitchens feature stove tops and microwave ovens, along with pretend foods. There are pots and pans to cook the foods, and dishes to serve the foods. There's a sink for washing the dishes. Small tables and chairs are just right for having friends over for pretend dinner. Your daughter is likely to incorporate her baby dolls in this kind of play, extending the reach of imagination and imitation.

Play appliances include vacuum cleaners, lawnmowers, washing machines and dryers, hair dryers, mixers, tool sets—just about anything you have in your household comes in a toy version. Such toys let your daughter imitate the workings of a household. Though they sometimes get a bad rap for being genderized, they are nonetheless items we all use in everyday life and boys enjoy playing with them, too.

Again, what matters is the freedom your daughter has to explore and play with these kinds of toys in ways she chooses. When she's playing with a group of friends, she may well head out to mow the lawn while one of the boys vacuums or bakes a cake. Or maybe she'll choose to bake the cake. These are all valuable role-playing experiences, with her ability to choose being at the core.

Beware the "Dumb Down"

Child development experts criticize toy manufacturers for strategies that "dumb down" toys for girls. A science set marketed to boys may feature chemical reactions that produce changes in color or form, or even "explosions." A science set marketed to girls may feature recipes for perfumes and body lotions. In responding to criticism about such matters, manufacturers generally take the position that they produce and sell what kids want and parents buy. But it's an interesting chicken-and-egg scenario: do parents simply buy what manufacturers produce?

Left to their own choices, kids themselves play with a wide range of toys. Boys as well as girls play with dolls and stuffed animals, and girls as well as boys play with trucks and building sets. But is a boy likely to want a "science" set that contains recipes for body lotions? Probably not. Does such a product teach the same things as the product that generates chemical reactions and explosions? Probably not.

Look Beyond Marketing

Child development experts suggest parents look beyond marketing and packaging to determine what creative and learning opportunities a particular toy offers, and how those opportunities match your daughter's interests. Manufacturers and retailers have a single shared objective: to get you to buy the toy. You have a much broader objective: to provide safe, fun experiences for your daughter.

Removed from its packaging, what is the appeal of the toy? Can you envision your girl playing with it? What's the first thing she'll do when she gets her hands on it? How long will the toy hold her attention? Does the toy's design let her play with the toy in various ways? Will she come back to play with the toy in different ways as she grows up, or is the toy narrowly age-specific?

It's important for you to understand both what interests your daughter and what messages you, as her parent guiding her development, want to cultivate through the toy choices you make for her. (And as she gets older, the toy choices she makes for herself.) Does she like to take things apart to see how they work? Legos and similar toys might indulge that interest. Does she like to play dress-up? Activities that engage her in play-acting and drama can stretch her. With a little imagination on your part, you can broaden as well as focus the appeal of just about any toy. Make sure to watch and listen to your daughter as she plays, so you understand *her* interests. It's all too easy for us as parents to buy toys *we* like.

Girl Play: Older Childhood

Toy	What She Learns Through Her Play
Action figures	To think of herself as strong, courageous, and capable; empowerment
Baby dolls	More elaborate care-giving role-playing; pretend parenting; deepening structures of attachment (a favorite baby doll becomes a constant companion); concepts of sharing when playing with a group of children
Barbies/Bratz/ role-playing dolls	The chance to "try on" different roles and experiences through play scenarios; practice social skills and interactions; engage in extended imagination and creativity
Board games	Reasoning, counting, strategy, and other skills of logic; social interaction skills; concepts of fair play
Dress-up	Stepping into roles on more of a real-life scale; extended creativity and imagination; experimenting with actions and behaviors; social skills and cooperative play
Building sets	Coordination and fine motor skills; conceptualization; extended creativity and imagination; broadened thinking and exploration of real-world experiences
Puzzles	Complex coordination skills; spatial orientation; logic and reasoning; abstract concepts
Word games	Language skills; letter and word recognition; basic reading; speech skills

Toy	What She Learns Through Her Play
Books	Reading aloud to her from storybooks helps her focus her attention for extended periods of time; listening skills; attention to details; basic books she handles herself let her create stories from pictures and develop basic letter and word recognition
Arts and crafts items	Open-ended creative exploration; coordination; dexterity; attention to details; follow instructions; ability to conceptualize an idea and create something tangible from it

Virtual Play

Digital is the new landscape for play. Electronic games and toys specifically target girls as young as three years old. Sometimes the attraction is simply color (pink or purple); other electronic toys feature characters (like Dora the Explorer and Care Bears), and of course Barbie. Boy themes, by comparison, may feature Batman and SpongeBob SquarePants.

The Sims, in which players create and "play" with simulated people, is credited with being the first full-scale interactive computer games designed specifically with girls in mind. The game's initial concept was for a virtual dollhouse. The Sims games have grown in sophistication and complexity, with increasingly life-like interactions. Sims characters have careers, build houses, earn money, get married, and start families.

Child experts have mixed opinions about electronic toys and computer games. Many worry that these limit the ways in which a girl can use her imagination as well as reduce her physical activity, especially in early and middle childhood. But games like The Sims also encourage analytical as well as conceptual thinking. As with anything, moderation is key and probably the answer. Playing computer games helps your daughter become comfortable on computers and develop skills in using computers. In our technical society, this is crucial. Yet it's important for girls to get outside to run, jump, ride their bikes, and otherwise engage their bodies in good, physical fun.

Get in There and Play Along!

Nearly every interaction you have with your daughter has the potential to be a moment of play. This is really important for her, because play is how she learns. And it's really important for you, because it engages you and your daughter at your daughter's level. Sometimes adults feel they don't know how to play. But you don't need to be elaborate. Take your cues from your daughter, and before you know it you'll both be laughing and having great fun.

The Least You Need to Know

- ◆ You have great influence over the ways your daughter plays, no matter what toys she plays with.

- ◆ Your daughter has her own unique interests and tastes, and it's important for you to provide her with toys and play opportunities to support them.

- ◆ Help your daughter broaden her experiences and interests through play that stretches her imagination.

- ◆ Electronic toys and computer games are popular with girls of all ages, although child experts are of mixed opinions when it comes to their value in play.

- ◆ Your daughter wants and needs for *you* to play with her.

Chapter 5

Confident Child of Mine

In This Chapter

- Living the promise of "everything"
- When generations collide
- When I grow up, I want to be …
- Carrying the torch

Previous generations of parents grew up fighting for the promise that girls can do and be anything they choose. Women, especially, jostled for position and balance in this new dynamic, feeling their way through the changing expectations and standards that defined their generations. They exploded past barriers and shattered stereotypes. They won the promise.

Now we're raising a generation of girls to live that promise. These girls don't even think about the earth-shattering changes that came before them. They simply expect to be able to do and be what they want. No restrictions, no doubts, no holds barred. How wonderful! But is it? Success, sometimes even more so than the struggle, has its challenges.

Girls Can Do Anything

What will your girl be when she grows up? Maybe she wants to be a surgeon, a welder, a pilot, a lawyer, an astronaut, even president of the United States. She may want to paint or write or dance or sing. Maybe she's more interested in taking apart her bicycle than riding it, or designs and makes clothes for her dolls while her friends are still learning to tie their shoes. She might want to have six children, four dogs, and nine cats. Maybe she can name all the constellations she can see from her backyard on a clear night, and wants someday to see them herself from space, up close and personal. All are within her reach.

So which should you encourage her to reach for? There's a fine line between nudging your daughter to expand her horizons and pushing her into experiences that don't interest her. We want our girls to have the best of everything. When we look at our daughters, "everything" might mean opportunities we—especially moms—may not've had when we were growing up, particularly in education and careers. It might mean leading our daughters into interests that are important to us. And under the most ideal of circumstances, it might mean paying close attention to what our daughters say and do, so we can identify and support their interests and goals.

> **Girl Pearls**
>
> I was always very interested in science, and I knew that for me, science was a better long-term career than tennis.
> —Sally Ride (1951–), former high school tennis champ, former U.S. astronaut, and first American woman in space

For our daughters, "everything" can be confusing and overwhelming. Our girls are growing up in a world that's changing even *within* their generation—quite a remarkable circumstance, given that they're not even out of high school yet. Girls today have more options than ever before—and they know it. They also feel more pressure to succeed and compete, starting even as early as preschool. (We talk about school pressures and challenges in Chapter 6.) Gary sees a fair number of young girls in his pediatrics practice who have a lot of stress, anxiety, and depression in their lives because they don't have the skills—understandably—to sort out their feelings.

Bumping Into the Past

The rub for today's girls is that they do still come up against traditional feelings and expectations. Change across generations is a slow and unsteady march. Perceptions about what it means to be "a young lady" still run the gamut. Grandparents may have one set of expectations, parents another, and your daughter and her peers undoubtedly yet another.

When our daughters bump into these differing expectations, it can be quite a jolt. Some of their collisions are the same kinds of collisions generations have been having with each other from, no doubt, the beginning of human existence. But others are distinctly unique to this generation of girls.

A frequent intersection is where boy meets girl. Every day, Kathy sees confident high school girls intently focused on goals they can see and articulate. They're taking physics, advanced-placement English, and trigonometry. They're leaders in school government and volunteers in the community. They've got everything going for them—in the classroom.

> **LOL**
>
> Quizzes are in with young teen girls. Not the quizzes in history class. These quizzes are all about current affairs: hers! Websites like quizzilla.com, ruhotquiz.net, quizarama.com, and dozens of others feature fun and revealing quizzes on topics from attitude to romance.

Yet when a school dance or other social event rolls around, tradition still has boys asking girls to go. Although girls are much more willing to bypass convention and go with a group of their girlfriends to minor events—and more accepted when they make this choice—tradition comes back full force when it comes to major events like prom. If our daughters could remake the classic film, *Pretty in Pink*, Molly Ringwald's character wouldn't go to the prom alone at the end of the movie … she'd go with a bunch of her friends.

One shift Gary sees is that both girls and boys are realigning how they behave in social settings, tending to hang out in groups rather than in the girl-boy pairings that characterized earlier generations. A girl today may still "go together" with a boy (even in elementary school!) but the "together" part is more likely to mean the whole crowd of friends, not just the couple.

Life Without Borders

Today's girls encounter far fewer limitations, simply because they are girls, than did previous generations. If your daughter wants to take woodworking, she can take woodworking. If she wants to take physics, she can take physics. If she wants to take ballet lessons, she can take ballet lessons.

The box that confined earlier generations of women is now mostly gone. In its place is a wide-open field. We've encouraged our daughters to think big, and they do. Most preteen girls today genuinely believe there's nothing beyond their reach. How great is that?!

The balance for parents is between encouraging our daughters' dreams and helping them shape realistic expectations around what making those dreams come true might involve. There are no cookie-cutter answers; even you can't know which of her dreams will manifest and which will evaporate. Things are changing so dramatically and so rapidly, none of us can even know what careers and other opportunities actually await her only a few short years from now!

Reality Gap?

Careers on the Official "Hot" List*	Careers Preteen Girls Dream of Having**
Accountant	Transplant surgeon
Airline pilot/copilot	Scientist
Firefighter	Humanitarian
Civil engineer	First woman professional baseball player
Computer software engineer	Fashion designer
Construction manager	Physics professor
Personal finance advisor	U.S. president
Dentist	Star of a reality TV show

Careers on the Official "Hot" List*	Careers Preteen Girls Dream of Having**
Insurance claims adjuster	Architect
Pharmacist	Environmental ecologist
Physician/surgeon	Artist or writer
Industrial engineer	Blogger
Plumber	Forensic pathologist
Loan officer	Photographer
Police officer	Wildlife refuge worker
Lawyer	Behavior analyst
Registered nurse	TV news anchor
Management analyst	Power forward

*U.S. Bureau of Labor Statistics (www.careervoyages.gov), careers likely to grow in demand by 2016.

**Collected from various sources including blogs, forums, MySpace and Facebook pages, and overheard in conversations among girls.

The Family Tradition

Changing expectations and roles have reconfigured our society. More families than not have both parents working outside the home. More families than ever in history have a single parent who carries the full load of going to work and raising the kids. Women and men have nearly an equal presence in higher education and in the workforce. This was nearly an impossible dream only 30 years ago, when one in ten women had a college education and one in three had a job outside the home.

Families today might include three or four generations of women—also a first, as each generation lives longer than the one before it. The women across these generations—great-grandmother, grandmother, mother, daughter—share traits with each other, to be sure, but also bring their own set of experiences and expectations into the picture. Though this can give today's girls an amazing foundation upon which to build their lives, it can also challenge them to stand up for their decisions without flinching.

Is It Okay to Want to Be a Mom?

Not so long ago it seldom crossed a girl's mind to think she would be anything other than a mother herself when she grew up. If it did, she didn't tell anyone about it but instead nurtured her dreams in secret. Sure, some women became teachers, secretaries, and nurses, but until the dawn of the women's movement in the 1960s the "average" girl expected she would follow in the footsteps of her mother and have babies of her own—even if, like Marlo Thomas's *That Girl!*, she decided to have an interlude of a career as an actress in New York City first. It was a home life not a public life that defined the dominant social role and highest aspiration for women. It's been a long struggle to change attitudes, perceptions, and opportunities for girls and women—a long journey from Helen Gurley Brown's *Sex and the Single Girl* to Sarah Jessica Parker's *Sex and the City*. So much so that today, even girls who don't know what they want to do when they get out of school nonetheless believe they'll do *something*—and "just be a mom" is rarely at the top of the list.

What mom-models do you see on television these days? Not many! There's little interest in preparing girls to become mothers. We, today's parents, railed against the box and now the box is gone. In its place is a focus is on cultivating the interests and abilities of each girl as an individual, helping her to shape her life the way she wants it to be. Today's girl isn't necessarily rebelling when she announces at the dinner table that she's never going to marry and never going to have kids. She might simply be stating her vision of her future. (Chapter 20 discusses potential motherhood.)

In Her Shoes

One notable exception to the dearth of mom-models on television is *Gilmore Girls*, which ran as an original series from 2000 to 2007 and now airs in syndication. With a storyline centering around a single mom and her daughter, the Emmy-Award winning show has featured guest stars including singer/songwriter Carole King; CNN's Christiane Amanpour; and the first woman to serve as U.S. Secretary of State, Madeleine Albright. These famous appearances aside, the show focuses on the relationship between mother and daughter, Lorelai and Rory Gilmore.

She's also watching you, mom, a lot more closely than you might realize. You are her live-in mom-model, and she keenly assesses what works (from her perspective, of course) and what doesn't — and she's quick to call you on it. Long gone are the days of being seen but not heard; today's daughters seldom hesitate to share their opinions about whatever's on their minds, including your parenting skills. While this fosters exactly the characteristics you want to see in her when she's 22, it can be a bit tough to swallow when she's 10.

The Promise of Having It All: Can We Keep It?

In the 1970s and 1980s, many women tried to do it all. They went to college, competed for jobs, and established lifestyles dedicated to their chosen fields. Then they married and started families. The awakening was sometimes brutal. Could you be mom *and* business executive, doctor, lawyer, or banker?

The combination didn't work so well. Although abundant career opportunities had opened up, women generally felt they had to choose one path or the other. Keen observers that they are, our daughters have learned from our challenge, and often failure, to have both thriving home lives and thriving public lives *at the same time*. But they also learned from our successes, to be fair. They're smart, today's girls, and they want balance.

Most girls up until middle school have a broad range of interests that fill their daily lives. They project the manageable fullness of this into their future lives as grown women. Some feel confident they can indeed have it all. Others fear something's gotta give and they worry what it might be.

Some studies report that by middle school, half of girls know what they want to be when they grow up and are already tailoring the classes they take and the hobbies and other interests they pursue to support their aspirations. While we can't help but applaud their determination, we also have to wonder whether they're taking on too much, too early. Our generation created, then popped, the super-mom bubble. Are we fostering in our daughters a rebirth of the same pitfall, only earlier in their lives? It's not a question we can answer, yet.

Dads as well as moms influence and shape the expectations girls perceive. Our shrewdly observant daughters recognize where we do and don't have balance in our lives. They measure their own interests and expectations against this framework, and then make decisions that sometimes seem the wrong ones to us—like going to a movie instead of using the time to work on that history report that's due in three weeks or to do soccer drills as extra training for the big match coming up. Do we feel the need to step onto the podium for the time management lecture, or acknowledge that everyone needs down-time every now and again? Balance is a tricky issue.

In Her Shoes

In the United States women earn about 80 cents for every dollar men earn, across the career spectrum, according to the U.S. Bureau of Labor Statistics. Not exactly equity, though by law careers and jobs may no longer explicitly exclude women. According to the U.S. Census Bureau, women's income levels most closely match those of men in technology careers and in the trades—where, ironically, women hold a significantly small percentage of jobs.

A Bigger Challenge

Today's generation of girls enjoys unprecedented equity, both in history and in the world community. It surprises them to learn that their mothers (if those mothers are of a certain age) weren't allowed to wear pants to school when *they* were girls but only dresses, and that in many parts of the world girls are not allowed to go to school and face other, more serious challenges simply because they're girls. We want, and need, to celebrate the possibilities that exist for our daughters. Yet we also want and need to cultivate in our daughters a sense of commitment to working to extend those possibilities to other girls—including, someday perhaps, to their own daughters (uh-huh, that's right—to your *granddaughters)*.

The Least You Need to Know

◆ Today's girls have educational, career, and other opportunities unprecedented in history.

◆ Half of girls already know what they want to do when they grow up by the time they enter middle school.

◆ Some traditions from past generations still linger, creating challenges and sometimes conflicts for our daughters.

◆ Our daughters learn from our experiences.

Part 2

Girl Power

As your girl starts preschool and elementary school, you'll want to stimulate her creativity and intelligence while you're laying the groundwork for self-confidence and a curious nature. At school, girls become more aware of body-image issues, food issues, and that living an active life is a conscious choice—and they learn that being fit and adventurous is not the sole purview of boys! And what about boys, anyway? This is the age where girls first begin to deal with boys, with teasing and competition. Teachers and mentors begin to influence your daughter now, too.

Chapter 6

Pretty Smart

In This Chapter

- What girls need to know *before* they get to kindergarten
- Girls love to read—but what they're reading might surprise you
- Digital learning: does it stack up?
- The measures of knowledge

Your girl is such an inquisitive creature! She wants to know *everything*—what's that? how does this work? can I touch it? She learns like she's a little sponge, soaking up all kinds of tidbits of information. Some, perhaps, you'd rather hadn't come her way, at least not quite yet, but we won't go there.

It's fun, though sometimes exhausting, to indulge her curiosity. With a little guidance from you, nearly any experience offers some sort of learning. You can talk about colors, shapes, words, numbers—all as they exist in the world around her, beyond classroom concepts. Such continual interactions engage the two of you, and tremendously build her confidence as she lays the foundation for understanding her world.

Beyond Scissors and Paste

Back in the old days (when *we* were growing up), kindergarten was the first leap into any sort of structured learning. For many of us, it was the first foray away from home without mom's constant presence. But timid and teary soon gave way to emboldened and giggly as we learned to tie our shoes, sing the alphabet song, count to 100, cut with scissors and paste the results onto different colors of construction paper, drink milk right from the carton (okay, with a straw), and hang upside-down from the monkey bars.

Not so any more. Schools expect kids to know these things, and more, by the time they enter kindergarten. Academic competition—yep, *academic*—starts when girls are barely potty-trained. We've all heard, and maybe you've experienced, stories of parents frantically racing to get applications around to all the best preschools. Competition is fierce and your girl can't even talk yet! Waiting lists for top-notch programs can be a year or longer, and many want to "interview" your daughter before letting her in.

The 25 Words Your Daughter Needs to Know by the Time She Finishes Kindergarten				
a	but	in	of	to
at	can	is	on	up
all	for	it	said	we
and	have	me	the	with
are	I	my	they	you

Does your girl really need to leap from diapers to diagramming sentences? Well, the situation's not quite that dire. But Kathy, like most educators, will tell you that expectations—and standards—continue to climb. Thirty years ago, kids learned to read in the second grade. Fifteen years ago, in the first grade. Now, learning to read is a staple in the kindergarten curriculum. Many kindergarteners have a pretty good grasp on recognizing letters and even key words. And some already can read basic words and simple sentences.

Oh, Puh-leeze!

Can your daughter tell time on a clock? Not the digital read-out window nearly every appliance sports, but on an old-fashioned, round-faced clock with hands? A surprising number of kids—even in middle school and high school—can't. Many see an analog clock for the first time when they go to school. Your daughter may know time in terms of "3:45" but the concept of "quarter to 4" may have no context for her until she sees the hand positions on a clock's face and begins to associate time with fractions.

Read! Read! Read!

Ask any educator what's the single-most beneficial action you can take to give your daughter a head start and you'll get a single-word reply: read. Now, more than in any previous generation, girls must be good readers. Not that we're biased or anything, just because we're writing a *book*. Reading remains fundamental to *all* subject areas. And while there's no disputing the digital direction our society's taking, and despite all the hype and banter about how this is changing the ways we communicate and learn, *girls must be good readers* to use the technology that surrounds them.

Grrl Books

Move over, Nancy Drew, here come Blair, Serena, and the rest of the Gossip Girls. Twilight's Bella isn't far behind (though she's more of, ah, shall we say, a loner). Young girls—preteens and early teens—flock to these books in which the main characters are girls their age who face the same kinds of challenges and problems they encounter at school and at home. Well, except the vampires and werewolves who co-inhabit Bella's world.

The preteen/early teen girl is a hot target for publishers. Girls, moreso than boys, are voracious readers. They pass books around to the other girls in their circle of friends. Poke your head in your daughter's bedroom when she's got a few of those friends over, and you might think you've stepped into Oprah's book club. These girls might be young, but they've been reading a long time (thanks to your influence) and they mince no words when it comes to analyzing story lines and character traits.

Series fiction girls are reading today:

- *Gossip Girl*, Cecily Von Ziegesar
- *Twilight* saga, Stephenie Meyer
- *The Clique Summer Collection*, Lisi Harrison
- *Sisterhood of the Traveling Pants*, Ann Brashares
- *The A-List*, Zoey Dean

Fiction classics your daughter might enjoy:

- *To Kill a Mockingbird*, Harper Lee
- *Pride and Prejudice*, Jane Austen
- *A Wrinkle in Time*, Madeleine L'Engle
- *Number the Stars*, Lois Lowry
- *Because of Winn-Dixie*, Kate Dicamillo

Adults sometimes worry that the subject matter and tone of series books like *Gossip Girl* are too sophisticated, seductive, materialistic, or otherwise inappropriate for their targeted readership. But these books pull girls to them like planets in orbit. Whether we adults like it or not, the issues we feel are "too adult" are more a part of their world than we realize.

Does your daughter have some of these books on her bedside table or on top of the hamper in the bathroom? Pick one up and open it at random. Read a few lines. Anybody you know in real life leap instantly to mind? Of course! And if now you want to sneak away with the book tucked under your arm, we won't tell.

Better yet, read the books your daughter reads, openly—push the limit, even, and read them in front of her. Then talk about them. You'll gain astonishing insights into her life, we guarantee … and she into yours. These points of common connection, as narrowly focused as they seem right now, will come back to serve you well at future moments when the two of you are squared off in disagreement. And maybe, just maybe, you can get her to read some of the books you read and love. You know, those English-teacher faves by the likes of Jane Austen and the Brontë sisters. Those were pretty racy stuff in their day, too.

Don't Know Much Geometry ...

Don't believe for one instant that girls hate math or aren't as good at math as boys. Girls not only love math, they excel in math. And science. And other "technology" subjects. Girls love to figure out how and why things work.

Basic math concepts start with counting. Young girls love to count everything, from the steps they take, to the bites they chew, to the stars in the sky. (That last one will keep them busy until bedtime, for sure.) All kinds of play supports basic math skills—games that keep score, games like hopscotch. Sports like baseball and basketball introduce geometry, though your girl doesn't think about triangulation when she's whacking a bouncer past the shortstop or back-boarding through the hoop to score her "R" in a friendly (okay, somewhat edgy, because this girl likes to *win*) game of HORSE.

Don't tell her she's doing math. Let her enjoy her play. But file these moments away. Later, when she's growling and fumbling over a math assignment, haul them back out. Remind her how she stood just to the left of the baseline and eyed precisely the ideal spot on the backboard for the ball to hit and drop through the hoop, then ran to grab the rebound. "Wasn't that a scalene triangle with an obtuse and two acute angles, like your problem?" you can ask, sweetly.

 LOL

Remember the charming 1990s family TV show, *The Wonder Years*? Supporting character Winnie often carried schoolbooks around and wasn't at all shy about being smart. Turns out the same is true for the actor who played this character, Danica McKellar. McKellar's a math whiz in her other life and has written a book just for middle school girls: *Math Doesn't Suck: How to Survive Middle School Math Without Losing Your Mind or Breaking a Nail* (Hudson Street Press, 2007).

Edutainment

Revolutionary when it debuted on television in 1969, *Sesame Street* has become nearly synonymous with educational programming. The concept was both simple and radical: package tidbits of learning into commercial-like presentations. Throw in a cast of wild characters—not quite real but not quite animated (those ever-lovable Muppets)—and sprinkle around a bit of wry humor to catch the interest of adults, and, as the saying goes, a star is born. New episodes continue to air, making the show a remarkable phenomenon—and older, perhaps, than you!

It didn't take long for the concept to catch on. Every digital discovery, from the personal computer on, established itself in some way, shape, or form as a learning tool. Some stuck, like CDs that teach playing the guitar or learning Spanish on the computer. Websites feature interactive games that highlight math, science, history, and other subject areas. Your daughter can take a quiz to test her knowledge, then practice areas where her skills are weak. It's all right there at her fingertips.

Educators give edutainment mixed reviews. On the one hand, at least there's some useful learning that takes place. And it's not necessarily a bad idea to use an inert interface for tasks as rote as arithmetic drills or spelling practice. But the limited context of the digital blackboard restricts deeper understanding of base concepts. Learning tends to stick when there's something it can stick to, like real experiences and examples drawn from your daughter's life.

LOL

Though girls use computers as much as boys, they choose careers in computer fields more than five times less often. The percentage of women in computer technology careers continues to drop, and currently hovers around 10 percent.

It's deceptive to think of electronic engagement as "interactive." Sure, your daughter's responding to questions and entering responses or reactions with a keyboard or other device. But the interaction is, well, fake. There's no one there who's trying to think a few steps ahead of your daughter, to watch the expressions on her face to determine whether she's struggling her way to irrecoverable frustration, to talk with her about why she gets stuck at the same point every time.

If your daughter sits in front of the control panel or computer screen long enough, she'll make her way through every conceivable configuration of the problem. She may ultimately master the problem, but is it because she understands the process? That's important, because much of learning is all about patterns and the processes that drive them.

It's kind of like thinking you can learn to drive a car by practicing in a simulator. Even though you may master every move involved in driving, nothing in your make-believe world can prepare you for the crazy driver who just turned the wrong way onto the street and is headed straight for you but is busy looking for something he dropped on the floor.

Faux Reality

The make-believe approach extends beyond digital boundaries, though it's hard to know which borrowed from what. Many grocery stores have little shopping carts with banners or flags that brazenly proclaim, "future customer!" The idea is that your kids get to push their own carts and shop for the items they want to buy. Of course, when they roll up to the checkout stand, they're not buying anything. You are. It's pretty blatant marketing that targets parents where they're most vulnerable—in the whine section. Who wants to listen to "buh-uttt Momm-mm-mm!" when what you really want is to make it up and down the aisles and still have a balance left in your checkbook?

If you stretch your imagination, you can reach for the grain of value buried in this strategy. First, though, you have to step carefully over that stereotype—you know, the "girls just love to shop" sinkhole. Once you're clear of that obstacle, you might find some valid learning opportunities. For example, you could help your daughter learn to separate hype from health in product labeling, make choices, and manage money (even though, of course, it's not hers).

> **Girl Pearls**
>
> It takes a great deal of courage to stand up to your enemies, but even more to stand up to your friends.
>
> —J.K. Rowling, British author (*Harry Potter* series)

Shakespeare Must've Had a Daughter in School

We'd like to think our girls could escape the pressures of peers and cliques at least until they were, oh, say, 40 years old and had the skills of gracious sarcasm down pat. But no such luck. If your daughter dives into a *Gossip Girl* novel or heads for her MySpace page the moment she drops her school bag on the floor, you can bet she's had a testy day at the circus.

If school was only about academics, what an easy time of it we'd all have! Your daughter would dash off in the morning, full of excitement and energy, and then race home at the end of the school day to tell you all about everything she learned. You'd probably not hear the names of any other girls unless you asked about them.

But it's complicated, and lessons learned transcend literature and medieval history. School's tough on a girl's psyche. Not too many girls truly learn everything they need to know about life when they're in kindergarten, especially when it comes to dealing with other girls. Even when her friendships are strong and solid, for your daughter every day is a drama. Whether she finds herself cast in a lead role or as a supporting character with no lines, your girl invests a lot of time and emotion trying to figure out where and how she fits in.

Your daughter learns the fine points of friendship by working through her daily challenges on her own. Be there for her, by all means. Help her find the positive and the humor in her situations. Encourage her to talk through the possible actions she can take. Try to convince her that sometimes no action is the best action. Offer gentle advice (this is dangerous territory). But don't try to fix her problems for her. Don't talk to her friends, or her friends' mothers. Your girl is strong, smart, and capable. When she believes that to be true, there's no stopping her no matter what challenge arises.

Oh, Puh-leeze!

One circumstance in which you must step in, and quickly, is when you suspect your daughter might be struggling to deal with a bully. Take your concerns to the school—your daughter's teacher or the principal. We talk more about bullies in Chapter 8.

Measures and Standards

If there's one constant we all associate with school, it's tests and grades. For better or for worse, this is the system by which schools determine whether our girls learn what they're supposed to. In the ideal, it's a great concept, a scale of relative knowledge. In practice, however, it's a structure of stress.

Stressing Out Over Tests

You'd think that, by now, if we can transplant hearts and shuttle a woman into space every now and again, we could come up with a less stressful way to measure knowledge and comprehension in school. But the ritual of frantic studying the night before a test upon which half the semester's grade depends still prevails.

Does your daughter complain she doesn't feel well the night before or morning of a big test? She's not simply trying to get out of taking the test. As many as three-fourths of high school girls feel nauseated and may even throw up from the stress and pressure they feel about tests and grades. Some girls panic and forget everything they've learned when that test paper hits the desk in front of them. Other girls whiz right through tests without giving them a second thought. Maybe they're better prepared, maybe they have photographic memories, maybe they've learned test-taking strategies, maybe they simply handle this kind of stress in a productive way.

In Her Shoes

If your daughter seems to know the material but consistently does poorly on tests (especially in multiple classes), talk with the teachers or the school's guidance counselor for their input and suggestions. Schools deal with such issues all the time, and may be able to help you guide your daughter to better test performance.

Whatever your philosophy about tests, they're likely to stay in the school landscape for a while. You can help your daughter prepare by studying with her for the major tests and encouraging her to study on her own for quizzes and less important tests. Most teachers structure their classes and grading systems to accumulate a base of work from their students, rather than grading solely on the basis of tests.

Making the Grade

Girls worry about grades. Parents worry about grades. Even teachers have their issues with grades. Some girls are so driven to get straight As that even an A-minus feels like failure to them. Other girls are so accustomed to having low grades that they stop trying to get higher grades.

In a certain way, it would be nice to sit down with our daughters and say to them, "Look. It's great for you to work hard in school. But focus on the learning … forget about the grades! When you get into the real world, no one remembers whether you were an A-student or barely scraped together enough points to graduate." Not that we're suggesting you do this!

The reality remains that grades do matter while your daughter is in school. Are you the source of the pressure she feels? Sometimes the things we do to reward our girls for doing well in school backfire, instead causing stress. Even when your daughter makes the honor roll, make sure you recognize and praise her efforts beyond grades.

The Least You Need to Know

- ◆ Reading is the foundation for all subjects.

- ◆ Today's girls are avid readers, share books among their friends, and talk about what they read.

- ◆ Computers and other digital devices can offer educational experiences, but your interactions with your daughter remain among the most potent learning situations.

- ◆ While your daughter may learn academic subjects at school, she also learns social and other skills that she needs to succeed as an adult in the world at large.

Chapter 7

Girls at Play

In This Chapter

- Make fitness fun
- How active should your daughter be?
- Group and solo activities
- Maintaining a healthy body-image and weight
- Eating for strong bones and good health
- Your daughter's watching *you*

Where's your girl right now? Out riding her bicycle, climbing the plum tree in the neighbor's yard, swinging, stomping through the mud, or chasing the cat around the house? Great! Well, maybe not so great for the cat, but definitely good for your daughter.

Girls want to be active. Girls *need* to be active. They need to run, jump, skip, tumble, pedal, throw, catch, pull, push, and anything else that strikes their fancy. They need to build bones and muscles strong enough to carry them through eight or nine decades of healthy living.

Focus on Fun

Mention the word "exercise" and you're certain to get The Look. You know it all too well—hips thrust to one side, eyes rolled to the other. It's just not cool to sweat, especially in front of you-know-who. (Though, of course, you don't know who … this week.) And—gag! All they hear about in gym class is *exercise*. Enough, already. But your girl needs to be moving! Put movement in the context of fun, though, and look out—that girl's on the go.

There are endless ways for your girl to be active, from just playing in the backyard with her friends to organized sports. Some girls are eager to be on teams and thrive on competition. Others prefer activities they can do at their own pace without a particular goal other than enjoying what they're doing.

To Her Good Health

The National Association for Sport and Physical Education (NASPE) says every child two years and older should get a minimum of 60 to 90 minutes moderate to vigorous physical activity every day, most days of the week. This is mostly *aerobic* exercise—physical effort that gives the cardiovascular system (heart, lungs, and circulatory structures) a good workout. Aerobic activity is crucial for health. It helps every cell in your daughter's body work more efficiently. She needs this efficiency for her body to be its healthy best.

def•i•ni•tion

Aerobic activities increase the heart rate and breathing. This gets more oxygen to cells, helping them to function more efficiently.

It's okay if the total time of physical activity comes in small chunks of time that add up over the course of the day, and more is definitely better. What's moderate to vigorous? Anything that makes your girl breathe hard enough that she can't sing, though she can still talk about how stupid it is that she has to be doing this!

The key, of course, is to make what she's doing so much fun that she wants to do it—and as much of it as you'll let her. This is easiest when activity's always been part of your daughter's day. And yours. Kids love to imitate the adults around them, and are pretty shrewd when it comes to the "do what I say, not as I do" routine. You're not going to get away with telling your daughter it's good for her to walk to school if you drive yourself a block and a half to the corner store.

National Association for Sport and Physical Education (NASPE) Physical Activity Recommendations for Children

Child's Age	Amount of Daily Aerobic Activity	Kinds of Activities
1 to 3 years	30 minutes structured, 60 minutes free play	Tag, kicking a ball, simple running games, teeter-totter, monkey bars
3 to 6 years	60 minutes structured, 30 minutes free play	Games that involve running, jumping, skipping, swinging
6 years and older	90 minutes cumulative (minimum)	Games that involve 20 to 30 minutes of steady activity, jumping rope, swinging, climbing on monkey bars, swimming, martial arts, gymnastics, dancing, age-appropriate organized sports, bicycling, roller-skating, ice-skating, sledding, skiing, horseback riding, snow-boarding

Sometimes lost in the frenzy of how much and when is the underlying recommendation that kids of all ages should be physically active most of the time they're awake. The NASPE says your toddler girl should be inactive no longer than one hour at a time unless she's asleep. Older kids should be inactive no longer than two hours at a time unless they're sleeping. Puts a different spin on the television debate, doesn't it?

Digital Dilemma

Texting. Cell phones. Instant messaging. Computer games. Video games. When it comes to technology, your girl's got it all right at her fingertips. Although the digital era is mostly a good thing, it definitely has its downside. As in, it keeps her down, backside parked on the couch. Talk about multitasking! Your girl can have a dozen or more different conversations going—and still be playing a game of Sims on her computer.

Oh, Puh-leeze!

Nintendo's blockbuster interactive game console Wii offers the add-on product WiiFit, turning fitness into digital fun for those who can't resist the lure of technology. Can WiiFit really make your daughter stronger and healthier? Well, we (and most child development experts) think she'd have more fun out there in the real world, interacting with real people. As parents have no doubt been saying since the beginning of time, "Go outside and play!"

And even the old-fashioned television claims time better spent on more active pursuits. The American Academy of Pediatrics (AAP) estimates that 90 percent of kids two years and under watch at least four hours of television each day. Even when this includes educational programming, it's too much, says the AAP, which recommends no more than two hours of tube time daily. More time than that and your girl's not getting the exercise she needs. (See Chapter 6 for a discussion about electronics and learning.)

Structured Activities

What an endless amount of energy your girl has—when something catches her interest. Structured activities, from games to sports, motivate that interest. Some girls can hardly wait to hit the ground running, while others need more nudging.

There's really nothing that should be off-limits to your daughter simply because she's a girl. She might choose a mix of traditional and nontraditional activities. She needs you to support her choices, even if they're not the ones you'd make for her. That said, there's nothing wrong with encouraging her to try new and different activities. Just don't push her into things she really doesn't like.

Group Fun

Team sports are not just for boys! From Little League to field hockey, basketball to soccer, and even lacrosse and flag football, girls are on the field and in the game. Girls like the excitement of the action, the camaraderie of the team, and the thrill of competition.

Most organized athletic activities for youth emphasize participation and safety above winning. Your daughter should feel good about her team no matter the outcome of a game, match, or season. Being on a sports team lets her push her limits while learning how to support others. It's very confidence-building to catch a pop fly, score a goal, or make a perfect pass.

The best teams build confidence by encouraging each girl to reach for her best and supporting the steps that take her there. Not everyone will catch that pop fly, score the goal, or nail the pass. But the effort of trying is itself achievement, and the team dynamic should support that. Coaches and other adults should set good examples through their own behavior.

Go to her practices and games. You may not be able to make all of them, but make it enough of a priority that your daughter knows you're there for her. Get to know her coaches. Help your daughter develop healthy habits for hydration (getting enough to drink), nutrition (eating the right foods to support her energy needs), and rest.

Solo Adventures

Maybe your girl's more the solo type, preferring to be off on her own. There are lots of activities to keep her busy. She might enjoy swimming, bicycling, or skateboarding. Dance and gymnastics. Tennis. Track. Martial arts. Even walking the dog.

Many such activities can be things she does just for the fun of it, or can be group- or team-oriented. Maybe she just wants to take dance lessons, or maybe she enjoys performing in a dance recital. Maybe she'd like to join the swim team, or maybe she'd rather splash around in the pool. Whatever her path, the more active she is, the healthier she is.

Push or Back Off?

It's easy, when your daughter's enthusiastic and you're encouraging, to stray beyond the boundary when it comes to pushing her to achieve. She sort of knows her limits, but not really. And her ambitions may cloud her judgment, especially when she's good at what she's doing.

We all know the dreaded "sideline parent"—the mom or dad who has all the strategies or whose kid isn't getting enough playing time if she's not on the field the entire game. And we know you're not one of those parents, right? Because if you were, your daughter would tell you.

But sometimes you do need to take a stand, and you should feel confident in doing so. You might need to question a coach's approach, or step in to take some pressure off your daughter. This is not only okay, it's your job as a parent. Take it seriously, even as you cheer yourself hoarse!

Shape-Shifting

Your daughter's first fascination with herself comes when she recognizes that the baby in the mirror is she. Nothing was the same after that. Life slides along pretty uneventfully until she loses that first baby tooth and recognizes, with a jolt, that she's changing before her very eyes. As exciting as it is to be growing up, it's also scary.

Young girls are sensitive about how their bodies look, which is an ever-changing picture as they're growing and maturing. Some girls might grow four inches taller over the summer, returning to school to start a new grade and to find themselves the tallest in the class. Other girls are on the slower end of the growth spectrum and are the smallest. Of course *you* know that by senior year in high school everyone pretty much evens out, but she can't see that far ahead. Kids just don't like to be different, and at times she feels like the only one who looks the way she does.

In Her Shoes _____

Show your daughter pictures of you (both mom and dad) when you were growing up! She's more keenly interested in what you were like as a kid than she'll ever admit. Seeing what you looked like when you were her age helps her to see what it means when you say to her, "This is just a stage; you'll change again before you know it."

Boys fret and worry about how they look, too; much of such anxiety is simply the process of growing up. But our society puts great emphasis on appearance for women, which pressures many girls to meet standards that are unhealthy and often unachievable. Television, movies, magazines, advertising, and even video and computer games present exaggerated images of women.

Though all you have to do to see the huge disparity between reality and fantasy is spend a half-hour at the mall, it's nonetheless challenging for your daughter to make the distinction.

A Body in the Image of Health

It's not necessarily a bad thing for your girl to think about her appearance. After all, what she sees in the mirror is how she looks to the world beyond herself. But this should be only one of many factors that feed her sense of self.

Encourage your daughter to be active and engaged in physical and social activities that interest her and enable her to shine. This helps her shift focus from how she looks to how she feels. Emphasize healthy choices, and make them yourself so she has an in-home role model. Point out women who look healthy and vibrant in varying situations, with a sideways comment about why.

Does your girl obsess about her appearance? Talk about it! Maybe someone said something hurtful to her and she just can't get beyond it. Maybe she's just unsure of herself. As the adult, you can glean insights from the tidbits she chooses to share that can help you reassure her and help her feel confident about who she is as a whole person, not just a flash in the mirror.

The Weighty Issue of Weight

One in three American girls weighs more than is healthy. We've moved from the perception of baby fat as cute to the recognition that overweight kids are at risk for some adult-size health problems. Weighing in from his perspective as a pediatrician, Gary notes that in his practice today he sees six or seven overweight girls for every underweight girl.

def•i•ni•tion

Body mass index (BMI) is a standardized measure of weight and height that estimates the relative proportion of body fat. BMI scores correlate to health risk resulting from too much or too little body fat.

Your healthcare provider can help you determine the boundaries of healthy weight for your daughter, within the context of where she is from a development perspective. The *body mass index (BMI)* standard for adults doesn't quite apply in the same way for kids; doctors instead use a percentile standard. This is because there's a wide range of "normal" in the rate at which kids develop and mature, especially when it comes to muscle mass.

Your girl may stay an "Olive Oyl goyl" until she's 14—hovering around the fifth percentile (meaning 95 percent of girls her age weigh more than she does; she's on the low end of the weight norm)—or be able to out-press the boys in weight-training class in the eighth grade (meaning 15 percent of girls her age weigh more than she does; she's on the high end of the weight norm)—pushing the eighty-fifth percentile. Many kids go through stages of looking alternately chubby or gangly. Either can be within the range of healthy.

Most girls make it through these tumultuous growth periods with a strong sense of self-confidence. Some struggle to be comfortable with their bodies. Eating disorders can surface during such struggle. *Anorexia nervosa* and *bulimia*, conditions driven by an unrealistic desire to be thin, affect girls far more frequently than boys. These conditions are always a background concern for the parents of girls.

But today's more common eating disorder, especially among younger girls, is *obesity*. An estimated one in six American girls under the age of 12 years is above the ninety-fifth percentile, putting her health at risk.

Pediatricians are seeing conditions more commonly associated with middle age in youngsters whose weight is out of control—type 2 diabetes, high blood pressure, high blood cholesterol, arthritis, and even heart disease.

def•i•ni•tion

Anorexia nervosa is an eating disorder in which a person eats significantly less than is necessary to support good health. **Bulimia** is an eating disorder in which a person eats but then uses measures such as self-induced vomiting or laxatives to purge the food. **Obesity** is an eating disorder of excessive eating, resulting in body weight that is 20 percent or more above a healthy weight. All three conditions significantly affect health in both the short term and the long term.

It's important to approach weight issues from the perspective of health, with compassion and love, and in low-key, supportive ways. You want your daughter to be healthy and happy. Your daughter's healthcare provider can offer suggestions and advice.

Good Eats

U.S. food (and we use the term loosely) companies spend $1.6 billion dollars a year to entice your daughter and her friends to buy their prepared or packaged products and convenience foods. Or nag you into buying them. How do you compete with that? The industry is betting that you can't.

It's not that most of these products (fast food, convenience foods, and packaged foods) are inherently bad for her. It's that they all too easily become a larger part of her eating habits than is healthy. And even if they're not outright bad for her, some products have no redeeming nutritional value.

Let's be real. You can't keep your daughter from eating junk food.

Oh, Puh-leeze!

"Sit there until you finish your peas" isn't going to help her like peas any better. Instead, offer her peas (or whatever foods she refuses to eat) but give her lots of other choices, too. Turning a despised food into a battleground doesn't do either of you any good.

It's everywhere, even at school. But you can help her make healthier choices. Start when she's young, and stay consistent. The earlier in your girl's eating experience you incorporate nutritious foods, the more readily she'll keep them on her menu as she gets older.

Picky Eater?

Does your daughter hate salad, green beans, Brussels sprouts, yellow cheese, eggs, or other foods? We all have our likes and dislikes. It's natural for her to have favorite foods and try to slip others to the dog.

Kids are most open to new foods when they're first learning to eat foods they recognize—between about ages two to four years. Between the ages of four and eight years, however, kids become more assertive—in general, and especially at the table.

Full Enough

The only time a clean plate matters is when it's in the cupboard. It can be hard to get past the "waste not, want not" mode, when it comes to leaving food on the plate. But the clean-plate club is not in need of new members. Young toddlers eat when they're hungry and stop eating when they're full. It's a great model, though it does eventually run head-on into issues like schedules and meal times and all that.

There are two things you can do to help your daughter eat the right amount of food: put only what is the recommended serving size on her plate, and let her be done when she's had enough. Even if it looks to you like she's barely grazing, it all balances out over the course of the day (or even the week). As long as she's meeting growth and development markers, she's getting plenty to eat. It's important, too, to associate food and eating habits with health and nutrition, and to resist turning meal times into battles of control. Later in her life, these control issues have the potential to play into eating disorders.

When the Problem Truly Is Not Eating Enough

We've spent a lot of time in this chapter talking about the dangers of your daughter eating too much, so that she lays the foundation for a lifelong struggle with weight gain and being overweight. And indeed, the challenge of maintaining a healthy weight is not only a problem for girls, but for the entire family. The popularity of seeing parent/child teams on the reality weight-loss show, *The Biggest Loser*, illustrates how closely parents and children have to work together to lose weight and be more healthy.

However, for some of our girls, the temptations surrounding food are the opposite ones. It is not eating too much, but *not eating enough* that is the problem. For these girls, not eating becomes a way of exerting control over their world (and this includes their lives at home). By not eating, or by binging and purging, a girl takes absolute control—or so she believes—over her body and what happens to it. And in her mind, she draws closer and closer to the idealized images of reed-slender women she sees in fashion magazines and throughout our popular culture. Indeed some runway fashion models *are* teen girls themselves.

How do you tell if your girl may have this kind of eating disorder? Is she just naturally thin? Or might there be something else at play? You'll need to observe her carefully, and listen closely to what she says about food. Quiz her friends on what kinds of foods they eat, and about outings to restaurants or anyplace where food will be served to see what they say about it. Chances are if your girl has an eating disorder, one or more of her friends do as well.

What do you do if you suspect an eating disorder? Begin with a visit to your family pediatrician. Eating disorders can be difficult conditions to resolve and will require the assistance of your pediatrician and other specialists who can work with you as a family. Don't be afraid to intervene in your girl's life to get to the bottom of any unhealthful eating patterns you suspect, as your tenacity as a parent is what may make the difference. Untreated eating disorders have the potential to become life-threatening to your child.

Oh, Puh-leeze!

Unfortunately, there has been a recent explosion of Internet sites, message boards, and girl blogs extolling the virtues of anorexia and bulimia. Keep a careful eye on where your girl is going online so that you can limit her exposure to these sites and prevent their harmful messages from influencing your girl when she may be vulnerable to unhealthful messages about food and body image.

Make sure to give your girl the care and attention she is craving, however vehemently she might resist your efforts. (Remember, control is an issue in these disorders.)

Strong Bones

Childhood and adolescence are the times when your girl's laying the foundation for her future health. That includes the critical but often overlooked inner structure that supports it all, your daughter's bones. We tend to think growing kids get all the vitamin D, calcium, and other nutrients they need because, well, they *are* growing. But growth alone doesn't give you a peek inside to see how good that growth is. Your girl will continue to grow because her body's programmed to do so. It takes the right mix of nutrients for her to grow a healthy, strong body.

The bone structure your daughter builds now will carry her through the rest of her life. In a certain way, she can "bank" bone density by building lots of it now, when bone growth is at its most active. Later in life, when she's older even than you are now (we know, it's a stretch for both of you to think in such of a way), her bone bank will help protect her from bone loss.

Doctors are seeing an alarming rise in preteen and teenage girls with *osteoporosis*, however. We've long thought of this condition of weakened bone structure as one that only affects older women. But changes in the ways we eat, coupled with couch-potato syndrome, are factors contributing to the rise in osteoporosis among the younger population as well.

In younger girls, the cause is most often a trio of not-enoughs: not enough calcium, not enough vitamin D, and not enough weight-bearing exercise. Calcium is the main ingredient of bone; vitamin D regulates how much calcium can get into the bones; and weight-bearing activity stresses the muscles and bones—and in this case, stress is a *good* thing—stimulating the bones to make more bone tissue.

def•i•ni•tion

Osteoporosis is a condition in which the bones lose density, causing them to become brittle and weak. This makes them susceptible to fractures.

Calcium

Dense is good when it comes to bones. Calcium gives bones their density and strength. Girls and boys need the same amount of daily calcium. But girls tend to be smaller in physical stature than boys, which means they tend to have smaller bones. This is broad generalization, but it has health ramifications down the road. And those raging hormones that define their teen years have roles beyond breasts and body hair—they're also key players in bone health.

Both girls and boys have both estrogen and testosterone in fairly equal proportion until puberty approaches. With puberty, girls have lots of estrogen and a wee bit of testosterone; boys have lots of testosterone and a wee bit estrogen. Testosterone helps build muscle mass. So with their higher amounts of testosterone, boys build bigger muscles. Which is good, because they need them to move around those larger, heavier skeletons.

Oh, Puh-leeze!

Back off the cola! Recent studies link cola soft drinks with decreased bone density. Researchers aren't sure why colas more than other kinds of soda have this effect, though they speculate it's a combination of the caffeine and minerals that interfere with the body's mechanisms for regulating calcium levels. A cola now and again isn't likely to do harm, but daily consumption (including diet and noncaffeinated colas) could have long-lasting effects on your daughter's bone health.

Muscle mass is important for healthy bones because the more stress against bones (again, this is the good stress), the more new structure the skeleton builds. So girls need strong muscles, too. We're not talking Arnold Schwarzenegger here; just your ordinary, barely noticeable muscles will do.

Estrogen has complex roles in how the body makes new bone. But even though girls have more estrogen, they don't build more bone because of it. During the years estrogen levels are high (the menstrual years), your daughter's bones are happy as can be. It's 40 or 50 years down the road that things shift, with menopause, when estrogen levels drastically drop. So, too, does bone density. So the bone your daughter builds now, in youth, is crucial not only for all the running around she does now but also in the future.

Recommended Daily Calcium Amounts for Children

Age	Calcium	Milk Equivalent
1 to 3 years	500 milligrams	2 cups (16 ounces)
4 to 8 years	800 milligrams	3 cups (24 ounces)
9 to 18 years	1,300 milligrams	4 cups (32 ounces)

Source: American Academy of Pediatrics (AAP)

One cup of milk—8 ounces—delivers about 300 milligrams of calcium. To meet her daily calcium needs, your 10-year-old daughter needs to drink about four cups of milk! Unfortunately, not too many 10-year-olds drink that much milk. And if they do, it's important that they drink a reduced-fat version. If your 10-year-old girl is drinking whole milk, those four cups come with 32 grams of fat—half the total fat she should consume in a day. Because of this, the American Academy of Pediatrics recommends that kids two years and older drink nonfat or low-fat milk.

Here are some other foods that give about the same amount of calcium as a cup of milk:

- 1½ ounces reduced-fat cheddar cheese
- 8 ounces low-fat yogurt
- 1 cup (8 ounces) calcium-fortified orange juice
- 1 cup goat's milk
- 1 cup soy milk
- 1 cup cooked spinach
- 1 cup cooked greens (collard or turnip)

Other foods that provide smaller amounts of calcium include sesame seeds, broccoli, green beans, mozzarella cheese, molasses, Brussels sprouts, asparagus, tofu, and oranges. Some products that are favorites with kids—like graham crackers—are coming onto the market in calcium-fortified versions.

Vitamin D: the Sunshine Vitamin

Without vitamin D, your daughter's body can't use the calcium she consumes. Vitamin D is a key player in calcium absorption as well as in calcium regulation. It helps keep calcium in the bones. This is why vitamin D is added to milk and other calcium-containing food products. There aren't so many foods high in vitamin D, but some foods that are include the following:

- Baked or broiled salmon, especially sockeye and Chinook
- Boiled or steamed shrimp
- Baked or broiled cod
- Eggs

Boiled, broiled, and baked are the optimal cooking methods. Breaded and deep-fried, not so good. Though this cooking method doesn't diminish the amount of vitamin D, it does add significant and unnecessary fat.

Exposure to sunlight also triggers biochemical reactions in the skin that produce vitamin D. Researchers believe as little as 10 minutes of sun exposure a day is enough to generate healthy vitamin D production. Counter-balancing this, however, are concerns about protecting the skin from damage the sun's ultraviolet rays cause. So when our kids go outside to play, we slather them in sunscreen. This protects their skin but also blocks the making of vitamin D.

Without adequate vitamin D, bones get soft and can become deformed (a disorder called rickets). The American Academy of Pediatrics now recommends a vitamin D supplement for all kids, so talk with your pediatrician or regular healthcare provider to make sure you've got your daughter covered.

Weight-Bearing to Build New Bone

Exercise and physical activity that put pressure on the bones—such as when the feet strike the ground—encourages new bone growth. Activities that get your girl running, jumping, skipping, hopping, and even just walking are all great weight-bearing activities. Games and sports often incorporate these in fun ways that don't even seem like exercise! Any activity that uses muscle force against resistance—think of pushing bicycle pedals or pulling oars—stimulates the bone growth. Many weight-bearing activities are also great for aerobic improvement, which strengthens the hearts and lungs.

Working out with weights is a good way to strengthen both bone and muscle, too. Some girls like doing this in a structured setting, such as in a class at school or at a community fitness center. Your daughter can use hand weights at home, or you can assign your girl household chores that involve carrying the laundry basket or various gardening tasks. (Carrying those bags of mulch requires muscles!)

As with all "exercise," the more fun it is, the more your girl will enjoy doing it and want to do it. Just be careful not to give her physical tasks that obviously are out of her fitness level. Less is more when working with weights in this way, and increasing weight slowly is better than carrying too much, too far, too fast.

Be the Example You Want Your Daughter to Follow

Your daughter looks primarily to you, her parents, for direction and guidance in how to shape her life. Make healthy eating and regular physical activity daily parts of your family structure. If you all do it, it's simply your lifestyle. Sure, other influences will come into play as your daughter gets older and goes out into the world. This makes the foundation you establish all the more important.

The Least You Need to Know

♦ Your daughter should be physically active for nearly all of her waking hours.

♦ Whether she chooses a group activity or a solo sport, it should be something she likes.

♦ Healthy food choices are especially critical for strong bones now and in the future.

♦ Start with your daughter's first "real food" meals to offer her numerous choices of vegetables, fruits, and healthy foods.

♦ Body weight is an important factor in your daughter's health and sense of self-confidence.

♦ Helping your daughter maintain a healthy weight also reinforces a healthy body image for her in that the goal is to look and be healthy; if you can teach her that, she'll know she will always look good.

♦ Make a healthy lifestyle your family's lifestyle.

Chapter 8

Discovering Boys

In This Chapter

- When your girl starts to notice boys
- What is it with boys, anyway?
- Naturally smart ... naturally not?
- Does equal mean the same?
- What parents don't know about what goes on at school and how it hurts their daughters

Until about fifth grade, boys are nothing special to girls. They're annoying sometimes. They're helpful sometimes. They're fun sometimes. Except for the lines at the bathrooms, there's not a lot of girl-boy separation.

Then around about age 10 or so, the dynamic starts to shift. There are girls' teams and boys' teams for sports that girls and boys used to play together. Academic demands intensify. And hormones begin to bubble. Girls start looking at boys in a different way. Not necessarily special, but different. It's the start of the Great Divide.

Hey, I Like Your Look!

When boys become B-O-Y-S, girls begin to change how they dress and act. Appearance moves to front and center. Girls are ahead of the curve on this one; they're thinking about what boys think of them, in a serious way, while boys are still shoving each other in the lunch line.

Boys don't start worrying about what girls think about *them* for a couple more years. They may notice the efforts girls make to get their attention, but are more likely to make fun of them than to compliment them. Throwing a football 50 or 60 yards, though—now that's going to turn their heads!

Can't We Be Just Friends?

Maybe your girl's BFF (best friend forever) since kindergarten is a boy. Now that they're in seventh grade, does that make him her BF (boyfriend)? Eww! No! They might stay BFFs, although the growing divide in their social circles might make it more challenging for them to remain close. Still, it's common for girls to have close friends who are boys in whom they have no boy-girl kind of interest. (See Chapter 11 for more on this.)

Sometimes "just friends" becomes a problem when the boy or the girl does get a boyfriend or girlfriend. The BF or GF may not like the amount of time the "just friends" spend together. Jealousy reigns in these early explorations; after all, these early relationships are where girls and boys learn to handle complex emotions.

Girl/Boy Competition: The Good, the Bad, and the Ugly

She's something else, your little girl—isn't she? There she is, the tallest one out on the soccer field, maneuvering the ball around everyone else like she's the only one out there. *Bend It Like Beckham*, how yesterday! She scores three goals in the final two minutes of the match, pushing her team ahead by one point. "Yea-eah-ahhh!" she shouts, thrusting her hands above her head. Why, then, does she sit silent in chemistry class the next day when the teacher calls for someone to come to the board and draw structural formulas for all the possible isomers of C_5H_{12}, when this is a problem she could practically do in her sleep? Ah, there you have it: the question that haunts and baffles the era of equality.

When kids are little, they're pretty equally matched in most areas of development. Kids are better and not so good at different things, but not because they're girls or boys. Parents, teachers, and other adults work hard to teach them to cooperate, share, and be fair when they play together—the "be" and the "no" basics: Be respectful. No biting, no spitting on each other or the ball. Be fair. No shoving, no cheating. Kids are smart. They get it, and they play nice. Mostly.

As they get older, the nature of play changes and competition creeps in. Games have scores, and scores mean someone wins and someone loses. We emphasize that it's more important for everyone to get to play than to win, but still we keep score. Kids are smart, and they catch on. They start playing to win. By about age 8 or 10 there are usually boys' teams and girls' teams. The rationale for separating the girls from the boys is that boys are bigger and stronger and play rougher, so it creates more fairness for girls to give them their own teams and leagues. Then they can compete on a level playing field.

It's an odd sort of fairness, and a fair number of experts question the extent to which this kind of separation sends the message that girls can't compete against boys and win—not only in athletics but also in academics. Like most such messages, it tends to become more deeply and broadly woven into the social fabric, even infiltrating arenas like the classroom.

In Her Shoes

From 1970 to 2008, boys have outscored girls on that precollege classic, the SAT test—even when there were more girls than boys taking the test. Girls, however, get better grades than boys in high school and in college.

It's not that girls shrink from competition. They welcome it—often fiercely so. Kathy and other educators find that it's the girls who will come up to fight for an extra point on a paper or argue about a grade. They want to do well, and will fight for it. Girls are just as competitive, if not more competitive, than boys. So what gives?

Math Is Hard!

Well, yeah, math's hard. So what? So is a back one-and-a-half somer-sault tuck from the 10-meter platform. So is French, unless it's your native language. So is writing a poem, shredding a riff on the guitar, swishing a three-pointer at the buzzer, and parallel parking on a hill. And while we're at it, so is raising girls!

Lots of things, especially when you first start doing them or haven't done them for a long time, are hard. But they're not hard just because you're a *girl*. They're hard because they require skill, study, and prac-tice. Now, just about everyone can develop a certain level of skill in just about anything, with enough practice. Some people will always be better—sometimes simply because they have more skill, but most often because they study more and practice longer than other people.

The academic equity issue comes to a head in math and related subjects—chemistry, physics, engineering, and even computer technol-ogy. Are boys truly better than girls in these subjects, or are other fac-tors at play?

In the Genes?

The fracas over girls and math started in the late 1980s when some researchers began to interpret data as suggesting that boys were better at math simply because they were boys. Something about that XY chromosome pairing, these researchers postulated, somehow translated into the ability to solve algebra equations. The XX pairing, these stud-ies further implied, somehow made girls better at English and history. Nature's complement kind of a thing—you know, the "two halves make a whole" concept.

Hmmmm.

The whole mess could've stopped in its tracks had someone, *anyone*, stepped forward to say, whoa there, doesn't that sound just ever so slightly like a sketch on *Saturday Night Live*? But no one did, and boys stayed in the lead by default. Instead, the studies inflamed the debate about single-sex education and drove girls from classes in math, science, and technology. Now, 20-something years later, we're coming around to look again at the same data. And guess what we're finding?

- Until high school, girls and boys perform about equally on standardized math and science tests.

- In high school, girls start choosing classes other than math and science.

- Girls who opt out of math and science classes in high school then struggle in these subjects when they take them in college. (Why this would surprise anyone is a mystery—if you haven't been doing something, what are the odds you'd excel at it until the effect of the learning curve is satisfied?)

The reverse appears to be true for boys, by the way. Boys who opt out of English, history, and similar subjects may struggle in these courses in college. So the final, unsurprising conclusion: sex has nothing to do with academics.

 LOL

Even Barbie got a piece of the action in the math debate when some of the talking Barbie dolls that debuted in 1992 uttered the now-infamous phrase, "Math class is tough!" Though it was one of 270 randomly selected phrases (with each doll speaking only four phrases), it became a flashpoint just about as fast as the words came out of Barbie's computer chip. C'mon, Barbie, we thought you could do *anything!*

The Equality Conundrum

As parents, we want the doors of opportunity to open wide for our daughters. More than that, we want to shove them through those doors, to *make* them succeed. But what happens when they don't *want* to do what we want them to do, what they're good at, what will serve them well when they're adults?

Some pundits dare to suggest, risking wrath on all fronts, that girls don't take "hard" classes like math and science not because they're not smart enough, they don't want to compete with boys, or even because the classes are difficult, but because they simply don't like math or science. It's an interesting position.

Equality doesn't mean everyone or everything has to *be* the same. It means they have the same *opportunities*. Biases, of course, run much deeper than the opinions that support them. Like the roots of weeds in your garden, they twist and turn and double back to sustain their own survival. We're looking at centuries of beliefs and practices that've kept girls out of classes in math and the hard sciences. It's tough to step back and think it might come down to, huh, maybe she really doesn't *like* math.

Do Boys Like Smart Girls?

New studies, along with re-analysis of previous studies, raise yet another explanation: girls don't take math and related subjects, or don't do well in them when they do take them, because they believe boys won't like them if they do better than boys in these subjects. Algebra, trigonometry, physics, chemistry—these are "hard-wired" subjects in the context that there's no waffling when it comes to the right answers—unlike literature, for example, in which answers are often interpretive.

In reality, girls do just as well as boys, if not better, in math and science classes when these classes interest them enough to overcome any social stigma associated with doing well in them. Today's girls are coming up through an educational system that's seen significant change over the past 20 years, and they're the first generation to fully experience these changes from kindergarten on. And in reality, boys *do* like smart girls— what a great way to spend time with someone when your pick-up line can be, "Hey, can you help me with this chemistry problem?"

In Her Shoes

Men outnumber women in math, science, and technology careers by as much as 20 to 1 in some fields, a gap that continues to grow.

No Boys Allowed

So what if there were no boys in school? The girls-only school first entered the academic landscape as a way to educate girls who were refused admission to school because girls just didn't go to school. Such schools have waxed and waned in popularity through the years, recently emerging as a girls-do-better-when-boys-are-out-of-the-picture solution to some of the challenges of educating girls. Some girls do indeed learn and thrive in such an environment, enough so that it's a viable solution for them.

Those who support all-girls schools say a key advantage is that girls feel more freedom to excel in classes where boys might otherwise dominate—like math and science. Others point out that changing the dynamic in mixed-gender classrooms would accomplish the same thing. Critics of sex-segregated schools argue that such settings interfere with the development of normal and necessary social skills (although most girls-only schools arrange with boys-only schools for social activities). The real world, after all, is a male-female mix. And other factors that interfere with learning don't go away just because there are no boys around. Teachers must still work to balance opportunities across knowledge, interest, and ranges.

Bullies

Boys mostly bully other boys, but boys bully girls, too. Boy bullies tend to be more physical and direct in their attacks on girls, just like they are in picking on other boys, and they tend to act alone. A boy bully isn't as likely to beat up a girl, mainly because there just aren't many bully points in that. But he might rush into the seat she's about to take, slam her locker door shut just as she reaches to put her books in, or crowd ahead of her in line, or jostle into her in the hallway. Or he might instead commandeer her iPod in study hall or filch her math homework.

The boy bully can be cruel in what he says, too; not to imply that his entire M.O. is physical or that girls have any lock on mean. The bully boy may spread nasty rumors, scribble a girl's phone number with a suggestive message on the locker room wall, use crude nicknames, and attack a girl's reputation on whatever levels he can. Especially when he's the most popular girl in school's BF. Or wants to be.

Equal Opportunity Bullying

Girls can be bullies, too. Girl bullies mostly pick on each other, although they may pick on boys, too. Your girl knows who the bully girls are in her school, and she's probably worked out her own ways for dealing with them when they turn their attention her way. Which, inevitably, they do, like the velociraptors in *Jurassic Park* that suddenly detect an unwary potential meal who wanders into the field of their senses.

And you could probably pick out the bullies in your daughter's school, too, if you could make like a fly on the wall. They look pretty much like all the other girls, when they're sitting there in class. But when the bell rings, there's no mistaking who they are—they gather their books, get out of their seats, and merge toward each other as though they're joined at the circuitry somehow. And talk about oil and water—as they move together, everyone else moves away.

Girl bullies hunt in packs. Their weapons of choice are snubbing, *outcasting*, innuendo, gossip, and rumor. They use them in calculated and compounded ways. They choose their prey for all kinds of reasons or for no reason at all. No one's safe, not even the girls in the pack. Even boys—especially boys who are shy, different, or keep to themselves rather than hang with a group—are at risk.

def•i•ni•tion

Outcasting is the bullying tactic of treating a girl as if she doesn't exist.

Get a Clue!

Think your daughter surely would tell you if she was being bullied at school? Think again. Although more than three fourths of girls experience bullying at least once during middle school and high school, few of them tell their parents. Those who do often struggle to get their parents to understand what it means. This is not the kind of bullying we grew up with—the big brute of a boy beating up kids for their lunch money. And it's not just about some misguided miscreant saying mean but meaningless things. This kind of bullying redefines ruthless.

There are three general levels of bullying, though the torment can start at any one of them:

◆ Just kidding. Sometimes bullying starts with teasing, some harmless fun with a prank or joke that gets a reaction so beyond expectation that the pack just can't resist doing it again. And again.

◆ Yeah, well, she deserves it. When the mean girls turn on one of their own, there's not a lot of sympathy from anyone. It's hard to feel bad for someone who's made quite the hobby out of making other people's lives miserable. The "deserves it" girl is sometimes someone whose "crime" is that she brings grief upon herself for persisting in being different.

◆ Ouch ... that's really brutal! Nothing redeems this level of attack. It horrifies even the girls in the pack who carry it out—not that that stops them.

How do you know whether your daughter's the target *du jour*? Talk with her every day about how things are going at school. Ask about her friends, by name. Pay attention to names that suddenly drop from her radar screen ... friends who no longer call or come over. Listen between the lines when she talks about things that are happening to other girls, especially when she talks about mean tricks and such.

Experts say girls who are being bullied should do their best to ignore the attacks and avoid their attackers to the extent they can. Sometimes this tactic works; even bullies get bored when the entertainment value of their efforts drops. It's a harsh and backward reality that the one being bullied bears the burden for turning things around, but there you have it.

Take *every* opportunity to reassure your daughter of her strengths and talents. Though your daughter (and even you!) may wish she had a slew of sarcastic put-downs to hurl back, this approach seldom has the desired effect. Instead, it either escalates the bullying or turns your daughter into the bully.

Cyber-Bullying

Camera phones. Text-messaging. MySpace and Facebook. IM. Chat rooms and forums. Even e-mail and the most antiquated electronic device of all, the telephone. Your daughter's world is digital, and it doesn't always reach out to touch in the ways we adults might expect.

There are two key factors that ratchet up the body count when it comes to *cyber-bullying:*

def•i•ni•tion

Cyber-bullying is the use of e-mail, text and picture messaging, instant messaging, and other digital means to harass, intimidate, or embarrass another person.

♦ Messages can reach endless numbers of people just about as fast as a girl can create them. Which is astonishingly fast—forget the typing test, today's girls can do more with only their thumbs than most adults can do on a full QWERTY keyboard. Of course, it helps that there's an extensive language of shortcuts (more about this in Chapter 17).

♦ Once on MySpace, always in cyberspace. She might *think* her posting stays where she sends it, but that's about as likely as her coming down to breakfast dressed in a plaid skirt, white blouse, bobby socks, and saddle shoes. Kids forward, copy, repost, and otherwise share everything that catches their attention.

Today's sticks and stones are cell phones that take pictures and send them to dozens of people with the click of a button (even right in class!) and web pages that let anyone anonymously say anything about anyone else. The damage and hurt they cause is immeasurable. For more on cyber-bullying, see Chapter 17.

Oh, Puh-leeze!

Bullying's not just a problem your daughter faces in school, but one that could well follow her into the workplace. About a third of women face bullying at their jobs, often from co-workers but sometimes from bosses. Workplace bullies who are men make life miserable for male and female co-workers alike, studies show. But when the shop or office bully is a woman, then so, too, are her targets—nearly exclusively.

What's a Girl (and Her Parents) to Do?

We like to encourage our girls to work things out among themselves, so they learn these skills. You're not always going to be there to bail her out or fight her battles, after all. But even the most self-confident girl suffers when she's a bully's target. It's hard enough to deal with all the other stresses of growing up, school, and social relationships. Bullying goes beyond the realm of spats between friends; there's a dysfunction at work here. You can be pretty sure that if your daughter could've worked things out, she would've. So if she's being bullied, you've got to come to her rescue.

You're the parent—step up to the plate. Go to the school. If it's only one class that's involved, talk with the teacher. If it's bigger than one class, meet with the principal. Ask for an investigation and an action plan. (Know, though, that schools can't always tell you what they find or do; laws and school policies safeguard the privacy of matters involving juveniles.) This is usually enough to at least draw attention to the situation—and not the kind of attention bullies like. Consider, too, working with an outside counselor or psychologist if the problems are intense or causing more significant issues like anxiety or depression.

> **Oh, Puh-leeze!**
>
> The most popular shows on television are "reality" shows in which the entertainment value comes of efforts to win at any cost, laughing at and making fun of others, and pushing people to their breaking points. Little wonder bullying is such a problem among young people!

When It's Your Girl Who's the Bully

Bullying is such a prevalent problem, we want to think girls who are bullies have parents in the background who are either oblivious or horrified but don't know what to do. No one really wants to say, "That's my girl, and she's quite the bully!" Truth is, bullies simply have parents. Perhaps even you.

Every girl, at some time or another, isn't very nice to another girl. Might be her best friend, might be the new girl, might be some girl she's never even met before who just happened to be in the wrong place at the right time. But it happens. Sometimes you suspect it's happening with your daughter, though more often the school calls to tell you it is.

Sometimes bullying is such the standard in a girl's environment that she feels she has to bully or be bullied. This is a serious issue for the school to address and resolve. Maybe she's retaliating for the ways she's been bullied, or feels bullying is the only way to get the "respect" of other girls. And maybe she doesn't realize other girls perceive her behavior as bullying.

Again, it's time for you to step up to the plate. Maybe you need to have your daughter talk with someone—a school counselor, perhaps, or a psychologist who specializes in therapy for this kind of behavior. Talk with her yourself, too, to establish expectations, as well as to let her know you're there for her.

The Least You Need to Know

◆ Social expectations and biases about girls and boys affect the ways girls learn and the ways they view education.

◆ The challenges of educating girls have, in the end, more to do with finding what interests and motivates each girl as an individual than a one-size-fits-all solution—or than worrying about where the boys are.

◆ Today's generation of girls has to deal with an extraordinarily cruel and ruthless bully culture that thrives because it stays just below the radar screen of parents and teachers.

◆ Cyber-bullying is a unique and especially damaging phenomenon with far-reaching consequences.

9

Teachers Matter

In This Chapter

- ◆ Teachers are key in shaping your daughter's perspectives and interests
- ◆ Where do male teachers fit into this picture?
- ◆ Getting to know her teachers
- ◆ What teachers wish you knew
- ◆ Heading off trouble

What does your daughter want to be when she grows up? Whether astronaut or veterinarian or anything in between—and even if she changes her mind every week—her path to her dreams and goals starts with the morning school bell. Her teachers are her guides and her mentors, even if she doesn't quite see yet. But you do.

Teachers are often the first role models your daughter directly encounters outside her family. They get somewhat of an automatic endorsement every time you say "the teacher." So your daughter pays close attention to these other adults who are now in her daily life. Your daughter's teachers—in school as well as in other settings— influence your daughter's perception of herself and her capabilities.

School Daze

Your daughter learns as much about how to get along with others, including other adults such as teachers, in her first years of school as she does about identifying story plots in her favorite books, classifying polygons, and finding Rhode Island on a map. Her teacher is her guide to the world beyond the familiar, and gets to know your daughter pretty well over the course of the school year. Meanwhile, your daughter's sizing up the teacher, too. Is the teacher anything like mom, dad, and other adults she knows? Maybe a little, maybe not so much. Until fourth or fifth grade, your daughter likely has the same teacher in the same classroom all day, for every subject. Odds are high this teacher is a woman—not even 1 in 10 elementary teachers in U.S. schools is a man. Your daughter might have a different PE teacher, or art teacher, or music teacher—the specialty kinds of classes. To your daughter, these teachers might seem more like relatives who visit often but don't stay long enough to become truly familiar. This may make the teacher seem more exotic or mysterious—especially if it's a man. But it's the one same teacher who handles everything from the three Rs to playground spats and scraped knees who becomes the cornerstone of your daughter's early experience in school.

In Her Shoes

In the United States, 91 percent of elementary school teachers are women. In middle school and high school, it's about 70 percent. The ratio has been steadily tipping toward women since 1974.

Beginning with fifth or sixth grade, your daughter may have a homeroom where her school day starts and ends, but go to different classrooms for specific subjects. Because each teacher now has three, four, or even five times more students, individual relationships with students are more fragmented and narrowly defined. Your daughter learns that she may have to ask questions rather than wait for the teacher to explain something she doesn't understand. The transition can be unsettling for some girls, although for many it's more of a grand adventure to be able to traipse down the hallways going from one classroom to another. But it's the way of middle school, high school, and beyond. It's good practice for her.

By middle school and through high school, your daughter has a different classroom and teacher for every subject—and she's quick to form opinions about them all. But not necessarily they about her, at least not in the way she's been used to. Your daughter might be fifth period, fourth row, third seat to the teacher for the first few weeks of school. Her teacher might instead know that your daughter has three hamsters named Wynken, Blynken, and Nod that live in a hamster condo in her bedroom—her answer to "what pets I have" on her getting-to-know-you questionnaire—yet not remember *her* name! Some girls struggle with these kinds of changes, finding it a challenge to form connections with others and particularly with other adults.

Male or Female Teacher: Does It Matter?

To a great degree, whether a teacher is male or female does not by itself affect whether your daughter can (or wants to) learn in the classroom. Far more important seem to be the universal characteristics of being enthusiastic, caring, creative, and knowledgeable in the subject being taught. These factors strongly influence how interested your daughter becomes in the subject, and how much effort she's willing to put forth to succeed or excel in the class. But not simply because the teacher is male or female.

Young kids—girls and boys alike—don't seem to pay all that much attention to whether a teacher is a man or a woman. Instead, they key into how much fun they have in the teacher's class. Core subjects are still basic, and most kids don't as yet have many real-world experiences to shape their views as to whether school subjects are "girl classes" or "boy classes." The teacher, male or female, can maintain that balance.

By the time your daughter starts taking courses in specific subjects, she's also starting to develop a sense for whether she expects to have a male or female teacher. Does she sit down in her American literature class and think, "Whoa, dude, a woman teacher"? Nah. Does she take a seat in her physics class and think the same thing? Well, maybe so. Two thirds of her teachers are women, still—the ratio doesn't swing the other direction until she gets to college—and she's more used to seeing male teachers in science and math classes.

In Her Shoes

Research shows that if a student can connect to someone in the school as a mentor or advisor, the child is more likely to want to do well or at least not drop out, even if he or she is struggling. Many schools have formal mentoring programs that team girls with each other as peer mentors, and with teacher-advisors who can support and encourage school work as well as dreams and plans for the future.

Transforming Experiences

When your daughter finds a teacher or other adult who she looks up to, respects, and wants to be like, and the teacher takes an interest in your daughter, the result can be profound. Women who are successful in their careers and lives nearly always point back to that one adult teacher or mentor who made a huge difference when they were growing up. (Men, by the way, tend to give their own efforts more credit.)

Those who study such things call these connections transforming experiences. A girl sees a woman doing something she didn't believe was possible, and suddenly an entire landscape of opportunity opens to her. Teachers are often in the position to be such connections, either through direct example or by presenting girls with new ideas and perspectives.

Does this mean your daughter's male teachers can't be role models for her? Well, not in quite the same way. Your daughter probably doesn't want to be *just* like one of her male teachers—she may want to do something the same way he does it, or can craft her vision of how she could be like him to fit her image of herself as a woman. But it's difficult for her to envision herself emulating his success in the same way she might envision that with a woman teacher or mentor.

Get to Know Your Daughter's Teachers

Quick, say out loud, right now, one thing you know about one of your daughter's teachers beyond the teacher's name. Got something? Great.

Nothing coming to you? Well, okay … can you at least name your daughter's teachers? First and last names? When you know your daughter's teachers, you can start to build a foundation for dialogue with your daughter about what goes on in school—and with the teachers, to stay up with your daughter's assignments, projects, and progress. Teachers often lament that parents behave as though their kids enter some sort of alternate universe when they head off to school in the morning and where they stay until they return home in the afternoon. Conversely, parents who are not connected feel it's almost impossible to bridge the gap between home and school.

Back-to-School Day/Night

This event is for you, the parent. Your daughter can tag along—and often it's insightful for you if she does. (Although few kids do this, so don't feel hurt or offended if your daughter declines.) But back-to-school events are mostly for and about parents. The school gets to showcase its classrooms and environment. You get to meet your daughter's teachers, see the classrooms where your daughter will spend most of her day, and learn about your daughter's courses and their requirements.

If there are handouts, take them. Even if they make you feel like you're the one about to slide into one of those weird, one-armed chairs. The handouts tell you everything you need to know about the teacher and the class, including a *syllabus*, the teacher's expectations for classroom participation, the teacher's grading structure, and major projects or assignments that'll be due throughout the school year. So when your daughter says to you, "But we just got the assignment last week!" you know better.

def•i•ni•tion

A **syllabus** is an outline that describes the course, learning objectives, in-class activities, out-of-class assignments, homework, and key due dates.

Teacher handouts also may include information about how and when are the best times to contact the teacher by e-mail or phone. Some teachers keep the level of information general, both to encourage parents to contact them with questions and to accommodate the inevitable changes that occur as the school year unwinds. Find out if the teacher has a website or a page on the school's website, or uses an electronic platform like Blackboard that allows the teacher to post assignments, information, and sometimes even grades.

Go every year, and go even when you went to the same one last year because your daughter has an older sibling. Maybe it'll be the same stuff, maybe it won't. As you would tell your daughter, though, you won't know if you don't go. Chat a little with the teacher, too. Try to connect in some way over the subject matter the teacher teaches. This shows that you're paying attention—this is more than "that class in the room with the big windows." And you give the teacher more reason to remember your daughter, because you become a tangible, real-life person.

What Teachers Want Parents to Know

Communication runs both ways. Here are seven things your daughter's teachers wish you knew:

1. What you say about teachers and school influences your daughter more than anything teachers say or do. Think an assignment is too hard, pointless, absurd? Take it up with the teacher directly, and not in front of your daughter. You might still feel the same way about the assignment, but at least you'll know why the teacher gave it.

2. No matter what her age, your daughter needs experiences beyond school to give her lessons a practical context. This is why schools schedule field trips. Just as when she was a toddler, look for opportunities to expand your daughter's learning out in the real world.

3. What matters more than grades is that your daughter puts forth her best effort. Not everyone can get straight As, and making that a goal for your daughter might be unrealistic. Plus, it's very stressful for her. Encourage good academic performance, but if your daughter's not getting the grades you think she should get, schedule a conference with the teacher.

4. It helps teachers to know if your daughter's having a problem in school or in her life that could cause changes in her behavior in

the classroom. You don't have to give a lot of details or explanation; often just a "heads-up" mention is enough.

5. Your thoughts, opinions, and comments as a parent and as a stakeholder in the school district matter. Speak up! Remember: even teachers appreciate recognition for good work, and change only happens when people make it happen. In the end, there's no such creature as "the school."

6. Call or e-mail teachers when you have a concern. Set up an appointment for a face-to-face meeting if you've got a big concern. (Your daughter doesn't like sitting next to Susie because Susie hums when she works on her assignments—small concern. Susie steals your daughter's homework and turns it in as her own—big concern.) Even though teachers can be hard to reach (you can't really just ring up in the middle of class), they want to hear from you and to stay in touch. E-mail is usually the most efficient approach for questions with straightforward answers or to schedule a meeting.

7. This is *your* daughter. Teachers take their roles in her life seriously, but *she's your daughter*. You're the one who needs to know what happens every day at school, cheer her when she's down, rally to her defense, and recognize and praise her many successes. What a profound change you'll see in your daughter if you make a point of praising her for one tangible thing every day—not, "You did well today" but "You did a great job on your paper about Napoleon; I learned a lot by reading it, and you have an exciting writing style."

In Her Shoes

Take a field trip yourself—to your daughter's school. You'll have to first sign in at the office, but otherwise you should be able drop by to observe any of your daughter's classes and teachers. Most teachers welcome such parent involvement, although your daughter might be less than thrilled (even mortified) to have you show up at school. This tends to go more smoothly when your daughter's still in elementary school. By middle school and high school, you're better off using less obvious methods—like e-mailing teachers or checking their websites.

Academic Success

Teachers give their all in the classroom and even beyond to educate, encourage, and support kids. But in the end, the single-most important influence on your daughter's success in school is you—her parents. Your daughter needs *your* support and encouragement *every* day. Ask her what homework she has, and sit with her for a few minutes, every now and then, when she's working on it. Engage her in discussions about school projects and assignments that help her connect them with events in the real world. Make homework a priority over chores, social activities, television, and even extracurricular activities related to school.

Making the Grade

There's no end to the debate about grades. Love 'em or hate 'em, they're nonetheless the way schools measure achievement. Grades can be a source of astonishing pressure, especially for girls. Parents often push (okay, nag) their daughters to do well in school. But sometimes their daughters don't want the attention being "smart" draws to them, or might want to take classes that aren't quite as academically oriented as their parents prefer.

Talk with your daughter, often, about grades. Not, "What's your grade in Spanish?" but, "How are you feeling about your work in Spanish class and are you happy with the grade you're getting right now?" She's so much more likely to lay it all out there about where she struggles in the class and what she likes best. You'll get a good sense for whether she's working to her ability—which might be a B or a C—or whether she's slacking. Talk with her teacher, too. If there's a gap in their perceptions big enough to *conduzca un camión por*, it's time for the three of you to meet.

We put a lot of pressure on our girls because we want them to have every opportunity. But not everyone can get straight As. When your daughter is truly doing her best, working to the fullest of her ability, that's got to be good enough.

> **Girl Pearls**
>
> At school I was always trying to con my teachers into letting me act out book reports instead of writing them.
>
> —Laura Linney, American actor

Houston, We've Got a Problem

Three weeks before the end of the school year is not when you want to learn that your daughter's failing World History. Not only is there little to no hope for pulling her grade back from the abyss, but there's also the unpleasant domino effect for the next semester ... or worse. You might be the last to be finding out, but you can be sure it's not news to your daughter—no matter the drama of her response when you confront her about it.

Teachers don't want grades to come as a surprise. They want you and your daughter to know exactly where your daughter stands. Your daughter's academic performance (not to be confused with the Oscar-worthy drama you might get during a discussion of grades) helps teachers to detect learning disabilities as well as your daughter's strengths and interests.

Gone, for the most part, is the black-covered, wire-bound notebook hidden in the second drawer of the teacher's desk. It's a web-based world. Teachers post grades online. Usually access to view them is by password; ask your daughter for hers so you can look at her grades, too. The teacher may also have a parent-access password that's in the packet of handouts you got on back-to-school night.

Make sure you know when interim progress reports come out, so you can check the mail. Attend scheduled parent-teacher conferences. And don't hesitate to send a "Hey, how's my daughter doing?" e-mail to the teacher once in a while. Random acts of checking in help keep your daughter on the straight and narrow with her schoolwork.

Other Mentors in Your Daughter's Life

Lots of people besides teachers influence your daughter: the librarian at the town library where your daughter volunteers, perhaps, or an adult who works with community youth groups. These people may have long-term, ongoing interactions with your daughter and her friends. These are your daughter's mentors, and they help your daughter by encouraging her, often simply through the example of their own lives, to follow her ambitions.

Sometimes encounters occur by chance, and need not be ongoing. Maybe your daughter now wants to be a physician because she made a connection with the doctor who treated her in the emergency department when she broke her collarbone. Perhaps the doctor would take a few minutes to answer some questions for your daughter, or show her around the emergency department. Your daughter will remember this interview for the rest of her life. And who knows … maybe she'll come back someday to practice emergency medicine at this same hospital.

The Sisterhood of Family and Friends

Who are the women in your daughter's daily life, and how do they support and encourage your daughter? Do they reinforce your messages and priorities? Aunts, grandmothers, and close family friends can be strong influences on your daughter. And she's likely to listen to them in ways she won't listen to you! Especially in late middle school and early high school, your daughter's efforts to find her own way of doing things—not like this has ever been a problem for her, but it intensifies when she's transitioning from childhood to womanhood—often translates into that "how could you be so stupid?" look when you, her parents, offer suggestions and advice.

Let the same concepts come from other women she admires and respects, though, and it's like an entirely fresh and profound way of looking at things. Mine this for all it's worth. Someday your daughter will make the connections in her head and recognize you weren't so stupid after all, but for right now what matters most is that she gets the right messages to motivate and focus her.

Dads Matter, Too!

There's no question that girls look to women as their role models; it's only natural. (Boys look to men … same premise.) But that's not to say the men in your daughter's life have little to offer. Dads—and dad-figures like uncles, grandfathers, and sometimes even older brothers—are important to your daughter's evolving sense of herself and to her confidence about her abilities to succeed both in school and in the world. Dad's interest and encouragement can be the boost that pushes her to try new things or persist in mastering subjects that challenge her.

Sometimes Trouble

Sad and sorry to say, we've always got to be on the alert for what we'll collectively call predatory behavior when it comes to the interactions of adults in the lives of our daughters. Even with the web of safeguards and procedures in place to thwart bad influences, they sometimes manage to slip through.

Stay connected and involved on a daily basis with what's going on in your daughter's life! Ask her about classes, school projects, teachers. Be present in your daughter's life in ways that everyone knows you're watching. Your daughter is less of a target when those who might prey on her know you might pop up at any time. When the alarms on your parental radar screen do go off, pay attention. You've got a lifetime of experience behind your intuition, and you're probably pretty good at reading people. It's just that you'd like to feel you can turn off this radar when it comes to trusting the people in your daughter's life. We all want to feel we can trust them, unequivocally. We can't. Not blindly.

And we also can't emphasize enough that most of the adults in your child's daily life—teachers, mentors, advisors, youth group leaders, church leaders—are 110 percent trustworthy. Like you, they'd hurl themselves in front of a charging momma bear to save your daughter—in a heartbeat, and without a second thought. But they, like you, understand the new dynamic of what it means to work with kids today. They've been screened, assessed, interviewed, and investigated. None of us likes that this is the way things are, that we have to "prove" we're good people before we can interact with kids. But we all know this is the way things are, and we accept the screening and the checking because we want to do all we can to keep our kids safe. Do some nefarious adults slip through? Sadly, yes. No system is foolproof.

 Oh, Puh-leeze!

We do a great job educating our daughters about "stranger danger" and other hazards. It's harder to teach them that the people they know and trust to help them might not be who they seem. Encourage your daughter to talk with you about all of her interactions with adults. She may not get it that there's a problem brewing, but you might.

You're the Hall Monitor

Your regular contact with the mentors in your child's life is the best way to pick up the danger signs that all is not what it seems to be. Unfortunately, it's easy to assume everything's okay. You don't want to be running your daughter's life. But you do want to stay plugged in.

What can you do? Maintain a constant presence. You don't have to be at all the meetings or events, but drop in for one or two at random. The element of surprise is often enough itself. Talk to your daughter after meetings and events. Gauge her demeanor and tone as you're listening to what she's saying. Sometimes you've got to ask all around a question rather than asking the question directly. But by letting your daughter simply talk, you'll get far more information.

If you suspect anything untoward, take your concerns to the school, youth organization, church administration—even the police. Insist on a full investigation, and remove your daughter from contact with the person until the situation is resolved. Sometimes parents want to make excuses for behavior they know is wrong. But the life that suffers most is your daughter's.

Cultivating Confidence

We can't—and don't want to—have our girls running from one tree to another, metaphorically speaking, afraid for what unknown dangers lurk out in the open. We want our daughters to feel safe, confident, and strong as they venture further toward independence. We need to encourage them to be savvy as they step out into independence.

The Least You Need to Know

◆ A teacher's interest and encouragement can open your daughter's eyes and mind to new possibilities.

◆ Your daughter is likely to form stronger bonds with a woman teacher she admires because your daughter can look at that teacher and say, "I want to be like her."

◆ Girls who form strong bonds with teachers and other adult mentors are more confident in themselves and their abilities to achieve their dreams.

◆ Despite systems and procedures in place to screen adults who work with kids, sometimes one slips through with nefarious intent.

◆ Talking with your daughter every day about her schoolwork, teachers, and other adults is critically important to keeping these interactions safe and positive for your daughter.

For the First Time

First period, first friends, first dance, first date—middle school is an exciting time of new experiences for your girl. In these chapters, we'll look at girls' emerging sense of individuality and uniqueness, even as she struggles with the notion of what it means to "fit in." What kind of young woman does your girl aspire to be? What messages about modesty, sexuality, and, well, womanhood does society send to girls who are growing up? Let's look with a beginner's mind at this time of initiation and transformation as your girl experiments with new experiences, feelings, and expectations.

Chapter

First Period

In This Chapter

- What's up with her?
- How much does she know that's not quite so? A self-quiz to clue you in
- Puberty's but a stage …
- Should she or shouldn't she—wear a bra, that is
- She's a woman now

There's *nothing* to *wear*. (Never mind the piles of clothes on the floor that seem to propagate of their own accord.) There's *nothing* to *eat*. (What about the $187.63 you just spent at the grocery store?) Everyone is so-o-o-o-o-o-o *annoying*. (You, most particularly.) I hate you! Can you give me a ride to school? Otherwise I'm gonna *miss* last *bell* and then I *might* as well *just stay home*. (Oh, please, no … where are those car keys?)

What's up with her these days? In a word: estrogen.

Yep. Estrogen, that most womanly hormone. It's surging, and it's pushing and pulling your daughter to the threshold of, well, womanhood. It's reshaping her body, remodeling her mind, and swinging her moods. Someday maybe you'll look back on this time as funny or even poignant, but right now all you dare hope for is to make it through the next five minutes with your sanity intact. (Good luck with that.)

Puberty Strikes!

It may seem that your daughter simply emerges one morning from her bedroom a woman, like a butterfly from a cocoon. But puberty is really a process, a transition that extends over about four to six years. Most girls are at least apprehensive about the changes beginning to take place in their bodies. Their flight to the unknown, exciting threshold of womanhood is inexorable. Yet puberty is also a unique experience for each girl.

The Talk

Maybe you've worried since your daughter's first gusty wails about "the talk." You know, the one where you sit by your daughter's side, take her hand gently and lovingly in yours, and explain the facts of life and all that. Not! By the time you feel ready, your daughter could give *you* the talk. Our girls grow up faster and at a younger age than we realize, pushed by a culture that exposes them to far more facts—and falsehoods—of life than we ever had to consider.

"The talk" really should be not an anxiety-riddled event but rather an ongoing dialogue you've been having with your daughter since the first time she asked why boys get to pee standing up and girls have to sit. Or what breasts *do*. Or why you have hair *there*. And of course, where do babies come from? The best preparation you can give your daughter is to help her understand the natural and wonderful progression of life, as she both experiences and observes it.

We're much better, as parents, about this today than were parents 20 or 30 years ago. Dads no longer pace the hallways, awaiting the call for pink or blue. They're right in the thick of things during childbirth, often first to hold the newborn and cut the umbilical cord. And it's not uncommon for siblings to gather around as well, welcoming the newest family member at first breath.

Still, many parents face the advent of puberty with a mix of dread and pride. That sweet little girl is growing up, and with the transition comes a whole new set of challenges and increasing independence as she makes her way into adulthood. Girls themselves, on the other hand, tend to be more concerned about whether they look like everyone else as their bodies are beginning to change.

Truth or Myth?

There's a lot of misinformation about puberty floating around out there. How much of what your daughter hears or believes is actually true? How much of what *you* know is fact … or simply not so? Check it out with this quick quiz. Check "truth" or "myth" for each of these statements.

1. Shaving causes leg and underarm hair to grow back faster, thicker, and darker.

   ____ Truth

   ____ Myth

2. Girls don't need to start shaving their underarms and legs until they're in high school.

   ____ Truth

   ____ Myth

3. Girls don't need bras until they're at least 12 years old.

   ____ Truth

   ____ Myth

4. Most girls start their periods around age 12.

   ____ Truth

   ____ Myth

5. Once a girl starts her periods, she won't grow any taller.

   ____ Truth

   ____ Myth

6. Girls don't start their periods until they weigh at least 100 pounds.

   ____ Truth

   ____ Myth

7. A girl's first period might not appear to be bleeding.

   ____ Truth

   ____ Myth

8. The typical period passes about a pint of blood … the same amount as when you donate blood.

   ____ Truth

   ____ Myth

9. Girls should avoid strenuous physical activity during their periods.

   ____ Truth

   ____ Myth

10. Periods come once a month.

    ____ Truth

    ____ Myth

11. A girl should not take a bath or go swimming during her period.

    ____ Truth

    ____ Myth

12. Some girls grow "moustaches" and "sideburns" during puberty.

    ____ Truth

    ____ Myth

How many "truths" did you mark? If you found three, give yourself a pat on the back. (Well, if you got the *right* three.) Here's how the mythology of puberty shakes out:

1. *Myth.* Genetics determines how fast, thick, and dark hair grows. All shaving does is remove visible hair at the skin-surface level. However, hair all over the body does tend to darken and thicken

in the transition from childhood to adulthood. Because that's when girls start shaving or otherwise removing body hair, it's easy to get the false impression that shaving affects the growth of body hair.

2. *Myth*. The shaving of women's underarms and legs is a cultural convention, not a matter of health or hygienic need. Women in much of the world beyond the United States and some parts of Western Europe do not typically shave or otherwise remove body hair. That said, if you, mom, and your daughter's friends shave their pits and legs, your daughter is likely to feel great pressure to do so herself. Because shaving does not change the characteristics of body hair (see statement 1), there's no reason to keep your daughter from shaving when she wants to start. Just make sure she knows how to properly use a razor.

3. *Myth*. Another matter of need versus convention. While girls don't actually *need* bras at all, the time to start wearing one is a) when breast buds appear, or b) when a girl says she wants to wear one … even if it seems she doesn't need one.

4. *Truth*. The average age for girls to start their periods is 12—when they're in seventh grade. However, the range of normal runs from ages 9 to 17.

5. *Myth*. Girls tend to reach their adult height between ages 14 and 16, although they can continue to grow taller even into their early 20s. A girl who starts her period when she's 15 or 16 years old may indeed be done growing, but not because of her periods.

6. *Myth*. Many girls do weigh between 100 and 120 pounds when they have their first periods. However, quite a few weigh less or more. Body fat percentage, more so than body weight, is one emerging factor. A low percentage of body fat (less than 12 percent) tells the body it's not capable of sustaining another life and triggers the mechanisms that shut down the menstrual cycle. Girls who are intense athletes sometimes drop below this threshold and their periods stop. Girls who have low body weight (and corresponding low body fat) because they're very athletic may start menstruating at a later age than other girls. The eating disorder anorexia nervosa may also delay or stop menstruation.

7. *Truth.* Yes, a girl's first period may not look at all like the bleeding she expected. Instead, it may be a brownish, sticky discharge that lasts only a couple days.

8. *Myth.* It sure looks like a lot of blood. But it's not: only 2 to 4 tablespoons each period—about an ounce to an ounce and a half is the average.

9. *Myth.* A girl's period is a normal and healthy function of her body. There's no reason to limit any activity because of it. Tampons are a good choice for girls who participate in sports. Girls can use tampons from the time they begin menstruating, although many prefer to start with pads because pads are easier to deal with. It's important to talk with your daughter about changing tampons frequently, making sure they're completely inserted, and what to do if the string disappears.

10. *Myth.* Periods can be from 21 to 45 days apart, though the average is 28 to 34 days. For the first year or so, periods can be wildly erratic in all aspects of their timing, from when they arrive to how long they stay. After a year or so, the cycle stabilizes to be more or less predictable, though not necessarily monthly. Stress (physical and emotional), illness (like colds and flu), and intense physical activity are among the factors that can influence the menstrual cycle.

11. *Myth.* Bathing and swimming during periods are perfectly fine—and bathing is certainly desirable, given that the typical period lasts about six days! Most girls prefer showering to sitting in the bathtub. A related myth is that menstrual bleeding stops when a girl (or woman) is in water, like a bath or pool. It does not. Girls who want to swim during their periods need to use tampons to absorb the menstrual flow internally. But there are no adverse health effects associated with water and menstruation.

12. *Truth.* Those surging hormones are not yet in balance, and when they overshoot their mark they may cause excessive hair growth on a girl's face and also on her arms and legs. This generally lasts only a short time, until the hormones rebalance themselves. Rarely, unusual puberty reflects an underlying medical cause. So don't

hesitate to talk with your daughter's pediatrician or regular health care provider if you have any concerns about your daughter's development.

Oh, Puh-leeze!

Generally speaking, a doctor should evaluate a girl who has her first period before age 8 or who hasn't started her period by age 17. Although either can be normal, both approach the extremes of the range. A number of hormonal and other health conditions (such as pituitary or thyroid disorders, or certain genetic conditions) can affect the onset and progression of puberty. But also consider seeing your doctor if your daughter seems overly worried. Some reassurance from someone other than "my parents" is often very helpful.

What Girls Worry About

As their bodies are beginning to change, girls have a lot of worries and concerns. The more they know about these changes, the better able they are to anticipate and adjust. But even so, no matter how much they research (even if that just means grilling mom), it's hard to truly *know* what it feels like to have periods if you've never experienced one. Girls pick up fragments of information from their moms, aunts, and older sisters, as well as their friends who've already started their periods. They may be afraid periods will hurt, or worry that they'll lose too much blood. A girl may ponder whether a period starts and stops like a faucet, because adult women are always "running to the bathroom" when they've got their periods.

So keep the dialogue open with your daughter during this time of transition. Take advantage of opportunities that bring up these topics, like TV shows and commercials, or shopping trips to Target or the grocery store. Even if she acts like she doesn't want to talk or isn't listening, you can be sure she's paying very close attention not only to what you say but also to how you act.

Those Wild and Wacky Hormones

The hormonal changes that transform your daughter from a little girl into a young woman start earlier than many parents recognize. What do you think ... seventh grade? Sixth grade? Fifth grade? Take one more step back: those hormones start bubbling somewhere around age 9 or 10 ... fourth grade. Most of the early changes stay behind the scenes, though, sometimes with the only hint that they're going on being those out-of-the-blue outbursts that cause you to look at this girl of yours and ask (sometimes out loud), who *are* you?

Genetics, ethnicity, and environment all play roles in how—and when—your daughter develops. Medical science defines five stages of puberty. Knowing what they are can give you a timeline of sorts for your daughter's march through this progression. Remember, though, that age ranges are broad and average ages are just that. What's more important is to note your daughter's age when she enters a stage, and then look at how long that stage generally lasts. Some girls step right through the stages in precise order and timing; other girls may linger in one stage or shoot through another.

The Five Stages of Puberty

Stage	Average Age Stage Starts	Stage Lasts About ...	Key Characteristics
1	8 to 10 years	2 years	None visible, although hormonal changes are and underway ovaries are enlarging
2	10 to 12 years	1 year	Breasts begin to form bumps (often one breast then the other)
			Pubic hair begins to grow
			Growth spurt of about 3 inches in height in a year
3	12 to 14 years	1 year	Further breast growth
			Underarm hair begins to grow
			Hair on legs begins to get thicker and darker
			Pubic hair grows thicker, darker, and more coarse or curly

Stage	Average Age Stage Starts	Stage Lasts About …	Key Characteristics
			Clear or whitish vaginal discharge at times
			Another growth spurt that may be 3 inches or more in a year
4	12 to 14 years	1 year	Breasts have adult shape though are smaller than adult size
			First period
			Growth slows to an inch or two in a year
5	15 to 16 years	1 year	Breasts are adult size
			Periods become regular, with monthly ovulation
			Reaches adult height

Some girls can't wait to announce that they've finally sprouted a few "pubes." Others girls tell no one of the changes taking place in their bodies, and may even go to great lengths to minimize or hide them. Wherever she is on the spectrum, though, nearly every girl worries about whether what's happening in *her* body is normal. It's hard to be on the early end of things—the first to wear a bra and start her period. It's equally stressful to be on the late end of things. Though kids today are more broadly accepting of differences and diversity, sometimes they still tease—and teasing can feel hurtful and even cruel. The more relaxed you are about the changes your daughter's experiencing, the calmer she will feel.

In Her Shoes

If your daughter's breasts appear to be different sizes, or if one starts to grow but the other doesn't, don't panic. It's normal for one breast to start developing first, and also for breast size to continue to be uneven through the development stages. Even many adult women have one breast slightly smaller than the other.

Some girls want to know every little biochemical detail about what's happening in their bodies and why. Other girls want to know only what they'll experience (such as enlarging breasts and menstrual bleeding) and what it will be like. Nearly all schools provide some kind of teaching about personal health matters. However, health classes in school range from excellent to woeful in the information they provide. If you've always been closely involved with your daughter's classes and teachers, you'll know where her school aligns along this spectrum. Many schools send home forms for parents to sign for any classes that have content about sexuality, so this is one heads-up for you. Take a close look at the curriculum, and talk with the teacher if you have questions about how the class covers topics.

Breasts and Bras

Breasts start to develop early in puberty, about two years or so before the first period. Girls who are on the early end of the development spectrum may feel uncomfortable or embarrassed to have breasts when none of their friends do. Girls who are on the far side of the curve also may feel uncomfortable or embarrassed because everyone has breasts but them. Some girls want to have big breasts because they feel it makes them popular. Other girls would gladly trade their large breasts for a smaller set, tired of being teased and feeling different. But in only a few short years, the dust finally settles and most girls become comfortable with what they've got.

And right away, girls worry about when they should start wearing bras—and particularly bras with cups. The answer is really pretty simple: a girl can start wearing a bra when she feels she needs to. Wearing or not wearing a bra has no effect on how breasts develop. The basic bra (sometimes called a training bra, for reasons no one seems to know … her breasts are training for what, exactly?) is more like a half-cami than a bra, and more for modesty than support. Other "starter" options include full camis with shelf bras and light-activity sports bras. These styles provide low-key coverage.

A bra with cups is a bra with a mission: to support and protect. It holds the breasts so they don't bounce around. An underwire bra takes this mission very seriously, providing extra support for larger breasts (and added "boost" for smaller breasts). The bouncing part doesn't so much affect the structure and growth of breasts—breasts are not going to get bigger or sagging just because they're free. But they are likely to feel uncomfortable during activities like running or even walking, and most teenage girls are not keen on displaying their breasts so flagrantly (although you might sometimes think otherwise, looking at clothing styles). They tend to prefer some degree of modesty, or at least a carefully constructed illusion of immodesty.

Is your girl a water child? If so, you'll want to help her find swimwear that she's comfortable wearing—and you're comfortable looking at her wearing. Bathing suits designed for beach strolling and pool-side lounging may have halter-style support or actual cups. Suits intended for actual swimming may at best have a shelf bra though often only a lining. Make sure she actually tries on the suit that's caught her eye, so she can see how it looks on *her*. Even if she wants to flirt with being revealing, she doesn't want to fall out of her top—and she doesn't have to be big-breasted for this to be a concern.

I Don't Want to Wear a Bra!

Ever since singer Madonna pioneered intimate apparel as outerwear, girls have had the freedom not just to burn their bras as a political statement à la Gloria Steinem '70s style feminism, but to manipulate *how* they wear bras ... and *why*. This generation of girls is free to wear bras for their own reasons, and so the wearing or not wearing of bras is liberated for today's girls from other considerations or expectations imposed by society. Bravo!

What if your girl doesn't want to wear a bra? (Indeed, savvy girls already reject pantyhose ... as savvy women have for quite some time!) Well, there's really no harm to your breasts in going braless. Wearing a bra or not wearing a bra is more a matter of personal preference than any kind of health matter. A girl may

LOL

How many bras does your daughter own? The average American adult woman has six, with the most popular color being basic black. Girls often like their bras bright and colorful, though, giving rise to an endless variety of solids, stripes, and even polka dots.

resist wearing a bra for any number of reasons. She might not be sure how to find the right size, or feels a bra makes her bust looks too big or too small. She might feel shy or embarrassed about shopping for a bra. Maybe someone's teased her at school. Perhaps the prospect of growing up scares her just a little … or a whole lot. Or maybe she just doesn't want to wear a bra for no particular reason—at least that she's going to share with *you*.

It's okay to honor this braless streak. Because bras are part of the American cultural norm, most girls eventually do wear them. Some moms just buy a few bras of different styles—from cami to sports bra to traditional bra—and slip them into the underwear drawer with the hope that eventually their daughters will just put them on one day, and that'll be that. Often, that's exactly what happens. (And what if you find a stealth thong among the panties? Sigh … Slip a package of thong-size menstrual pads in her drawer, or confiscate the thong!) But if she's bra-resistant, it doesn't hurt to try to talk with your daughter about what's worrying her. It might be something you can relieve with a few comforting words.

I'm Never Taking This Bra Off!

What if your girl's on the opposite end of the spectrum and doesn't want to take off her bra, even at night? On this one, there are some potential health issues. It's not really a good idea to wear any item of clothing all day and all night, especially one that fits tightly against the skin, as bras do. At best it's likely to cause some chafing and skin irritation, which is not very comfortable. Some girls are self-conscious about their blossoming breasts. If your girl is one of them, maybe you can coax her to switch to a cami under her jammies. Some girls experience breast tenderness, and feel wearing a bra helps protect their breasts from further irritation. Again, something less restrictive, like a cami, might be a better alternative. If your daughter insists on wearing a bra even at night, try to get her to at least put on a fresh bra when she changes into her nightclothes.

Beyond the Bra as Functional

We did bring up Madonna earlier, so we'd be remiss not to comment on bras and other foundational clothing as items of fashion. Some girls will want to expand into strapless bras, cleavage-boosting bras, and even bustiers. Breasts have a sexual connotation; it's natural for girls to want to explore this dimension of their emerging womanhood. Your role as parent, of course, is to keep this exploration appropriate. As with other areas of her life, your daughter's trying on different roles. She might wear a bustier Madonna-style simply because to her it seems funny or outrageous or no big deal. Same with those bust-boosters—she just wants bigger breasts because all her friends have them. Though you want to keep a cautious eye turned her way, your daughter has her own set of limits. And wherever those aren't defined quite clearly enough or she steps beyond them, peer pressure will pull her back. Chapter 13 talks more about fashion and boundaries.

The Big Day

The day a girl starts her first period is a big moment in her life. She's been preparing for a few years now, looking forward to this day with excitement and a bit of trepidation. There's no going back, that's for sure. Childhood is now behind her, even though she may act more like your little girl than ever before (read, *tantrums*) until she becomes more comfortable with this monumental change. Doctors call this first period *menarche*—the start of menstruation.

def•i•ni•tion

Menarche is the medical term for a girl's first menstrual period.

Hopefully you've been helping your daughter become emotionally ready and practically prepared for this big event, and she's been talking with you about what she's feeling as the time approaches—maybe she's been queasy or crampy, or unusually irritable. When she lets you know she's started her period, it's good to review the basics with her—like how often to change her pads, how to dispose of used pads, and how to handle pad changes at school or other places away from home. For all the "head smarts" she might have about what it means that she's starting her period, she doesn't really know what to do or how to do it because she's never done it. The more direct and matter-of-fact you are in helping her find her way, the more quickly she'll be at ease with this new experience.

It's also good to eyeball the girl to see if she looks like she's feeling uncomfortable, and offer some suggestions for relief if that seems to be the case. Her first period might be little more than two days of light bleeding, or she might have cramps and other discomforts. Let her tell you how she feels. Then you can respond in positive and supportive ways.

Many cultures celebrate a girl's first period as a rite of passage, with ceremonies and special events. You might want to have some sort of celebration with your daughter, to help her feel that this change in her life is something special. Not a big announcement or anything like that; that would be certain to embarrass her. But maybe a fun lunch with her mom, aunts, and older sisters—a "welcome to womanhood" event.

Period Products

Chances are your daughter has a good handle on period products—and likely even a supply of them—well before she has her first period. Girls talk. They share their likes, dislikes, and preferences. And girls watch the older women in their lives. Daughters generally know what products their mothers use, and may even have experimented with them. (That's why there aren't as many left in the box as you thought you remembered.)

LOL

Think Tampax was the first tampon? Not exactly. Thousands of years ago, ancient Egyptian women rolled their own, so to speak, of sea sponges, wool, and grasses. Tampax, however, was one of the first tampons to become available in the United States, debuting in the early 1930s.

In the beginning, most girls use pads. It's easier, although medically speaking, it's fine for girls to use tampons even from their first periods. Girls who are active in sports, especially swimming, may prefer to use tampons from the beginning. But some girls (and even some moms, too!) are a bit squeamish with the idea of putting something into their bodies—and getting it back out. For this reason, most girls start out using pads, until they get comfortable with the whole idea and process of periods.

But I Just Had My Period!

For the first year or so that she's menstruating, your daughter might feel that all she does is wait for her period to come—and it's either late or early. In the beginning, the menstrual cycle is irregular. Your daughter may have her first period, then not have a second period for two or three months. Or she might start bleeding again in three weeks. The range of what's normal is quite broad. But things will settle into a more predictable pattern after a year or so, as her hormones stabilize.

We talk about periods being monthly, but this isn't quite accurate and is often confusing or frustrating to newly menstruating girls. The typical cycle—from the first day of one period to the first day of the next period—is 24 to 28 days, with the period itself lasting five to seven days. But girls often get confused about how to count the days of their cycles. A more practical approach, especially in the beginning, is to help your daughter learn to pay attention to the signals her body sends, so she can anticipate her period based on what's happening with her body. As she becomes more familiar and her body settles more into a routine, then she can more easily correlate her periods with the calendar.

Dads and Periods

Some girls are perfectly comfortable talking about their periods and anything else in their lives with their dads. But if your daughter's not one of them, that's okay. It's not that she doesn't trust you, or feels she *can't* talk to you about such matters. It's that the whole period thing is all pretty new to her, on top of all the other changes taking place in her body over which she has no control, and she'd just as soon not have to talk to *anyone* about it. And a lot of dads might say, "Right back at you!" This time during which a daughter is transitioning from little darling to young woman is especially awkward for both dads and daughters.

When there's a mom or a big sister or an aunt who can step into the picture, most everyone breathes a sigh of relief. If you're a single dad or a dad primarily responsible for your daughter's care, you've got to be the one. Regardless, stay matter-of-fact. Menstruation, after all, is a natural process and you know at least a little something about it. Today's girls are pretty self-sufficient, but until she can drive herself and has a source of income beyond her allowance, she needs you to at least keep her stocked with period products.

What's Up with the Period Pill?

Gary often gets questions from both moms and girls about whether there's a pill that can just stop periods. There is: it's the so-called period pill, which is really an oral contraceptive (birth control pill) that you take all the time instead of 21 days on (active) and 7 days off (placebo). Many doctors believe these continuous birth control pills, as they're called, cause no harm. They say there's no research to support a biological reason a woman needs to have regular periods, unless she wants to become pregnant.

Other health experts question the long-term affects of altered hormones within the body. Though so far no research suggests there are any adverse effects from long-term hormone suppression, the approach does change the body's natural rhythms. Some people further question the message it sends to young women that their periods are nothing more than inconvenient interruptions of their lives and activities. And the reality remains that suppressing periods is, of course, contraception. Chapter 18 talks in-depth about the pressures girls face today to become sexually active.

The Least You Need to Know

- Puberty is the transition from childhood to adulthood, lasting about four to five years for most girls.

- Girls worry about the changes taking place in their bodies, even when they know the changes are normal.

- Breast development is usually the first sign that a girl has entered puberty.

- A girl's first period generally comes about two to two and a half years after her breasts begin to grow.

- A girl can wear a bra when she feels she wants to … and go braless if it suits her; bras are more about culture and fashion than about health.

- The range of "normal" ages for a girl's first period stretches from 9 to 19 years, although most girls have their first periods around age 12.

Chapter 11

Best Friends Forever

In This Chapter

- ◆ Girls gotta have friends
- ◆ When parents should step in ... and back off
- ◆ Groups rock—and rule
- ◆ Friendships that challenge
- ◆ Your daughter's boy friends

They laugh together, cry together, share their deepest secrets, and plot new adventures. They have sleepovers and pass notes to each other in class. They IM, TM, and VM. They're on each other's MySpace friends' lists. Mostly they love each other; sometimes they hate each other. You might think they're siblings except they get along too well and go to different homes most nights.

These are your daughter's peeps—people—and her BFFs—best friends forever. They matter in your daughter's life as much as you do, and sometimes even more. Girls just gotta have fun ... and that means *friends*. And girls tend to form friendships that last over a long span of time—years, decades, and even a lifetime. Or until one crosses a line from which there is no stepping back.

BFFs are like beautiful meadows where wildlife roams free—you've got to watch your step.

Girl Friends

Every girl yearns for that one special BFF among her peeps who is the one friend she can trust above all temptations and enticements, the one friend she can tell *everything* and be confident that what she says stays in confidence. Ah, don't we all! And many of us are fortunate enough, now that we're adults, to have such friends—some of them the friends we made when we were our daughters' age.

Girls are drawn to one another in friendships for various reasons. Maybe your daughter admires the brashness of a friend because she herself is less outspoken. Maybe it's your daughter who's the bold one, and she seeks friends who are quiet and calming. Maybe the bonds of friendship center on common interests like reading, music, fashion, or sports. Just as often as you might know why your daughter chooses her friends, you might have no clue. She and her BFF might be so much alike that they finish each other's sentences or say the same things at the same times, or pick up the phone in anticipation of it ringing; they may text each other simultaneously, where one sends the answer as the other sends the question. Or your daughter's BFF might be someone who seems, to you, to have little in common with her. But somewhere, in some way, they've connected with each other. Will they truly be best friends forever? Maybe!

In Her Shoes

Friends are important for many reasons, not the least of which is that girls choose their friends themselves. No one can mandate friendship—not parents, not teachers. Adults can tell kids to play together, but they can't make them be friends. Forming friendships is one of a girl's first expressions of her own interests and desires.

Girls want for their friends to all like each other, too, and they'll work hard among themselves to resolve disagreements and differences that threaten group alliances. They build tight networks of their collective BFFs, expecting all to remain loyal within the circle of friends. When one has a problem, all work to find a solution. Girls, far more so than boys, are determined to talk things through and work things out among themselves to preserve their friendships. (Getting a boy to *start* talking is often as challenging as getting a girl to *stop* talking. Sounds cliché, but it proves true!)

The Parent Trap: Bolstering or Butting In?

How—and how much—should you try to help when your daughter seems to be having trouble with friends? Hard as it is to watch someone we love struggle and flail, it's exceedingly important for your daughter to learn how to manage the relationships in her life by herself, without interference (however helpful) from you. That said, it's also exceedingly important for you to step in there for your girl when she needs your help—and for her to know you'll do so.

You need to know what makes your girl tick, and to know when she really *does* need your intervention and when the better part of valor is to simply listen to her. Sometimes the process of talking is all she needs to help her work things through, and she'll come to the right solutions on her own. Sometimes you can ask questions to lead her to solutions she hasn't yet considered, or lead away from those that are more likely to make things worse. Sometimes you can share your observations—with due caution and nonjudgmentally; this is a minefield where the wrong words can explode in unexpected ways. And once in a great while, you might be able to make a suggestion.

But you can't solve your daughter's friendship problems for her—even if they take you back to a similar place in your own childhood and you now know what you wish you would've known then. Hard as it is to watch her flail and suffer, you've got to let her learn, for herself and in her own way, how to navigate these sometimes-treacherous waters. This is the time in her life when she's supposed to learn these lessons; now is when she figures out what it means to be herself, share herself in ways that preserve and support who she is, and shelter herself from those who would have her instead be who they'd like her to be.

This is what adolescence is all about: learning to be an adult, to work through problems and make choices that are sometimes hard to make. She'll scream at you that you don't know what it's like. (Hah!) And you'll scream in your own head (though not out loud … that might scare you both) that you didn't know you'd have to go through all this again—and it'd be worse the second time around because now it tears at two hearts. But you can use what you now know to help your daughter figure things out, because part of what you now know is that the more things change, the more things stay the same. At the core of it, the challenges your girl has with her friends are the same challenges you had with yours: things like trust, honesty, loyalty, teasing, and competition, to name a few. Only the trappings of the times are different.

Oh, Puh-leeze!

Sometimes problems that appear minor to you are very major to your daughter. She's waving a huge red flag if she suddenly loses interest in a favorite activity, no longer wants to go to school, starts skipping classes, or begins getting in trouble at school. It's time for you to get involved—sit down with her for a serious talk and maybe talk with teachers and others at the school. Small squalls blow over in a few days. Anything that lasts longer needs your attention and perhaps your intervention.

It's Not Always Easy to Make Friends

Some girls make friends everywhere they go. They're not necessarily one of the "pops"—popular girls—but other girls—including the pops—like them. They're outgoing and genuinely interested in other people. They make others feel comfortable. Every girl wants such of a friend. But not every girl makes friends so easily. For most girls, making friends is a process that takes effort and time—and more of both, the older they get. Some girls are even so shy that they avoid new situations and people. Challenging situations up the ante for girls who already struggle to make friends—moving to a new neighborhood or transferring to a different school or friends who move away, changes in the family situation like divorce or the birth of a new sibling, and even personal health problems.

As parents, we want to jump in to help our daughters find the friends they crave. We mastermind playdates and sign her up for every club or activity she expresses a passing interest in. But like setting up blind dates between our own adult friends that we just *know* will hit it off, the odds are not very good that we'll succeed at pairing our daughters with their BFFs. We see a blend of what we want to see and what our daughters want us to see about them. Sometimes what your daughter does best—say, playing the violin or writing poetry or mountain hiking isn't what she wants to do most. So your trying to craft friendship opportunities within such talents doesn't serve her very well.

Take a week to observe your daughter, as you might if she were a niece come to stay with you for a while. Try to see and experience her as a young woman separate from your experience of her as a little girl. What makes her laugh? What does she do and say to make other people laugh? What does she do when she thinks you're not watching? What are her favorite books, movies, foods, sports, video or computer games, and television shows?

LOL

In the 2003 movie *Freaky Friday* Lindsay Lohan and Jamie Lee Curtis star as daughter and mother who literally switch places one mysterious Friday the thirteenth. Though the film plays the out-of-body adventure mostly for laughs, both characters learn they're more alike than different. Oh ... and if you're a film buff and you're thinking, wait a minute, didn't Jodie Foster get a Golden Globe nomination for her role as the daughter? Good job! The first *Freaky Friday* film, based on the same 1972 novel by Mary Rodgers, featured Foster with Barbara Harris as the mother, and it hit movie theaters in 1976.

The Anguish of Betrayal

Your daughter heads off to school cheerful and eager, but comes home in tears. Her BFF is now someone else's BFF and, by the time your daughter arrived at school, had already moved her things out of the locker she and your daughter had shared. They've been locker partners since fifth grade—"forever" through the lens of youth—and your daughter is disbelieving and devastated.

It might well turn out that your daughter goes to school tomorrow or the next day and finds her locker partner's moved back in. Or your daughter may herself find a new BBF by dinnertime. Sometimes the ups and downs of teenage friendships can be dizzying, and all you can do as a concerned and loving parent is hang onto the rail—sometimes white-knuckled—while you watch.

Let In, Left Out

Little matters more to tween and teen girls than fitting in, being part of a group. This has always been true for girls, but today, groups provide girls a sense of belonging and security unlike previous generations. Today's girls bond around various factors and common interests, but what's conspicuously absent is a preoccupation with dating and boys. The focus is more likely on where the girls want to go, and do. When a girl group is together, like in the hallways during class changes or at lunch in the cafeteria, it seems to move all as one. The girls who belong walk in step, jostle each other in unison, laugh in harmony. Other groups acknowledge them—smiles, head tosses, finger lifts—in passing, and may even smile as well because the positive energy is contagious.

As much as groups are about inclusion, they're just as much—and sometimes even more—about exclusion. Negative energy is also contagious, and much harder to overcome. Groups can be the source of enormous anguish when they turn their collective backs on one of their own—or those who want to be part of them. Their "rules" are mysterious and often unspoken though everyone knows them. Rigid yet fluid, so no one ever really knows them. Groups rock—and rule.

It's My Party and You're (Not) Invited

Girls learn very early in their lives that the ability to include or exclude someone else is a great power. Some learn to wield this power with equally great skill, while others dabble in it just enough to every now and again get what they want. At its best, this power lets girls be their best selves—kind, generous, collaborative, encouraging. At its most troubling, it establishes boundaries that might as well be brick walls. No girl wants to be on the outside, even when she doesn't want to be on the inside, either.

Parents and teachers often attempt to mitigate potential inclusion/exclusion. Many schools allow private party invitations to be passed out only when everyone in the class receives one. Others don't allow—officially, at least—such invitations to be passed out at school at all. Parents of younger girls may insist that an entire group be invited, including boys (ew!), because it's fair. Parents of older girls may encourage a smaller group, without boys (oh, c'mon!), because it's manageable.

Invitations—inclusions—are not only about parties and events. They're about everything from seating in the cafeteria to participating in the daily gossip. And of course, it's not practical or possible for everyone to be part of everything. Sometimes, too, as the parents you're the ones who nix the invite.

But *Everyone's* Going!

How great ... your daughter finally got invited to the big party after the big game, the movies in a town an hour's drive away, or the slumber party. She's long coveted this inclusion, and now she has it in her grasp. Only one problem: you've said no, she can't go. We're presuming you have a reason for your decision, because you know how important this is to your daughter. But of course, no matter what your reason, it's not going to be good enough.

So is your reason truly valid? If so, stand firm and be kind. Explain the reason to your daughter, even if she puts on a great show of not listening. (She can hear you through that door she just slammed, even if you whisper.) If, after you search your thoughts and your heart, you realize either your reason's not valid or you could work things out to let her go, don't be afraid to change your mind. Just be clear in explaining how you've arrived at your change of heart.

Sometimes your daughter gets invited to something everyone's excited about, and she acts excited, too, but she really doesn't want to go. Some girls will act out in ways that get them in trouble. They *want* a parent to step in and say no, you can't go now. It might surprise you to think about your daughter's behavior and come to the conclusion this could be partly an explanation for actions that otherwise make no sense. She may look, talk, and walk like a young adult but she's not quite there, and sometimes those inner child behaviors simply take over.

Let your daughter know you're there to take the heat as the "heavy" if she doesn't want to do something all her friends are doing but she doesn't want to just say no on her own. It's tough when she wants nothing more than to be accepted, to be part of the group, but then doesn't want, or quite know how, to say she doesn't want to do what the group's doing. But if you're the one who says no, who can argue with her about it?

So step in and be the parent! Everyone knows there's no reasoning with parents. Parents are always making stupid rules and decisions, and all kids know it. Let your daughter tell her friends you've said no, she can't go. It could be the biggest favor you ever do for your daughter.

In Her Shoes _____

Work out a code word or phrase that either you or your daughter can use to get out of a situation, no questions and no hesitation. Choose something that sounds plausible, yet is not a word or phrase you're likely to otherwise use. Your daughter can then call you when she gets in a bind and know that when you hear the code, you'll come pick her up. Likewise, you can use the code to tell your daughter, "We're out of here, right now."

Dealing With Mean-Girl Tactics

Every school has them, and every girl knows who they are. Mean girls make life frustrating for many and unbearable for some. They gossip, spread rumors, exclude, and play cruel pranks. (We talk about bullying behavior in other chapters so we won't go down that path here—we'll instead keep our focus on the "ordinary" mean-girl stuff.) Though as parents we might look at these tactics and think, whatever is the purpose of that?, the result is actually quite clear: power. And power can be quite intoxicating.

What do you tell your daughter? *Just ignore her, no one will even remember by tomorrow, you didn't want to go to the party anyway?* Well, easy for you to say! But your daughter can't ignore her, her hurt will be every bit as real to her tomorrow (and maybe even until she's your age!) even if no one else remembers what happened, and even if she doesn't want to go, she desperately wants to be the one to say no!

It's no quick or easy task to figure out how to handle words and actions intended to hurt—because they *do* hurt. No amount of platitudes can dilute the pain of being the only one not invited to the after-game party or having a BFF turn to someone else. Often the most helpful we can be for our daughters is to let them know it's okay to feel disappointed and angry and frustrated—and that we feel the same ways, too, sometimes, even as adults—and then to help them decide how they'd like to deal with those feelings in ways that help them feel better about themselves.

Retaliation, however tempting and however high on anyone's list, is not one of the better options! Often what helps most is simply letting your daughter dump everything out on you, in her own words and with little comment from you beyond "uh-huh" and "tell me more about that," about how she feels and why. Then she starts to analyze and understand her reactions—and you also gain insights into how she thinks.

All this said, we do want to point out that mean girls, though they exist everywhere (you might even work with the adult version), they're truly a minority across the spectrum of tweens and teens. Most girls do say mean things about each other at some point. Then they apologize and make up. It's part of the process through which we all learn to shape and express our less-than-positive feelings.

Getting to Know Your Daughter's Friends

Who are your daughter's peeps, her BFFs? How much do you know about them? Where do they gather, and what do they do? If they view your home as their home away from home, good for you! The more your daughter and her friends hang out at your house, the better you get to know not only the friends but also the dynamics of the friendships. You can observe how the girls relate to one another, see who is the leader of the group (or how leadership rotates with different situations), and get a sense for what these friends have in common with each other. Are they doing homework together or filling out the quizzes in the latest issue of *Teen Vogue*? Do they talk to you when you enter the room or does everyone fall silent when you approach?

The underappreciated advantage to getting to know your daughter's friends is that they also get to know you. You might someday walk into the room to hear one of them whisper, "We can't do that, your mom/dad'll get really upset!"

When Friends Bring Out the Worst in Each Other

Sometimes all that comes from a particular friendship is trouble. It's not that the friend is a bad person, or even does bad things. It's just that sometimes people bring out the worst, instead of the best, in each other. Call it personality, call it circumstances, call it the thrill of being bad. Sometimes, girls just bring out the dark side of each other.

You've experienced this in your own life in same way, no doubt. And likely it's nothing tangible at first that makes the connection for you. You just have a sense that something's not what it appears to be with these friends. In the interest of balance and supporting your daughter's independence, you probably take a wait-and-see attitude. But the longer you wait, the more you see what you wish you didn't. Go ahead, you can groan.

Separating your daughter from friends who are less-than-positive influences is no easy task. Unless you luck out and you've just been transferred to a job in another country, you walk a fine line in how you handle splitting them up. Make too big a deal about the friend and you're likely to only increase her appeal—the whole forbidden fruit kind of thing. Ignore the friendship in the hope that it'll just fall apart on its own and you run the risk that it won't. So what's a concerned parent to do?

Unfortunately, there's no clear-cut, universal answer. Much depends on the particular circumstances. Start by taking a step back to look at the situation from a fresh viewpoint. Why, exactly, are these friends undesirable? Is your daughter failing classes or getting in trouble at school when she's with these friends? Has your daughter made radical changes in how she dresses and acts since she's started hanging with these friends? Or do you just not like these friends, for reasons you can't quite put a finger on?

When you can identify specifics, you have firmer ground to stand on with your daughter. The older she gets, the more difficult it is to shape her friendships, so your chances of having influence are much better when you've had a strong relationship with her all along. Sit down somewhere—maybe take her out to coffee, to underscore your perception of her as grown up—and express your concerns clearly and objectively. Try not to accuse or judge.

If you can focus on specifics—grades, your expectations—you're more likely to find common ground and keep the conversation positive. No matter how resistant she might appear, she does hear you. If your track record with her is that you're straight up (and right more often than not), she'll find her own way to change. Don't expect overnight miracles, but do stay attuned to what happens every day. Make sure she knows you're there, you care, you want the best for her—and you're going to persist.

Oh, Puh-leeze!

Sometimes, of course, you've got to step in with full parental authority to protect your daughter from risky situations. Drugs, drinking, shoplifting, joyriding, vandalism, and other activities are not only illegal but also fall into the "guilt by association" snare. Even if your daughter can successfully make the claim she was only there, not participating, sometimes simply her presence makes her complicit. The consequences are often devastating and far-reaching. Say "no" and back it up. You might have to become your daughter's shadow for a few weeks or even months, but it beats accompanying her to see a parole officer—or worse.

Boy Friends

Not *boyfriends* … friends who are boys. Many girls have friends who are boys, kind of like big brothers by choice. Maybe they've grown up together, or find themselves sitting together in a class both either love or hate. What bonds them in friendship isn't so important as that they enjoy simply being friends. Boy friendships are easier when girls are younger, although many girls continue these friendships into high school and beyond.

Boys approach friendship differently from girls, which is one reason many girls like to have friends who are boys (and vice versa). The factors that are so frustrating in friendships among girls often don't exist in boy-girl friendships. A girl can talk and have fun with her guy friends mostly free from the trappings of both girl-friendships and romantic relationships. She can explore her interests outside any boundaries of conventional expectation—she might collaborate with her guy friend to build a robot for a science fair, for example.

Sometimes "he's just a friend" can take an unexpected turn when the sense of common interest blossoms into attraction—especially if only one of them feels that way. You might see the signs of this long before your daughter does; although as a general rule you want to keep this observation to yourself. It's usually better to let them work this through themselves. As with other friendships, it's most important simply that you're there when your daughter wants to talk.

Encourage New Experiences

You can't force your daughter into friendships that please you, of course. She chooses her friends because they make her happy. But you can look for opportunities that play into your girl's interests and passions. And you can help her to understand that she's coming into a time in her life where nearly anything she wants for herself is within her reach.

The Least You Need to Know

- ◆ Friends are sometimes more important than family.

- ◆ It's part of growing up for girls to both make and lose friends, even though they may not quite see it that way.

- ◆ A challenge for parents is knowing when to step in and when to step aside when their daughters are struggling with friendships.

- ◆ The friendships your daughter forms now may last a school year or a lifetime, but both are equally important to her.

- ◆ Girls can have wonderful and lasting relationships with boy friends—friends who are boys.

Chapter 12

First Dance, First Date

In This Chapter

◆ Testing the waters of adulthood

◆ Trust and expectations

◆ Trying on clothes, trying out roles

◆ So, yeah, we're going together ...

On Tuesday, she's casual and disinterested when you ask her about the dance coming up on Friday. (You noticed it on the school calendar when you were looking to see when was the next early-dismissal day.) On Wednesday, she guesses she'll go because most of her peeps are going. (But she doesn't have anything to wear, so you'll have to take her shopping.) On Thursday she comes home from school a girl possessed: *he* asked if she would be there and said, "Yeah ... um ... well ... okay, good, then" when she said she was thinking about going.

Whether she feigns nonchalance or lets her excitement shine, her first school dance is a big deal. A very big deal. Maybe even a heels-and-dress big deal—or at least new jeans. Whatever she wears, she's choosing it to impress *him*. Yep, him—even though she's going to the dance with her group of girlfriends and probably bringing the whole girl group home for a sleepover at *your* house, this event is mostly, at least in theory, about boys.

Girl, Transformed

Your daughter's first real dance—or any other boy/girl event—is a touchstone in her emerging sense of herself as a young woman, a big-deal social event she'll remember for all her life. It's her first official foray into the adult world and the first toe in the water of the ageless mating ritual. Your daughter doesn't view it this way, of course—and might even be horrified were you to present it to her in this way. Maybe you don't quite see it this way, either! But you can bet the school recognizes the many dimensions of the first dance, which features more rules than song sets.

The Trust Factor

Your daughter's first dance marks an important turning point for you as a parent, too. Until now, you've had a fairly good degree of oversight when it comes to where your daughter goes and whom she goes with. But with her increasing independence comes less direct control for you. You've now got to trust her to be out with her friends and still hold true to her values and your expectations. You might feel like you want to stay right here, parked in the parking lot, until she comes back out. But you can't—for your sake and for hers. She'll be fine, and so will you.

The first dance is often the first test of trust in this way. It's an exciting moment for her, when she and her friends pile out of the car and wave good-bye to you without a backward glance as they disappear through those decorated doors. Even though it's the same building where she spends six or seven hours a day, it's fun and exciting to be here in this new context.

Find out when the dance starts and ends, and make sure you or someone you trust (there's that "T" word again!) will be there to drop her off and pick her up. Does the school make sure kids stay at the dance once they arrive? Most middle schools don't let kids leave the dance unless they call their parents to come pick them up—and then usually require the child to wait with a chaperone for the ride to arrive. This keeps her safe as well as limits her ability to say she's going one place (the dance) and actually going somewhere else (a friend's house).

> **Oh, Puh-leeze!**
>
> Schools send home a flurry of materials about dances, sometimes including permission slips for parents to sign. These materials should tell you everything you want and need to know about the dance, from its scheduled hours to who'll be chaperoning. If any aspect of the event concerns you or there seem to be missing details, don't hesitate to contact the school for clarification.

Setting Expectations

You can't talk with your daughter often enough about your expectations for her behavior in social settings like dances. Not that you should bombard her with lectures such that her response is to turn up the volume on her iPod. But have a mantra you can repeat when the opportunity presents itself—something like, "Have fun … but no drinking, no drugs, no getting in anyone's car, no making out, and always check that there's no toilet paper trailing on your shoes when you come out of the bathroom … love you."

Say this often, consistently (same words), and when your daughter least expects it. Then she'll begin to assimilate it into her own sphere of awareness so that it becomes her embedded code of behavior across the spectrum of her daily experiences rather than only a warning she hears preceding special events like dances.

First, to the Mall

Your daughter's first dance means new clothes. There's no getting out of this one, even though most middle school dances are intentionally casual. So even if this is the case, it doesn't matter what clothes she already has. If anyone's already seen any item, it won't do for such a big event.

For most girls, this doesn't necessarily mean they have to have the hottest styles or the most expensive fashions—despite the advertising and media pressure aimed at girls like your daughter. It simply means they need something new, something bought specially for the event. Many casual dance fashions eventually find their way into the regular wardrobe rotation, sometimes in the most interesting of combinations, so even though it seems like you're spending a lot of money for a single event, your daughter's likely to get more wear out of the outfit than you anticipate.

Girls like to shop in packs when it comes to picking clothing and accoutrements for social events. You get the invite to join the pack mostly because you're the wheels and the checkbook. There's also a sliver of honor in the request for you to take them: your daughter trusts you to behave yourself with her friends. Now there's a twist on perspective! But it's a very important twist as far as your daughter is concerned, because in her world just about the worst thing that can happen is anything that embarrasses her. And this is a meaningful excursion, so she's doubly anxious.

If you shop together with your daughter as a routine, she knows what you'll approve and what you'll intercept at the cash register. Your standards are clear. You might have a few disagreements on interpretations now and again, but you're able to work them out in low-key, adult-like ways. But your daughter hasn't shopped like this before. She needs your guidance in that same low-key, adult-like way you use so well for ordinary shopping but lots more of it.

The Right Outfit

Until now, her dress-up clothes have probably had the purpose of being appropriate for a particular setting where adults set the standard, like weddings and other family celebrations. It's kind of sweet when grandma says, "Oh, that shade of blue really brings out your eyes!" Not quite the reaction she'll be looking for from her friends at the dance, however.

Remember, these are *her* fashions and she's trying to fit in with everyone else, not stand out—that comes later, in high school. So have a few basic rules in mind, and then give her the freedom to choose what she wants to wear. Try to separate the little girl you know (and, in this moment, desperately crave) from the young woman standing in front of you saying, "Does this make my boobs look bigger or smaller?" And you thought things would get easier as she got older. The correct response to this query is, of course, "How do you want them to look, dear?"

Makeup

Whether or not makeup comes up will depend on how formal the dance is, what most of the other girls are doing, and what your personal philosophy is about it. Girls start to dabble in makeup often when they're in the fifth or sixth grade, though mostly at slumber parties and in other settings where no one really sees them. Makeup is part of our culture, so it's natural for girls to want to try it out.

If your daughter does, talk with her about why she wants to wear makeup and what kinds of makeup she wants to use. Help her make modest, low-key choices and teach her—or have someone whose taste and style you trust teach her—to properly apply makeup. Choose hypo-allergenic products; your daughter's skin has enough to deal with already. The adage, "A little goes a long way" is hard for young teens (and even some adults) to understand as it applies to them and their makeup. And if your daughter shows not the least bit of interest in makeup, that's normal, too, and she shouldn't feel pressured to wear makeup because her friends do.

> **In Her Shoes**
>
> Most schools have a clear dress code for dances that they send home as part of the information about the dance and also post on the school's website. It's good to have a printed copy of this with you when you go shopping for clothes, just in case questions come up.

It's very easy for young teens to look over-done with the makeup, partly because they don't know what they're doing and partly because cosmetic fashions designed for older women don't work in the same way on their youthful faces. Trends change fairly often, too, so what your daughter wants to do with makeup may surprise you but be nothing more extreme than the current fashion among her and her friends. (Or what she's seen in a magazine that she likes.) Black might simply be "in" as a color, not any sort of political statement. Lipstick, eyeliner, and eye shadow are the most common types of makeup that appeal to young teen girls. Chapter 13 talks more about makeup and other aspects of fashion.

The Big Event

If you could somehow get a peek behind the hallowed doors of the redecorated gym, your daughter's middle school dance might remind you of your first school dance. On first take, it looks more like some twilight zone PE class, with colored lights or a mirrored glass ball hanging from the ceiling to send sparkles of light around the room, flashing fragments of light and color from the basketball backboards and the high gloss on the floor—boys lined up on one side of the gym, girls gathered on the other, no one wanting to be first and no one wanting to be last to pair off. Music throbs the eardrums, usually with a DJ at the controls. Sometimes the playlist matches the decorating theme; often there's an attempt to play something of most everything to appeal to, and appease, nearly everyone (including parents).

Were you to somehow achieve the proverbial fly-on-the-wall vantage point as the dance gets underway, you'd see the alignments of kids break into clusters and start dancing. Yep … actually dancing. This is where things start to break from what you might remember. Every song your daughter listens to on her iPod has a music video she's seen; she knows exactly how to dance to the song. There might not be a lot of boy-girl pairing off, although boys and girls tend to drift toward each other as the dance takes on momentum and kids become more comfortable.

How kids dance is probably more a function of the school's rules than anything else. Most such rules encourage distance between dancers and discourage overtly sexual or provocative moves. And at this level, despite the influence of music videos everyone's still pretty much learning what to do with their dance moves. For many girls, this is the first public venue for what they've been practicing at slumber parties. Teachers and other adult chaperones (often teachers from other schools) walk among the kids, sometimes even dancing themselves, much to the amusement of students whose surprise at seeing this side of their teachers stops them like a pause button.

Some kids are even plugged into their iPods, even as the dance music blares all around them—it's hard to know which beat drives their moves. (Well, sometimes not so hard, but you're not really there and the other kids don't much notice.) By high school the whole dance thing is a very different story, which Chapters 15 and 16 tell. But for now, everything is new and exciting.

In Her Shoes

No one really knows what to expect of the first dance. Girls may talk to older siblings and friends to get a feel for how to dress and act, and often have a group approach to the entire event. Parents, take comfort: middle schools tightly regulate their dances, typically requiring proof of student status (like a student ID card or a report card) for admission and establishing both a dress code and a code of behavior. Once through the doors, kids must stay until parents return at the designated time to collect them.

Trying On Different Roles

Girls are trying on more than clothes for their first dances and other social events. They're also trying on different versions of who they are and who they want to be as women. Though most of them have crossed the biological threshold to womanhood, they've still got a fair amount of growing up to do. Their bodies and minds are changing and developing, and it's both an exciting and a confusing time in their lives as they try to figure out how they feel themselves and what to do with the reactions and feelings of others. From the way they dress to the ways they behave, they're stepping into their perceptions of being adults.

A big part of this exploration, of course, is sexual. Today's girls know a lot about sex, and they know it a lot earlier than we realize. From about the fifth grade on, most public schools incorporate some form of sex education in health classes. These classes take a clear turn into detail by seventh grade. This is good; kids should learn these things from reliable sources. They also learn about sex and other adult topics from sources that aren't so reliable, like TV, movies, and magazines. Many TV shows and movies popular with younger audiences portray teens as adult-like in the experiences and problems they face in their daily lives. Genuine adults—like parents—sparsely populate these shows.

That your daughter *knows* so much about sex, though, doesn't mean she really *understands* sex. It's like driving: you can read and watch movies about it, but you don't really get it until you get behind the wheel. Young teen girls are sitting in the driveway with the engine running, to extend the metaphor. But the idea of doing anything more is still pretty scary. Nonetheless, you should know, as parents, that sex—the act—is on your daughters' minds—and is a topic of great theoretical debate among their girl group.

As our girls hover at the outskirts of numerous firsts in their lives, experiences that have, in generations before, been private and even secretive—like first kisses, first loves, and first break-ups—are instead out there for everyone to see in every way imaginable. Texting, instant messaging, e-mail, and cell phone pictures and video can send the news around the school (and beyond) even before the event—whatever it is—ends.

LOL

Those who teach sex education classes hear it all. Here's one of our favorites, a girl's response to the question, Do you know what a condom is? Yes, indeed: "If you live in the East, like in New Jersey, it's a townhouse. If you live in the West, like in California, it's a condom."

This is an especially challenging issue when girls are at such a pivotal time in their lives. They think they know who they are but are still working out the details. The hormones that flood their bodies generate different ways of thinking about themselves and about others. Attractions start to take on sexual overtones—girls start thinking about boyfriends, not friends who happen to be boys, although most girls will continue to have friends who are boys.

Gay, bisexual, transgender, and other nontraditional lifestyles are much more open today than they've ever been, even to the extent that there's strong, sometimes in-your-face activism around them. Without getting into issues of whether this is right or wrong, moral or immoral, we simply point out that this openness exists. Physicians like Gary, who see girls who struggle with their self-perceptions and emotions, sometimes worry that the combination of openness and activism creates pressure in girls' perceptions of themselves at a developmental stage when confusion already reigns.

Parents who are well-established and comfortable in their own sexuality, as most adults are, often don't recognize how much their daughters might be conflicted about their sexuality. As with other issues that challenge your daughter as she comes of age, you as a loving parent can best help your daughter simply by being there to answer her questions and support her while she sorts through her impressions and feelings.

A Kiss Is Just a Kiss ...

These early teen years mark the age when girls are not only aware of their emerging sexuality, but they're also aware that others are watching. They don't quite understand the sudden interest but they're beginning to recognize that without doing much else except showing up, the altered environment of social events like dances morph them into intriguing beings.

Kids who've gone to school together for years are suddenly not the friends they used to be but are eyeing each other like they've never seen each other. Partly, this is true—they haven't ever seen each other in this context. They're not playing dress-up anymore; they're truly all dressed up. They look a lot like the adults they've been pretending to be. They find it a little bit exhilarating, a little bit scary, and a little bit funny.

That boy your daughter's known since second grade now looks at her with glazy eyes that make you want to sign him up to be the first teenage astronaut, because you know exactly what that look means. You know what's going through his thoughts and his hormones, even though your daughter notices only that he's paying a lot more attention to everything she says and does, and besides, she thinks he's kind of cute. You know exactly what's going on with your daughter's hormones and thoughts, too.

Most of the time, of course, you're not there to see these signals. You catch them only by accident. Your daughter's on her own with her new experiences, and she's probably not so interested in sharing them with you—they're exciting, and she doesn't want for you to put the kibosh on them before she has a chance to enjoy them.

> **Girl Pearls**
>
> I don't really have a style—I'm just me. My style is kinda whatever I feel like wearing. A lot of girls feel like they need to wear what everyone else is wearing. But it's good to have your own trend. People will start following it!
>
> —Miley Cyrus, American teen actress and singer

If you've been open and talking with her all along, you've already had discussions about what's appropriate and what's not. Is she thinking about that? Probably; forays into areas where suddenly those discussions become relevant are kind of scary, and your words are going to come back to her with new meaning. Is she thinking about whether she wants to kiss the boy? Maybe. Will she *actually* kiss him? Probably not.

Changes in Friendships

Moving from tween to teen and beyond means a shift in perceptions about friendships and social interactions. Maybe your daughter and her BFF used to greet each other with enthusiastic hugs and hold hands walking to school together. It's sweet that they love each other in this way, sort of like sisters. Then they leave the protected environment of elementary school and discover how others may perceive their friendship; that this is no longer so cool and is even suspect.

The older (adult and not-quite-adult), broader world girls now inhabit may look askance at these displays of affection. What was sweetly innocent even last year takes on new, and often befuddling, context. Your daughter might find herself the subject of speculation about her sexual orientation and her relationships with her girlfriends, and not even quite understand what the speculation means.

As young teens, girls are just beginning to sort through a lot of new feelings, including sexual. Your daughter may wonder … if she loves her best friend who is a girl, does that mean she's gay? It's always been a *good* thing that these BFFs do, in fact, love each other. But now the picture seems to have shifted, and how and why things are different is often confusing for girls. As parents we might bemoan the sexualization of *everything*. But we can't make it go away.

Gary cautions that as parents, we can't just close our eyes because what we see makes us feel uncomfortable or because we disapprove. Instead, we need to recognize that our daughters are searching for who they are and how to best express that. We need to talk with our daughters about what they're feeling and thinking, and encourage them to consider both short-term and long-term consequences of their decisions and actions— whatever those choices are. There's a lot of emotion flowing.

Our culture does allow broader latitude for how girls behave with one another compared to boys. Girls are more touchy-feely than boys, and social standards accept this. The positive side of this is that such latitude provides a cushion of ambiguity for girls that doesn't exist in the same way for boys. Two girls in middle school can still link arms when they walk or hug when they meet, and there's not necessarily any connotations of sexual orientation associated with their behaviors. It's normal, and good, for your daughter to have girlfriends she loves.

Kathy makes the point that it's essential for parents to support their daughters and follow their cues, even when it comes to same-sex attraction. What matters above all else, and profoundly at this age, is that daughters know their parents love them and accept them no matter what. Keep your daughter's best interests and happiness always in front of you. When your daughter knows she can talk to you about anything, you know you'll always be a part of her life—and that she'll share with you who she is, what she believes, and how she feels.

What Do You Mean, You're "Going Together"?

There you are, minding your own business, heading toward the broccoli in the produce section, when you come upon a gaggle of women you recognize as the moms of your daughter's friends. "Aren't the two of them so cute together!" one gushes as you approach, and they all laugh. Turns out, the joke's on you. Cute? Together? Who? Your daughter, silly, and her, um, boyfriend. They've been going together now for, oh, three or four days. Didn't you know? It's okay—take a deep breath, that queasy feeling'll pass. Have a cup of coffee to clear your head. And relax. It's not what it seems.

Going together and dating are very different concepts for young teens than for older teens and young adults. A pair of eighth graders might consider themselves to be going together and tell everyone (except their parents) that they're dating. Though it makes us gasp to hear them talk so casually about such an adult experience, it's not so much an adult experience for them as it is part of the many roles they're trying on. And it starts early, even in the fifth grade.

Often it's more of a paper romance, existing mostly in notes passed in school or in text and e-mail messages. Each might post pics of the other on their respective MySpace pages. Friends may post comments. But the two most likely never actually go anywhere together outside school, and may not even interact with each other in school. These pairings tend to form and disperse like bubbles on the water's surface, lasting a few days to a few weeks. Girls may have dozens of "boyfriends" over the course of the school year.

"Going together" like this is a safe way to explore the changing dynamic that girls and boys are starting to feel. A girl might announce she's going with a boy on the bus on the way to school, spurring a deluge of text messages such that everyone already knows by the time the bus pulls into the school. She might tell the boy directly … or not. The girl may then may break up with him during second period and by lunch have two or three offers from other boys—and even be "going" with one of *them* by final bell. Other "going together" relationships might last a week or even a month.

Adults tend to look at these "going together" relationships as flighty and superficial because they're so brief and seemingly capricious. This might surprise the girls and boys who are going together; they take their relationships very seriously. Too seriously, sometimes. Some health experts worry that girls especially face too much pressure to begin dating.

Though these early "going together" relationships are hardly dating in the conventional sense, they are laying the foundation for later partner ings that are more the traditional first stages of courtship. But young teens don't yet have the emotional maturity that intimate (not necessarily sexual, but simply sharing of themselves) relationships require. Their practice relationships may take them too deep, too fast. Again, the ideal circumstance is for you and your daughter to already have in place a solid and loving connection that lets you both talk calmly and easily about any subject.

The Least You Need to Know

◆ Your daughter's first dance is her first big step into the (more or less) adult world, and is an important moment for her as well as you.

◆ Friendships and attractions are beginning to shift in your daughter's life, and indeed the "boy next door" your daughter once snubbed may become suddenly fascinating.

◆ This is a time of confusion mixed with excitement for girls; your steady love and understanding are essential.

◆ "Going together" and "dating" are important at this age, but are much more general than the terms mean to you at your age.

Chapter 13

Modesty Rocks

In This Chapter

- Who sets the standards, anyway?
- Girls gotta be themselves … as long as they look like everyone else
- Makeup, piercings, and tattoos—not just for renegades
- Putting your values out there for your daughter to see

Not even old enough to drive, Miley Cyrus suggestively bares her shoulders and back on the cover of *Vanity Fair*. Store mannequins pose in necklines plunging so low they could be belted and skirts with less coverage than a washcloth. School dress codes find it necessary to prohibit lingerie worn on the outside of other clothing … or as outerwear by itself. Stilettos, miniskirts, thongs. What can, and should, girls wear?

Teen girls seldom view their clothing as being as outrageous or provocative as adults view it. They're just wearing what they like—which has as much to do with looking like each other as anything else. The ageless question, "Is *that* what you're wearing to school?" is likely to evoke the equally ageless and somewhat exasperated response, "It's what *everyone's* wearing!" The difference today is that, it seems, everything goes. But even if it's trendy, does that mean you have to let your daughter leave the house looking like *that*?

In the Image of ... Whatever's in *Vogue*

The media—magazines, advertisements, television, movies—and the fashion industry have long set the trends and standards that girls strive to emulate. Girls get a lot of their ideas about what to wear and how to look from what they see and read. With many of the fashion models, TV and movie stars, and performers that today's girls admire being themselves still teens, it's easy for a lot of girls to believe they should be able to look that way, too.

The problem is, of course, that fashion models represent an ideal that doesn't exist in real life, even if the clothes they're modeling do filter down in some variation to items real people can buy in regular stores. The current trend is toward models who weigh much less than is healthy, establishing unachievable expectations in girls who desire the same look. (And indeed, these are unachievable standards for most girls who would like to be models!) So how do you make the connection for your girl between a healthy weight and a fashion-forward look?

Magazines and other media have long presented the "ideal" in attire and image, launching fashion trends around the world. The *Ladies Home Journal*, first published in the 1880s, took on the mission of describing the fashions popular in the East (New York City, Philadelphia, Boston, and other sophisticated urban centers of the time) so clothiers in the frontier West could replicate them for their customers. The Sears, Roebuck & Company catalog served a similar mission, though not with quite the same panache.

Somewhere along the line, though, the purpose shifted from showing women how other women dressed to showing women how they *should* dress. And clothing fashions shifted from stylish to sexy, intimating that sexy was stylish. Not to be so prudish as to say that this can't be the case, but when is it too much? This is a tough line for parents to walk with their tween and teen daughters—especially with the popularity of shows like *Sex and the City*, now in syndication on TV as well as in the movies.

As important as what your daughter wears is what she does when she's wearing it; this is another—and often overlooked—dimension of modesty. Yet here, too, girls get mixed messages. Some of the most popular magazines among girls aren't much different from magazines that target adult women, with the teen version a spin-off of the adult version. Some, like *Cosmo* and *CosmoGirl!*, *People* and *Teen People*, and *Vogue* and *Teen Vogue* seem little different from one another right down to the names, cover designs, and content.

Even though many teen magazines feature one article in each issue about a contemporary issue or subject (often health-related, like the hazards of yo-yo dieting or the risks of cosmetic surgery), the balance of articles are about fashion, beauty, and using both to make themselves attractive to boys. One study determined that on average, over half the advertising of the major magazines that target teen girls had to do with cosmetics and beauty products!

Remember, you're the one in charge. You have the authority—and the responsibility—to say "no" when your daughter shows up dressed in something inappropriate. Even if she believes she's just being herself, she's sending mixed signals, too. And in her circumstances, those receiving her messages—the raging hormones otherwise known as teenage boys—lack the maturity to sift through to what she really means by how she dresses.

I Want to Be Pretty

There's nothing inherently wrong with cultivating attractiveness; after all, that's the essence of male-female bonding. It's great when girls feel strong and beautiful. But to turn inside out the old cliché that beauty is in the eye of the beholder, we want our girls to grow up feeling strong and beautiful from the inside, such that they like themselves, their bodies, and how they look simply because they do, not because they're trying to meet some outside (and unrealistic) standard. We want the beholder's eye to be hers.

Many experts believe the increasingly extreme gap between the portrayal of "ideal" in magazines and other media and reality leads growing numbers of young teen girls toward eating disorders, depression, and anxiety because they don't—and can't—match up to the "standard."

Some girls even desire cosmetic procedures, from liposuction to surgery, to help them achieve the look they believe they should have.

In his practice, Gary often talks to middle school- and high school-age girls about body weight and body image. He sometimes resorts to grabbing a teen magazine from the waiting room and handing it to a girl who insists she's fat even though her weight is well within the range of healthy from a medical perspective. "Show me someone in here who's normal," he instructs. It's the new Where's Waldo ... except this Waldo is nearly *always* impossible to find. Maybe it's a really good trainer, maybe it's micro-eating, maybe it's extraordinary talent with an airbrush. But it's not exactly the picture of good health. Nonetheless, these are the pictures that bombard teens today.

Oh, Puh-leeze!

The American Society of Plastic Surgeons reports that in 2007, nearly 40,000 teens had surgery to alter the appearance of their noses. Women of all ages accounted for 91 percent of the year's plastic surgery patients, undergoing 10.7 million procedures (1.6 million of which were operations). That's a lot of fooling with Mother Nature!

Stylin' Celebs

They're the top teen queens of today: Hilary Duff. Amanda Bynes. Mary-Kate and Ashley Olsen. Avril Lavigne. Paris Hilton. Nicky Hilton. Miley Cyrus. Aside from their entertainment value, what else do they have in common? Here are a few hints: Dear. Stuff. Abbey Dawn. Hannah Montana. Okay, the last one is a bit broad, we'll give you that.

These are the clothing lines of their respective celebs: Dear by Amanda Bynes, Stuff by Hilary Duff, Abbey Dawn by Avril Lavigne, and of course Hannah Montana by Miley Cyrus. So not only can your young teen watch her faves on the tube, but she can now dress just like her! For the most part, these teen stars take their clothing lines where their fans shop: Kohl's, Target, and Wal-Mart.

(Un)Reality TV

Magazines, of course, are not the only media influences that shape expectations and perspectives. Television has by far the most significant reach into the lifestyles of young people, from advertising to programming, when it comes to media influence. Increasingly, television shows purport to present "reality," filming real people engaging in real activities of real life. Well, unscripted, perhaps. But real? Probably not so much, despite appearances.

Shows that more creatively blur the line can be a mix of really great stuff for girls to watch and some confusion—for example, Disney's *Hannah Montana*, which drew about 3 million tween and teen viewers an episode during its 2008 season. In case you've somehow missed the Hannah Montana phenomenon, the series stars Miley Cyrus as Miley Stewart, ordinary teen during the day, and her secret alter-ego, rock star Hannah Montana.

Despite the oddly schizophrenic sense that comes from everyone pretending to be someone else, the show gets major points for the mostly realistic problems young teens face and how they work them out among themselves or with their parents. It's not real life, of course. But it gives girls new ways to think about similar situations in their own lives. And every now and again, what Miley/Miley/Hannah says or does is exactly right to say or do in real life.

LOL

The Disney Channel original series *Hannah Montana* premiered in March 2006. The comedy features Miley Cyrus and her real-life dad, country music star Billy Ray Cyrus (who plays—no surprise—her father on TV, too). Nominated for an Emmy as Outstanding Children's Program in 2007, the show won a Teen Choice Award for TV comedy in 2008. The show has also received numerous other nominations and awards, and spawned a sell-out national concert tour for character Hannah Montana—and, of course, Miley Cyrus—aptly titled the Best of Both Worlds Tour.

For the most part, today's girls have a pretty good handle on what's real and possible and what's not—even when they yearn for what's not. To evoke again the fly-on-the-wall perspective from Chapter 12, were you to somehow catch a glimpse into a slumber party or other gathering of young teen girls, you'd hear a lot of chatter and giggling about boys, clothes, and makeup. These are the mysteries that just lie ahead on their trajectory through adolescence. Some of their peeps (even, perhaps, among those at the slumber party) are further along, and maybe did kiss a boy at the middle school dance or regularly wear makeup to school.

But the tone in these settings is mostly one of curiosity, not necessarily of disappointment or envy (as it might be when discussing the latest issue of *Teen People*). The lives of all adults look exciting and glamorous from the distance still between these girls and adulthood, even—or perhaps more so—right in their own homes and communities. Sure, all those magazines and TV shows are intriguing, and wouldn't it be grand to live like that. Maybe, but maybe not so grand or different, in many ways. But girls know *Gilmore Girls*, *90210*, *Gossip Girl*, and even *Hannah Montana* aren't real, even if they sometimes seem far more interesting than real life or touch on issues important in their daily lives.

Counter-Couture

Teens rebel. It's what being a teen is all about—finding your own way to make it through an ageless transition. Every generation of teens does it; one of the most famous quotes of all time about the decline of youth, attributed to the Greek philosopher Plato (circa the 400s B.C.E.), is centuries old: "What is happening to our young people? They disrespect their elders; they disobey their parents. They ignore the law. They riot in the streets inflamed with wild notions. Their morals are decaying. What is to become of them?" Could've been an editorial in last week's newspaper!

Some of the fashions and behaviors teens adopt are simply their efforts, en masse as a generation, to distinguish themselves from other generations. As adults we might look at them and think, "But they all look the same!" When we do so, we've missed the point. They want to look and act like each other. They just don't want to look or act anything like us.

To this end, they blend styles in some very creative ways, sometimes in the effort to be both stylish and comfortably modest.

What's Old Is New Again

Ever look at your daughter and think she looks like she just stepped out of *That 70s Show*? Fashions come and fashions go … and then they come back again. For as original as the hottest styles today appear, look back 20 years and you're sure to see at least some of them. But they've passed the magical divide between old and vintage, and vintage is hot.

Stores that sell vintage clothing are increasingly popular—from thrift shops like Goodwill and Salvation Army to specialty boutiques featuring carefully selected and worn items (a little fraying and fading increase the desire). Although shopping these stores is a great way to buy trendy on the cheap, some vintage fashions fetch prices that would make their original sales tags blush. One advantage to buying vintage is that often the styles, for as contemporary as they look, are less revealing because societal standards weren't as accepting 20 years ago as they are now. That jeans rode on the hip instead of at the waist was radical in itself!

Regulating Attire

Fashion trends present ever-changing challenges for schools. As clothing styles become more revealing and suggestive, they become more distracting—though to harken back to the influence of the media, television shows and magazines treat them so casually as to imply such fashions are so common and so much the standard that everyone's used to them so they have no distraction value. Um … not! The fantasy factor sometimes plays out in some surprising ways.

Schools often attempt to mitigate media and fashion influences through dress codes and sometimes even uniforms (both public and private schools), especially in middle schools. These bans, most of which clearly apply to girls although they don't specifically say so (we're not so sure about the dog collars), appear on a compilation of middle school websites and give a sense of the kinds of issues schools face when it comes to how kids dress:

- No short skirts or shorts (length must be at least to the fingertips when the girl stands with her arms at her sides)

- No spaghetti straps

- No low-cut blouses, midriff-baring tops, tube tops, or halter-tops (no breasts and limited skin visible)

- No visible undergarments

- No overdone makeup

- No chains

- No pajamas

- No slippers or flip-flops

- No gang references or affiliations

- No references to alcohol, cigarettes, drugs, weapons, sex, religion, politics, or profanity

- Nothing see-through or skin-tight

- No exposed tattoos or piercings except earrings worn in the lower ear lobe

Quite the list! Would you've thought of some of these? It can be tough to balance letting girls (and boys) express their opinions and individuality without offending or intimidating others.

Some schools take a more open approach, with a dress code that simply asks for reasonable choices. Other schools require uniforms—a tightly defined range of clothing choices. Generally uniforms offer some options, such as limited color options—like dark green, navy blue, and khaki—and, for girls, usually a choice between slacks and skirts. When schools establish such tight guidelines, they usually arrange with area clothing stores to stock a wide range of sizes and plentiful supply of the kinds of items they're requiring.

While the primary objection most people have to stringent dress codes and mandatory uniforms is the protest that it restricts individuality, in practice it seems that even kids find it relieves stress about what to wear and dressing within the style circle. There's no shortage of opportunities for girls to flash the fashion outside the regular school day—including at school dances and other events. And parents appreciate any efforts that make their lives easier, not to mention less expensive! When everyone has to wear pretty much the same thing, a lot of issues simply fall away.

Oh, Puh-leeze!

A Texas teen made national headlines after being arrested for refusing to leave her prom. The reason school officials wanted her out? Her dress bared her belly and back, as well as revealed ... well, quite a lot of the rest of her body. The attire was deemed inappropriate and in violation of the dress code for prom. The teen protested, however, because she felt her prom dress was simply stylish. To be clear, it wasn't the dress that got her arrested, it was the disruption she created in her effort to attend the event. Police later released her without filing any charges.

Body, Adorned

Clothing styles are only one facet of the fashion dilemma that confronts today's teens. From the long-standing tradition of pierced ears to other body piercings and tattoos, over the past generation or so body adornment has become an intriguing blend of self-expression and fashion. For today's teen girls, often it's not so much a question of whether they'll get piercings or tattoos, but when and where.

No matter your own feelings about such body adornment, your most successful path of influence is to stay open and objective (not objectionable!) to your daughter's views and desires. Often, as with anything else, a girl wants a piercing or a tattoo because someone—a media star or girls at school—she admires has one.

"That's great, dear! But have you thought about how that might look when you're, say, 30?" is a response certain to get a startled pause. First, teen girls know the age of 30 lurks out there in their futures but it seems impossibly far away. Old, even, like their parents. Second, while it seems so obvious to us, as those old parents, that piercings and tattoos are *permanent* changes, they don't get it because everything in their lives, still, is transient.

Makeup

Makeup—eye shadow, eye liner, lipstick, nail polish—is the first foray into body decoration for most girls, and they often start experimenting even before they get to middle school. It's fun to try all different looks, knowing they can wash them down the drain when they tire of them or discover they look, well, somewhat monstrous. By middle school, though, a fair number of girls wear some kind of makeup on a regular basis.

Parents may have rules around the wearing of makeup—waiting until she's 16 is a common one. But parental rules don't necessarily trump peer pressure. If all your daughter's friends are wearing makeup, you can be fairly certain your daughter is, too, no matter how clean-faced she leaves the house in the morning. The girl's bathrooms at school are frenzied with activity in the 10 minutes or so before first bell in the morning, and again after last bell in the afternoon.

In Her Shoes

The most common—and strident—complaint about young teen girls and makeup is that the girls overdo it and look, by adult standards, gaudy. Overdone makeup has a strong societal association with, shall we just say, loose morals. If your daughter wants to wear makeup, help her learn how to wear it appropriately.

As with other fashion issues, openness and dialogue are a parent's best strategy. Some girls wear makeup to make a particular statement. Others wear makeup because all their friends do. A lot of girls have no interest in makeup. What are your daughter's interests? If she wants to wear makeup but you don't want her to, what are your reasons? Sometimes just saying your objections aloud helps you both get to the center of the issue so you can resolve any disagreements and move to a place of compromise that satisfies you both.

Piercings

It's long been traditional for girls to wear pierced earrings. Some parents have this done when their daughters are still infants. Others allow their daughters to choose to pierce their ears when they reach an age parents feel the girls can appropriately care for the piercings—8, maybe, or 12. Still others hold out for an older age, like 16. And some parents disapprove of piercings altogether, not permitting their under-age daughters to wear pierced earrings.

Both fashion and health are factors. Piercings require regular hygiene and care, especially in the first four to six months after while the piercing is healing. Most girls, until they reach late middle school, are content to remain fairly conventional with their piercings. That is, they confine them to their ears, although many girls have double sets of piercings, wearing two earrings in each ear lobe. Some girls even have multiple piercings that go up the cartilage. The fashion standard is pretty broad; girls are most likely to want what their circle of friends (and their moms and other adult women in their lives) have.

By late middle school and into high school, piercings start to show up on other body parts—belly buttons, noses, eyebrows, lips, and tongues. This is not a trend new to the current generation of girls but rather a trend that started about a generation earlier and that today has some-what of a mainstream acceptance, depending on where you live. For many girls today, having multiple piercings is not much different than, say, having a closet full of shoes. Their parents—you!—may also have multiple piercings.

The key question comes back to this: when is your daughter ready to take care of her piercings, wherever they are and however many of them she has? Some body parts are more challenging—like ear carti-lages and tongues, where wicked infections can rage almost without warning—and with enough risk for serious complications to sit up and take notice. Fashion sensibility, too, comes into play.

Oh, Puh-leeze!

Many states have laws that require minors to have written paren-tal consent before they can get piercings, tattoos, and other permanent alterations to their bodies. Of course, this is far from foolproof. Your daughter should understand, clearly and unequivocally, where you stand on this.

Tattoo: No Longer Taboo

Once upon a time, only gnarly sailors sported body ink. Women who dared dabble in permanently painting their bodies quickly found themselves outcasts, accused of all manner of lewd behavior and immoral sensibility. Not so any more. Body art is now state of the art when it comes to fashion. About a third of American women between the ages of 15 and 50 have at least one tattoo. Far from being manly, women's tattoos are typically graceful and feminine. For older women (that is, beyond their teens), tattoos often express independence and a sense of self that sends the message: I own my body.

Teens like to be simultaneously the same as and different from each other, which gives tattoos much of their appeal. Girls can get them, so they're the same in that respect, but each girl might get something different, which makes her unique. Tattoos come with risks that young people often either don't know about or don't believe can affect them. Such risks range from contracting hepatitis, HIV, and other infections from contaminated needles and inks to excessive scarring, infection, and tissue damage at the site of the tattoo. Because of these considerations, in many locations a parent must sign a release form if the girl is under age 18.

Girls are sometimes attracted to permanent makeup, like tattooed eyeliner. A lot of teens think they can just have such tattoos removed when they get "old" (like 30) and no longer want them. Even with advances in laser technology, though, tattoo removal remains (and is likely to remain) a painful and often incomplete process.

Family Values

We all have family values. Political wrangling has appropriated much of what this means, but at their core, family values are simply the standards by which we live our lives and teach our children to live theirs. Some people are really out there and very public about what that means to them; other people are quiet followers of the paths they've set and prefer to keep their beliefs and philosophies closely held. It's kind of like income, in a certain way: though we all know we earn money, some people are open about how much money they make, overtly or through conspicuous consumption, while others are low-key and private.

At their core, family values tend to center around love, respect, acceptance, and encouragement. The framework that supports these values might be religious or philosophical beliefs. Some people draw their family values from a long and beloved family history. Other people create their own values to provide the life and lifestyle they want for their families. It doesn't matter whether your family values run generations deep or started with you. It doesn't even matter how you define your family values. What does matter is that your family values shape the expectations you have for how your daughter lives her life.

It's a very good thing to be able to say, these are our standards. You can't be too clear about it. Your daughter may mime your words behind your back, but that's a good thing, too: at least she knows what the family values and standards are. When you're clear about what you expect, your daughter is clear about how to behave. She may not always do what you expect, but she knows the standards.

Engage your daughter in dialogue about values and standards. "Because I said so" is not a very good reason for very much, even though sometimes those are the words that slip from every parent's mouth (usually after attempts at reason have failed). It's far more effective for your daughter to understand why you value certain beliefs and behaviors. It's not only fine but necessary to draw a line between what's right and what's wrong, what's acceptable and what's not. Later in her life (like when she's your age) your daughter may choose to cross that line, but for right now it's a good and healthy thing for her to toe that line.

The ability to make choices implies an understanding of the consequences, positive and negative, of a decision. Kids don't have that understanding; we, as their parents, have to help them come to it. This happens only as they learn and accumulate information. So the more we explain, the more they learn. This isn't to say that we're explaining as a process of asking our daughters to follow our standards. It's not an option in that way, at least not yet.

In Her Shoes

Whatever we're continually exposed to over time becomes the norm—in fashion, in behavior, in lifestyle. Standards and values begin to shift accordingly. This is the primary concern with the proliferation of sex-oriented content on television and in advertising, coupled with the extended exposure today's girls have to this content.

Sex and Sensibility

How many references to sex do you think the typical teenage girl sees on TV? One study says 14,000 over the course of a year. *Fourteen thousand!* You've got to wonder how that can even happen. Or watch an hour of the television shows popular with teen girls to catch a glimpse of how it's possible. Everyone's having sex, often seemingly without discrimination or discretion. Although the story lines would have you believe there are emotional intertwinements that connect all these characters in ways other than through sex, it's more back-story stuff that you never really see.

Now, as adults we can sit through an hour of such drama and come away from it without much change in how we see our own lives. We might even be amused that such drivel manages to hold the attention of viewers at all. Because teen girls don't have nearly as much perspective and life experience, they can't. In numerous surveys, teen girls say that what they see on TV influences their perceptions about what's normal and how they should behave. (Hear your family values calling?) Groups like the American Academy of Pediatricians (AAP) worry that this influence pushes girls into experimenting with sex (even only kissing and making out) much earlier than they're emotionally, and perhaps physically, ready.

> **In Her Shoes**
>
> A growing trend across the United States is purity events that emphasize the values of modesty and sexual abstinence. Some events are formal, like Purity Balls, in which daughters pledge (often to their fathers) that they'll remain virgins until they marry. Other events are casual, with information and education their driving components.

Toning It Down

Girls can comfortably choose modesty and claim ownership of themselves without feeling that they have to give in to standards they don't agree with—and many have no qualms about doing so. They're able to feel comfortable about themselves and their appearance without chasing impossible ideals. Not so many girls are willing to be the odd one out, though they can be quite creative in establishing their own ways of fitting in.

Some girl-oriented organizations emphasize teaching girls how to dress to feel beautiful and confident without baring their sexuality. These might be community organizations for girls like Girl Scouts, church groups, and mentoring groups. Some of these approaches tap into the framework of family values in a very overt and structured way; others focus on practicality or professionalism.

Sometimes all a girl needs and wants is for someone (like you or an older sister or aunt) to step in and say, "Do you really think you should wear that? What are you trying to tell others about yourself?" Sometimes, the straightforward "You're not leaving the house dressed like that!" works, too. You might get some grumbling, whining, or even a toddler-style foot stomp. But you're also likely to get an outfit change, at least partial.

Though television and magazines may offer the impression that what it presents is all there is and widely defines girls and women, the reality is that the majority of girls and women live quite differently than these media portray. This is often as much the issue as what that portrayal is. What remains important with any standards of dress and behavior, however, is that girls are able to choose presentations of themselves that *they* like, that are true to their sense of themselves, and that enable them to feel at ease among their friends and classmates.

The Least You Need to Know

♦ The media—television, movies, magazines, advertising—is a far more powerful influence on our daughters than many parents recognize.

♦ Girls in their early teens want more to look like everyone else than to make statements of their individuality.

♦ Parents have great ability to influence their daughters' choices in fashion through reason and negotiation—and sometimes simply by saying, "No, you can't wear that."

♦ Piercings and tattoos are increasingly common among girls, and, as is the case with most such trends, are beginning to appeal to them at younger ages.

♦ Attire and presentation are important elements of family values.

Chapter 14

Girls in the Middle

In This Chapter

- ◆ The fun side of these middle years
- ◆ Finding shared interests
- ◆ Stepping out to make a difference
- ◆ Learning independence, a little bit at a time

For all that we fret and talk about the challenges of your daughter's early teen years, these years are also a delightful time in her life and in your relationship with her. She's old enough that you can begin to share common interests, find humor in the same situations, and otherwise get to know each other as she's becoming more like an adult.

Your daughter's ability to function more like an adult with independent interests and abilities than a child who needs constant supervision grows by leaps and bounds between the ages of 13 and 15. She knows more clearly what she likes and doesn't like, and why, and can express herself in rational ways (when she chooses). She's more like you and more uniquely individual than either of you recognizes. And she's growing in confidence as she finds her way.

On Common Ground ... for a Moment

It's such a breath of fresh air the first time you and your daughter laugh together at the same situation for the same reasons! After the stresses of the tweens, when anything either of you says or does diametrically opposes the other, how delightful to again stumble onto common ground big enough to hold the both of you. The pivotal event might be "getting it" together: the aha moment about a movie scene that has subtle humor or drama ... discovering that your daughter's chosen from your bookshelf Jane Austen's *Sense and Sensibility* ... saying simultaneously that you'd love to head downtown for a coffee ice cream cone ... swapping plates midway through lunch out to sample each other's sandwiches. Whatever the circumstance, it flashes like a lightning bolt through your collective consciousness such that you both see, for the moment, your similarities instead of your differences. It's a beautiful moment you want to hold onto forever. And you *will* hold onto it—both of you, though in different ways—long after the moment passes.

Engage with Your Daughter in Her Interests

You've always been a participatory parent, going to volleyball games and swim meets, guitar lessons and taekwondo classes. You've cheered her on and consoled her. She always knew she could count on you to be there for her, no matter what. She still knows that. But perhaps in her efforts to pull away and establish herself as independent and individual, she's shifted away from relying on you for this kind of support.

It's okay; it's part of growing up. But the connection is important for both of you. And like all growing and changing connections, you've got to remake this one to fit the current circumstances. If your daughter's still involved in school sports and group activities, great—you've probably still got a strong connection going, if only because she wants you to drive or supply refreshments.

But it's time to step back and look at your daughter through a fresh lens. What are her interests? Even if she's still involved in the same sports, her interest is likely more refined and specific. Rather than just playing volleyball, maybe she's become the team's lead setter. Maybe she's emerged as the strongest 400-meter breast-stroker on her swim team and no longer competes in shorter-distance events.

You're not looking to push your way into your daughter's life as one of her best friends. That's not your role. But you can, and should, be an active part of your daughter's interests. Read the books she's reading. Ask her to show you what's on her MySpace page. Better yet, have your own MySpace page so you can be on each other's friends lists and see each other's pages whenever you want. Text-message with her. See a movie she wants to see.

In Her Shoes

As your teen daughter matures and demonstrates increasing reliability, reciprocate by extending your trust in her. Establish progressively expanding boundaries for her, like going places with her friends or just hanging out. Keep your finger on the pulse of what she's doing, of course. It's always good for her to know you could show up at any time, and for you to do just that, every now and again. But resist the urge to overtly check up on her every time you let her go out. She'll learn responsibility better when she actually has to take it.

Encourage Your Daughter to Share Some of Your Interests

It's been a long time since your daughter did more than stifle a yawn when you took her with you to run errands or let her tag along when you went to play tennis. Once everything you did fascinated her. She tried her best to imitate you, hefting your tennis racket high above her head or dressing up in your work clothes. It was the stuff of great home videos (which the both of you may sneak away to watch, though not together).

Your daughter still watches everything you do—and likely with an attention to detail that might make you a bit uncomfortable if you knew its depth. She continues to learn from her observations, though likely tries on the parts that appeal to her when you're nowhere around instead of playing dress-up in the living room on a Saturday morning. She doesn't quite want you to know she's curious about what it's like to be you, but she does want to know about you.

Invite her to come along with you at times. It doesn't matter where you're going or what you're doing (as long as it's appropriate to take a young teen). The idea is simply that you get some together time with your daughter. Make a pledge to yourself that you'll use this time only for positive interactions with her—no lectures about grades or grilling about her friends. Let her take the lead. If all she wants to do at first is sit with her iPod, fine. But soon enough she'll get bored enough with that and start to talk with you about *something*. These are the kinds of conversations that give you the greatest insights into her life and her interests.

This is also the age when your daughter begins to gain a new understanding for your career or job. She's starting to think a bit about what she might want to do or be when she grows up. As she approaches the end of middle school, her teachers are talking more about class choices and how they relate to potential career interests. For the first time, your daughter can see that school will come to an end—either not soon enough or all too quickly, depending on her mood. But she's beginning to think, in small spurts, beyond algebra and Spanish.

In Her Shoes

National Take Our Daughters and Sons to Work Day, which takes place the fourth Thursday in April each year, is a structured event to encourage parents to share their work lives with their daughters and sons. The program originally started with an exclusive focus on daughters as a way to encourage girls to think about and plan their careers and futures.

She more closely observes work-related interactions you might have, like encounters with colleagues and co-workers at the mall or other social settings. She senses both your satisfactions and your frustrations, and tries in her head to work out how you feel as well as how she feels about them. If you love your work, she notices your passion and dedication. If you hate your job, she notices this, too.

For the Greater Good

Many middle schools encourage, and some require as an extracurricular activity that earns school credit, kids to participate in community service activities. Because this time in your daughter's life is all about belonging, this is an excellent opportunity to expand her horizons about what that means in a context beyond her circle of friends. Girls at this age may be resistant to trying new things, so maybe she can get a friend or two to volunteer, too.

Communities are desperate for volunteers in all kinds of activities and events, from community centers that have daycare and afterschool programs for young children to food banks and animal shelters. Many communities have departments or agencies that coordinate volunteer efforts. Your daughter's school can also provide information or steer you to the appropriate resources. Volunteer positions often require prospective volunteers to complete an application form. If she's under 18, the application likely requires your signature.

Getting out into the community stretches your daughter in ways she otherwise might not consider, broadening her sense of her role now and the potential that awaits her in the not-too-distant future. Instead of building Sims communities on her computer or watching TV on Saturday mornings, she could be making a real difference in the lives of others. And she could be making a real difference in her own life.

Opportunities to Learn

Many volunteer opportunities can serve the dual purpose of giving to the community and gaining insight and experience into potential career fields. The local animal shelter might be a good volunteer experience for a girl who wants to be a veterinarian. Animal shelter volunteers might help feed and exercise dogs and cats. A girl who wants to be a doctor, nurse, or other healthcare professional might enjoy volunteering at a hospital. Yep, you might've done this as a candy striper ... which you'll be pleased to know has advanced beyond the red-and-white-striped uniform. Hospital volunteers might help in the business office, pass out books and magazines, read to children on the pediatrics unit, or help out in the gift store. Girls who like to be outdoors and might want careers in recreation might volunteer to maintain trails in the parks or help with recreation programs.

Community volunteer opportunities for your daughter include the following:

- ◆ Animal shelters
- ◆ Big Brother/Big Sister programs

- Community centers
- Convalescent centers
- Day camps
- Daycare centers
- Food banks
- Hospitals
- Libraries
- Museums
- Public parks
- Recreation programs
- Senior centers
- Special events (parades, local fairs, farmer's markets)
- Thrift stores

Reaching Across the Generation Gap

Volunteer activities can also help connect your daughter with younger as well as older people. If she enjoys babysitting, your daughter might enjoy volunteering at a community-center daycare program. Does your daughter like to read? Perhaps there's a senior center or program for reading aloud to people with impaired vision or who otherwise can't read themselves. Or maybe your daughter would be good at teaching others to read, through library or community literacy programs.

She Wants a *Real* Job

Around the time they turn 13 or 14, girls begin to realize there is a potential to earn more money than parents are willing to fork out in allowances. They want to get jobs. Partly, getting a job moves your daughter closer, in practice, to independence and adulthood. Partly, it helps her develop a sense of accountability to others. Overall, getting a real job is a great boost for a girl's self-esteem.

Oh, Puh-leeze!

Most states strictly regulate working conditions for those under the age of 18. Some states don't allow employers to hire anyone under 16, or impose such stringent regulations that employers don't want to hire under 16. Make sure you know what your state requires, and also what, if any, effect your daughter's earnings might have on your family's state and federal tax obligations.

Letting your daughter get a "real" job (read: paying) while she's 13 or 14 (even 15 or 16) requires a good sense of your daughter's interests, abilities, and reliability. Having a job can teach your daughter valuable life lessons at a time in her life when she's most amenable to learning them: responsibility for being on time, commitment to both time and tasks, and managing money. It's also a good way to establish solid savings habits with an eye toward future needs—like college.

It's a great boost for your daughter's self-confidence, too, especially if she's had some struggles with peers and others at school. A job makes tangible your assurances that things will get better and there's life beyond school. For there to be life beyond school while she's still in school ... well, what a score that is! It doesn't matter how much—or how little—the job pays, or how much of her time it requires (as long as it doesn't interfere with her schoolwork). She's now edged past some of the challenges she's been experiencing.

Babysitting

Babysitting remains primarily the domain of the teenage girl who's not old enough to get a "real" job. It's a great introduction to working for many girls. But it's not for everyone. Some girls have no interest in caring for other people's children, and as parents we need to honor that.

For girls who do want to babysit, it's important to make sure they're capable of handling the responsibility of taking care of young children, and have the training to deal with possible emergencies—small and large. And it's crucial for you, your daughter's parent, to know who your daughter's babysitting for and for both you and your daughter to feel comfortable with the setting and circumstances.

Many middle schools, as well as community organizations like the American Red Cross, offer classes in babysitting that cover everything she might imagine and a lot she'd never think of about taking care of kids. Such classes teach basics like changing diapers, feeding, and burping babies as well as what to do if there's a fire or other kind of crisis. Babysitting classes also teach CPR and general first aid. Classes are especially good for girls who don't have younger siblings or cousins they've cared for.

Some communities require babysitter certification for babysitting to be "legal" for kids other than siblings when the babysitter is under a certain age. However, a lot of babysitting takes place as informal arrangements between neighbors who know each other, or friends. It's important that you know whom your daughter'll be babysitting for, how many kids will be under her care (more than two is generally too many) and that you're comfortable with the family and the home. Sometimes girls like to babysit in pairs, which isn't a bad idea as long as the parents who are leaving the babysitter in charge approve this in advance, especially when there's more than one child to care for. This is not an opportunity for your daughter to invite her friends over to socialize, however.

 In Her Shoes

Middle school is all about nurturing, with the focus on getting girls through the difficult transitions they might be encountering, and preparing them for the greater independence of high school only a year or two away. Even though girls in their middle teens might resist stepping out on their own, the more of it they do, the better prepared they'll be when such independence becomes the expectation.

Other Jobs

Paying jobs besides babysitting may be scarce for your girl who's between 14 and 16. For one thing, she doesn't have much in the way of qualifications and she has little or no experience to offer a prospective employer. Anyone who hires a teen girl is taking on the role of training her for the job, and many employers who need workers don't have time to do that. Opportunities sometimes exist for small business owners who need people to help out with nonessential tasks. Landscapers, tailors, café owners, and other service-oriented businesses sometimes hire younger people. We know more than one teen girl whose first job was at the public library as a page, shelving books (and what a great way to reinforce a girl's love of reading!).

Even if not too many opportunities are out there for your daughter, it's great experience for her to present herself as a prospective employee. At best she's only two or three years from wanting to do this in a more serious way. Any practice she gets puts her that much further ahead when she might face a competitive hiring situation. It also helps her develop her skills in communicating with adults about her abilities and interests, making her more confident about expressing herself and interacting with people beyond her own peeps.

Her Safety

No matter what your daughter does—whether a volunteer or paying job—her well-being and safety are most important. We wish we could say we lived in a Mayberry-kind of world, where all the neighbors looked out for everyone's kids and kids knew this network of protection was there for them. Sadly, such of a world lives only where we remember it: on black-and-white television.

Even when you know where you daughter's supposed to be, make sure she's there and she feels comfortable being there. Drive her to her volunteer position, her babysitting job, or her paying job. Let others see that you're on the ball and involved with what's going on with your daughter. Walk her in now and again, instead of always dropping her off. Occasionally show up early to pick her up. Ask her, every time, how things went. What did she do? Who else was there? What did they do?

You've got good parental intuition—use it! If something doesn't feel quite right to you, don't waste time (and potentially your daughter's well-being) trying to figure out what it is or whether you're overreacting. It's not quite right, and in the short term that's all you need to know to take action. It's much easier to laugh about it later than to forever regret a missed signal.

However responsible your daughter is, she doesn't—and can't—have the same sense of the world that you do. She doesn't have the experience.

Oh, Puh-leeze!

Do you have a code word or phrase that your daughter can use to alert you that she's in some kind of trouble? If so, remind her of this as she ventures into activities that let her be more independent. And if not, it's a good thing to do now. Then she'll know that no matter what the trouble, you'll come to the rescue—no further explanation needed.

In many ways, this is a good thing. She's open and eager in ways that you can't be. But it's also a bit of a risk in the context of her vulnerability. She might feel safe with a person because she knows that person from somewhere she trusts, or in a place that's always been comfortable. Most of the time, she's right to feel this way. Every now and again, though, she's not. It's a difficult challenge for us as parents to encourage our daughters to leap into the world with full gusto, yet teach them to at the same time be cautious.

To Her Good (Emotional) Health

These middle years—from tween to 16—are especially formative when it comes to your daughter's self-confidence and sense of her ability to blend who she is now with who she wants to be and who she might become. Her world is still mostly about potential, but she's beginning to see how she can shape her experiences to support her interests. This is a time of transition and transformation in her life unlike any other she'll experience—she's in neither childhood nor adulthood.

Even though fitting in remains more important to her than just about anything else, her friends are beginning to stretch their wings, too. And in certain settings, it's even becoming okay to stand out because her interests are stronger and she has greater faith in her abilities. It's great to win the state soccer title or the Math Challenge Bowl. She has her peeps in these areas, and they support her as much as you do.

You can support your daughter by helping her to find some kernel of the positive even when things don't go right for her. Encourage her to talk about her experiences and how she feels about them. Especially help her to understand that it's all part of learning and growing up to try something you thought you'd love, then find out you really hate it—and to try something you thought you'd hate and discover you like it even better than coffee ice cream.

The Least You Need to Know

♦ As challenging as the transitional years of middle school are, they also offer increasing opportunities to reconnect with your daughter in positive, enjoyable ways.

♦ Encouraging your daughter to pursue her interests, in school and out of school, helps her to expand her world.

♦ Girls who become involved in volunteering in their communities are able to move past limitations they might feel in school to feel proud of their abilities and efforts.

♦ A "real" job that pays money helps your daughter develop responsibility and broadens her ability to interact with other people.

♦ The more connected your daughter feels to situations and people beyond her friends and school activities, the stronger her self-confidence and sense of well-being.

Part 4

You Go, Girl!

Your girl is ready to test her growing freedom and set out on her own path. *She's* ready, but are *you* ready? To complete our task of raising this generation of girls, we need to examine the influences that are shaping the way they think differently than we do. We need to support her decisions as she makes her own peace with the tension between home and career, single and married, and when and *whether* motherhood will feel like the right choice. Guiding your girl is as easy and as hard as understanding her: hopes, dreams, fears, ambitions, and all.

Chapter 15

Going to High School

In This Chapter

- Not just a step up to the next grade
- Navigating the official and the unofficial rules of high school
- An F?! How did *that* happen?
- Bringing down the stress level

Talk about culture shock! There's nothing that can quite prepare your daughter for her first day at high school. She might as well be plucked from Earth by a spaceship and deposited on a mirror planet in a galaxy far, far away as get on that school bus and step out onto the high school campus.

Okay, maybe that's a bit extreme. But fasten your seatbelt anyway. This ride's gonna be bumpy, at least until your daughter reaches stable orbit in her new universe.

Brave New World

High school truly is another world, and compared to middle school it can seem quite harsh and inhospitable. In middle school, the focus is on helping kids do what they need to do to make it through, academically, personally, and socially. High school is all about independence and individual accountability.

It's likely to be at least twice as big, in terms of campus size as well as student population, as your daughter's middle school—often even larger. High school is the end of the secondary education funnel. School districts that have a half-dozen elementary schools may have two middle schools and one high school. Even when the population from middle school to high school stays about the same, it's a bigger, less regulated environment.

High school presumes a higher level of maturity among students. Given that maturity is a process that progresses over time, girls entering high school are lower on the scale than girls about to graduate high school. The gap is often overwhelming, and leads to much of the teasing, taunting, and even hazing that returning high school students (typically sophomores, juniors, and seniors) inflict upon incoming freshmen. Although behavior like this does cause you to wonder, at which end of the scale is the immaturity? And for the record, all high schools have explicit policies that ban such behavior. They try.

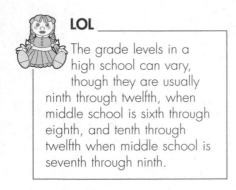

LOL

The grade levels in a high school can vary, though they are usually ninth through twelfth, when middle school is sixth through eighth, and tenth through twelfth when middle school is seventh through ninth.

I Didn't Sign Up for This!

Depending on the size of your daughter's school district, she might find herself attending a different high school than some, most, or even all her friends from middle school. This can be quite devastating, leaving her to feel alone and abandoned. She has to start over to make friends—not an easy thing to do when so many of the other girls are coming into high school with their long-time BFFs. Though they'll all make some new friends as they make their way through high school, it's tough to start out feeling that you're on your own.

Even if most or all of your daughter's peeps head to the same high school, odds are high they won't all have the same classes. They might be on different academic paths, especially as they move up through the grade levels. Depending on how the school allows kids to register for classes, they might not be able to get into the same classes even when they do have the same interests. Some schools register by alphabet, so girls whose last names start with "T" may not have the same choices as those whose last names start with "C."

Though it doesn't make much sense to us that our daughters might plan their schedules according to whether their friends are taking the same classes, the girls might now see why it isn't the best method. Fortunately most high schools have numerous offerings of the same courses, so there are enough classes to accommodate this dance. It's a good idea to sit down with your daughter before registration day to go over the class offerings and help her choose ones that match her interests and goals. At least then when she goes to her friends, she's already got a plan and they can follow *her*.

Mentors: Integrating into the System

Many high schools assign teachers and counselors to serve as mentors for incoming freshmen and other new students. The mentor's role is to help those new to the school to make the appropriate connections, from things as basic as finding the cafeteria and restrooms to reading their class schedules and understanding course requirements. Even as your daughter's entering high school as a freshman, her mentor will be asking her about her plans for after high school. If she hasn't given this any serious thought, she's going to be flustered and upset.

Most high schools offer appointments with guidance counselors for incoming freshmen and their parents. During these sessions, the counselor explains required (often called core) and elective courses, grades, and graduation requirements. The idea of so

In Her Shoes

High school girls don't yet have the maturity to see the long-term consequences of their actions. When you're 14, 15, 16 years old, the future is next summer! You don't see 20, 25, 35 years old. Mentors—and parents—can help girls look further into the future and make choices now that support what they want to be and do.

many choices likely both delights and scares your daughter. She's not used to having this kind of control over her school life, and may not know how to go about making her decisions. The counselor may want to establish a schedule during the meeting, or ask that you and your daughter discuss the various options and be ready to select a schedule the first day of school.

Peer Advisors: Learning the Ropes

An increasing number of high schools are turning to peer advisors to help make life tolerable for new students. Peer advisors are usually upperclassmen (juniors or seniors) who are themselves in good academic standing and who participate in a broad range of school activities. Sometimes peer advisors are members of the student body government; sometimes they're simply older students who want to help out younger students.

Numerous studies show that peer advisor programs improve behavior and academic focus. But your daughter's take on the peer advisor is likely to be far more personal: she should see this person as someone who can, and wants to, make her life easier. Though initially the school assigns peer advisors, your daughter can switch if she doesn't get along so well with hers.

Peer advisors are often kind of like big sisters, helping younger high school girls navigate the sometimes-treacherous (from a social perspective) waters of their new environment. Peer advisors give the low-down on teachers and classes, and the lay of the land about cliques, pops, and jocks. Your daughter and her peer advisor may never be friends, as such, but the peer advisor will often smooth the way in social settings and help with problems that arise with friends.

Remember, though, that peer advisors, for as helpful as they can be, are nonetheless students—and young—themselves. They might receive orientation from the school that covers some of the serious kinds of issues they should report to school officials, but they're not really hall monitors. Your daughter's peer advisor sees her role as helping your daughter work through her concerns and problems that relate to school, not reporting to anyone about them.

In Her Shoes

Hopefully, as a parent you've pretty much figured your daughter
out by now. You know her strengths and weaknesses, where she needs
help, where she acts out and how she shuts down, and what kind of
support she needs from you. It's your responsibility to bring down the
stress level by telling your daughter, you can't do everything and we
don't expect you to … but we *do* expect simply that you give your studies your best effort. Do your best, and that's all you can do.

Making the Grade(s)

In earlier grades, even middle school, your daughter's teachers established procedures to make sure kids got their schoolwork completed
and turned in on time. Maybe the teacher wrote on the board the
names of kids who still had outstanding assignments after the due date.
Probably the teacher held structured study sessions to prepare for quizzes and tests, and offered lunchtime or after-school help for those who
wanted or needed it. The emphasis was on helping everyone to at least
achieve passing grades on tests and coursework, and teachers took on
the responsibility of making sure that help was available.

Not so in high school. Teachers prepare information sheets about their
policies, procedures, and expectations and pass them out on the first
day of school. Typically, parents are asked to sign off on the papers, for
which the teacher awards credit to the student. The class summary tells
what major projects are on the syllabus, as well as what research they'll
require and what resources are available for students to use. The summary also specifies how the teacher grades assignments and whether he
or she accepts late work. (Surprise, surprise … work might actually be
due on its due date!) Failing a class might mean taking it again if it's a
required course, often in summer school.

Competition around grades can be intense, especially in the upper
grade levels, and many girls aren't quite ready for it. They might be
used to earning grades that factor in their effort as much as the actual
work, or allow for minor grammatical errors in papers for classes other
than English. Not the way it happens in high school, where teachers
generally expect a higher level of ability. This is a tough lesson for girls
who're used to getting good grades almost as a matter of routine.

Classes and even subjects are not so delineated by grade level as when we were in high school. Way back in the old days, by our daughters' standards, a freshman took only freshman-level classes and a senior took only senior-level classes. A student was clearly a freshman, sophomore, junior, senior. Today, most students take classes over a four-year schedule (or three-year schedule, in a three-year high school). The goal is to get all the needed classes by the year of graduation rather than year by year.

LOL

Each state has minimum requirements for the number of classes, and in which subjects, kids must earn passing grades to graduate. School districts have additional qualifications.

Classes often contain students across grade levels. An advantage to this is that the class is often more lively, as upper-level students are more comfortable speaking out. A disadvantage is that lower level students can feel pushed aside.

Grades Count

Grades matter in new and more significant ways in high school. They count now toward high school graduation requirements, which is the most important consideration. But high school grades also matter after high school. This is the beginning of the "permanent record," in a way—the report of her performance that follows your daughter through the next decade or so of her life. Colleges, technical programs, and even prospective employers use high school grades, activities, and achievements—the high school portfolio—in their decision-making processes. Certainly grades aren't everything; balance is crucial. But grades matter more now than they have before, which ups the ante on stress and pressure.

Is your daughter the studious type, spending hours preparing for tests and treating each assignment as though her entire future depends on the grade she receives? High school is likely to rock her world in some uncomfortable ways. Or is your girl laid back and casual about schoolwork, doing what interests her, when she's interested? High school is likely to rock her world in some uncomfortable ways, too.

Though a good student is a good student no matter the environment, the pressure of increased expectations in all classes creates a lot of pressure for girls who're used to making the honor roll every semester. Sure, in middle school she had six or so different classes and teachers, just like she does now in high school. But in middle school, teachers were more likely to coordinate with each other when it came to big projects and major tests, so as not to overload students. In high school, teachers expect students to figure out how to manage their class loads. Showing up unprepared for a trig test because she had to write a term paper for history isn't going to get a girl any slack.

The Trouble with Being in Academic Trouble ...

Kathy points out that all too often, girls (and boys, too) who slip into academic difficulty don't realize they've gone over the edge until it's too late for them to scramble back. They either slack or struggle all semester, often thinking that because no one's nagging them or asking them how they're doing, they're doing all right. Even doing none of their work, they somehow believe they'll still pass.

When your daughter stands in front of you and says, "I can't believe that!" when you ask her about the F on her report card, she's probably telling you the truth. She's genuinely just as shocked as you are (though how this could be defies adult logic), and very much in disbelief that her teacher failed her without even telling her (never mind the semester of weekly progress reports) or giving her a chance to make up missing assignments and failed tests.

If you can catch academic and school problems early enough, you can help your daughter work with her teachers to get back on track while it's possible to do so fairly easily. It doesn't take much to fall so far behind that you need to look at alternative solutions, though, such as tutoring, summer school, Internet classes, or enrollment in an alternative school instead of the regular public school. Are extracurricular activities—school-related or not—taking too much time and focus from academics? If so, don't hesitate to pull her back or even cut her off! Do it with love and a calm expression of your concern for her future, of course. But step in and be firm; as her parent, you are in charge.

In Her Shoes

Nearly all high schools use a progress report system of some sort in addition to official grade reports, so at least parents aren't caught by surprise even if their kids seem unaware that they're not doing well in class. These reports commonly come in the mail, so make sure you know the schedule (look on the school calendar) and watch for them to arrive.

It's crucial to get to the bottom of the problems so you can put the right solutions in place. Would the subject matter be easier for her if she went to class every day, or is she giving her best effort and still struggling? Does she do her assignments and turn them in but receive poor grades, or does she not turn in her work? Does she freeze when it's time for a test, even though she knows the material so well that she helps her friends study? Or does she not even know where her textbook is? Sometimes the issues are more social than academic—friends who are in her classes or not in her classes, personality clashes with teachers.

Beyond Grades: Bigger Issues

Bigger issues surface when girls become discouraged and feel that they're failures, not just failing a class or two. Anxiety and depression are distressingly common among high school girls, although they—and their parents—are often slow to recognize something's wrong.

Parents should be alert to the signs their daughters are struggling with school and other issues. Is your usually cheery and outgoing girl suddenly sullen and distant? Is she lethargic, disinterested, and clearly unhappy as a perpetual state of emotion?

Girls who are not doing well are the ones who are left to their own devices. School becomes a downward spiral and it's hard to get out. A girl fails a few classes, and suddenly she's down on herself. She starts questioning, *why should I keep going through this*? If she can't do the academics, she may turn to other ways to "excel," such as sexual promiscuity, drugs, or drinking.

The Pressure to Excel

Now more than ever, girls especially feel a lot of pressure to excel and succeed. They've been endowed with opportunities in education and careers that weren't available to generations of women before them. We—their parents—want them to make the most of these opportunities. Girls in the eighth grade may take classes that give them high school credit. Girls in high school may take classes that give them college credit. It's a heavy responsibility.

Girls do seem to have a bit better perception of the bigger picture than do boys, which is perhaps one reason parents and teachers feel they can handle more of an academic load and its resulting pressures. Girls in high school, more so than boys, often have a sense of what they want to do or be when they grow up. Boys at this age are often still in fantasyland, wanting to be in the NFL or the NBA. (Some will succeed in realizing these dreams; we're not dissing these ambitions.) Girls tend rather to have their sights on becoming teachers, doctors, nurses, engineers—whatever, but more grounded in reality. While this makes it more likely for girls to succeed, it also puts them under greater stress.

Oh, Puh-leeze!

High school graduation rates vary widely across the United States. At best, just over 80 percent of those who enter high school currently leave with a diploma; at worst, just over 20 percent graduate. Each state determines that age to which a child is legally required to remain in school. Kids drop out because they're bored, they fail to see the value of staying in school, or they have life circumstances that make attending school difficult. In most communities, kids who drop out can earn a high school diploma through a community college or an equivalency diploma (GED). Parents are an important influence on a child's interest and success in school.

Extracurriculars

Extracurricular activities used to be the kinds of things girls did outside of academics, for fun and to help maintain balance in their lives. Sports, school government, special-interest clubs, drama, band or choir—all kinds of activities. For many girls, these are things they still do for fun, and they have a great time participating in them.

With so many kids applying to college, colleges are looking beyond academics to try to choose applicants who appear well rounded and ambitious beyond grades. So increasingly, school counselors and parents push these "extracurriculars" because they look good on the transcript, not necessarily because they're interesting or fun. Many high schools require extracurricular activities, and may even award credit for them.

It's great for your daughter to be busy and involved in all aspects of high school. Just make sure she's doing things she wants to do, things that interest her, or that she wants to explore, not just things other people (ahem, even you) are telling her she needs to do. Encourage her to indulge her passions. And for some girls, extracurriculars are where they excel. We talk about boys dreaming of playing professional sports, but girls have these dreams, too—and also in other areas like science, art, politics, music, medicine, and drama. Girls dream big.

Sometimes too big. It sounds great to have all kinds of things going, especially when they're all related to school. And you want your daughter to enjoy her high school years to their fullest. But there's still only so much time in the day. As important a lesson as any academic one is to balance interests and efforts. If your daughter routinely gets home well after dinnertime and is so exhausted she falls asleep on the sofa still wearing her shoes, she's got too much going on in her life.

When she's well rested, sit down with her. Ask her to take you through a typical day, and write down what she tells you she does. Ask her to estimate how much time each activity requires. When she's finished, add it all up. Are you over 24? That's a problem! Help your daughter choose the activities that are most important to her, and let the others go. (And maybe take a look at your own daily activities, while you're at it. Are you unwittingly setting the pattern your daughter's following?)

Not Everyone Is College-Bound

For today's generation of girls, college is almost a given—we and they simply assume they'll go. From when they begin to walk and talk and interact with the world, we plant the seed that education is the path to success. And in the beginning, we have a broad view of what this means. We engage our girls in all kinds of learning opportunities before and beyond school that are fun and casual—going to museums of all kinds, libraries, aquariums and zoos, nature preserves, and historic sites.

Somewhere along the line, though, the path narrows and learning becomes primarily academic. The fun factor drops by the wayside. By high school our daughters are taking a lot of classes because they're being told they need to take them, not because the subjects interest them. High school becomes all—and only—about getting into college. Some high schools even offer classes that provide college credit, to give kids a jump-start.

But what if your daughter really doesn't want to go to college? (Gasp!) What if she wants a career in the trades or in a technical area? What if she wants to take a year or two after she graduates high school and travel the country or the world? What if she just wants to get a job? What if she doesn't really know what she wants to do with her life? (Did you, when you were her age?)

Wherever your daughter's passions lie, encourage and support them. Of course academics are important; high school remains the foundation for acceptance into most aspects of adult life, from further education (including vocational or technical training) to jobs. Supporting your daughter's passions helps her to move away from dependence on her friends, too, because she becomes more centered and confident in herself and her abilities.

 LOL

If your daughter complains that school starts too early and she can't be fully awake for her first few classes, she's not exaggerating. The natural cycle of teens runs a bit differently from our adult sense of timing. Put a group of teens in a room with no clock and tell them to sleep when they feel tired, and you'd find that they'll go to bed around three in the morning and sleep until noon!

Finding Balance

High school is a huge leap for our daughters. As parents, it's our role and responsibility to help them find balance as they move toward adulthood—balance in their academic workloads, balance in their personal and social lives, and balance in their desires and goals. No one can do everything, though teenage girls tend to believe they should be able to (and are expected to). Bring down the stress level for your daughter by regularly reminding her to take a break and relax. And always let her know that as long as she is doing her best, that is all she can do.

The details will fall into place as your daughter learns that when she explores each subject with her whole intent and focus, regardless of the grade, she's being supported by the adults around her in her quest to discover who she is, and what fascinates and inspires her. After all, school is about discovery, in all senses of the word. Your daughter will gain confidence and excitement as she begins to figure out what subjects hold her passion, and that her dreams are within her reach, so long as she continues to learn about herself and the world around her.

The Least You Need to Know

- Moving up to high school is moving into an entirely different world for your daughter.

- Girls, more than boys, worry as much about high school now as college in the future when it comes to classes, activities, and grades.

- Although college is now an expectation in terms of what comes after high school, the focus of high school as preparation for college sometimes puts extreme stress on girls.

- Parents can help their daughters keep a balanced perspective so they enjoy their high school years.

- Encourage your daughter to always do her best, regardless of whether the subject comes easily to her or not.

Chapter 16

Going Out?

In This Chapter

- ◆ Is she really ready to drive?
- ◆ She's on the road
- ◆ In due time: her curfew
- ◆ When her friends are driving

"I need the car tonight, okay? Everyone's meeting at the Dairy Queen, and then we're going midnight bowling."

Girls drive. Not just their parents crazy, but their parents' cars. Some girls have their own cars, which drives their parents crazy in different ways. Driving is a rite of passage into adult freedom and independence.

"I'll Drive!"

At last, she can ask for the keys and do more than turn on the radio. For your daughter, driving is power. Driving is freedom. Driving is the ability to go where she wants, when she wants. Driving enables her to truly be on her own—as long as *you* fill the gas tank.

For you, your daughter's driving is both liberating and scary. Liberating, because now you no longer have to listen to, "Pleeeeeezzzze will you drive me to the mall?" Scary, because your daughter doesn't yet know why she herself should be scared—or at least more humble—when she slides behind the wheel. Just like *WATCH OUT!!!* she doesn't see the car on her left that's about to blow through the stop sign.

Even the best of teen drivers isn't as good as she'll be, say, even five years from now. But she doesn't see it that way. "I've been driving for a *year* now, Mom. I know what to watch for. I saw the car. I knew it would stop. It had a stop sign."

This is how parents go prematurely gray.

Ready or Not

From your daughter's perspective, only two things matter when it comes to determining when she's ready to drive: the legal driver minimum-age requirement and the birthday when she reaches that age. As her parent, you have a third factor to throw into the mix: her level of responsibility.

Some girls can't wait to drive. They watch your every move when you drive, offering commentary on everything from how you hold the steering wheel to the three miles per hour over the speed limit registering on the speedometer. They ask questions—incessant questions—about how everything works, from shifting to the windshield wipers. They immerse themselves in the driver's manual like it's a new *Twilight* novel and beg you to ask them questions. Would that they devoted as much focus to their schoolwork! And come that magical birthday when they're legally old enough to get their learner's permit, they're showered, dressed, and ready to go to the licensing department even before you raise your head from the pillow to notice it's daylight.

In Her Shoes

Girls tend to be more willing than boys to wait until they're older, even 17 or 18, to get their driver's licenses. So by the time they do take the keys, they're in general more mature. Some girls might even be able to articulate that they fear driving because they always react emotionally to stressful situations.

Other girls let their "now I can drive!" birthdays pass with barely any acknowledgement of their import. They don't much care to wait in the car at all, preferring to tag along as you wind through the aisles of canned goods and boxed cereal. They'd even rather sit and watch you get your hair done. The driver's manual and brochures for driving schools just stay there on the corner of the kitchen counter, under the phone book and the junk mail. They don't even want to bring the car keys to you when it's time to go somewhere in the car.

Some girls see driving as their means to the freedom and independence they crave. They want to go where they want to go, when they want to go. And the less you know about it, they figure, the better … as long as you put gas in the car. Other girls like the status quo—having their parents drive them wherever they need to go, walking or taking the bus, or just not going at all but staying home instead to read or click away at the computer. Eagerness and reluctance are not very good measures of how ready a girl is to get behind the wheel.

And are *you* ready for her to take the wheel? It's a mixed bag! What a relief to finally not be driving her here, there, and everywhere—all the time. At last your day (and your night) returns to your own interests and needs. But when you're driving your girl everywhere she wants to go, you're getting in a lot of together time. Even if she's only sitting there plugged into her iPod, the potential is there for her to let you behind the curtain of her daily life for a few minutes.

But when she's in the driver's seat, first of all you don't want her doing *anything*, like complaining about her math homework or planning what to wear to the homecoming dance, that distracts her from driving. All other issues aside, she's got your life in her hands! And second, you're increasingly less likely to be the one in the passenger seat beside her, particularly after she gets her license and can drive on her own. Even if you wanted her to talk while she was driving (which you don't), you're losing this time together. It's okay … you'll find other ways to share and stay connected.

Learning Curve

Hard to say whether it's the learning to drive or the actual driving that most worries parents. Like everything else, though, we take the plunge and believe we can effect the best possible outcome. Though driving school may pump new drivers onto the roads in a couple months, it takes many more months (years, even) for those drivers to be fully comfortable and competent. Experience comes with time and practice, as you know all too well.

In Her Shoes

Growing numbers of high schools are abandoning driver's education programs to the private sector. This puts the burden on families to enroll their teens in, and pay for, private driving lessons. In some communities a shortage of qualified programs means teens might need to wait to obtain their driver's licenses—which is not an entirely bad thing, looking at the statistics that 16-year-old drivers have four times as many accidents as 18-year-old drivers.

We talk a lot about the influences of your daughter's peers on her decisions and actions, and certainly that rolls over into driving. But when one of your daughter's friends, attempting to persuade you to let your daughter ride in the car with her when she's driving, says to you, "I always go five miles an hour over the speed limit because the police never stop you for that and I can get there faster," where do you think that comes from? Not her peers! The most significant influence on your daughter's driving habits is reading this book right now: you. Your daughter's been watching you drive for a few years now. She knows all your good habits, bad habits, and frustrations. If that makes you uncomfortable, it's time to clean up your act!

Keys, Please

It's a liberating moment when your daughter starts to drive. She can take herself where she needs to go, including to and from school and to run her own errands (and, occasionally, yours as a bargaining chip for borrowing your car). You're no longer on tap as her sole chauffeur. No more worries about missing the bus ... unless she's expecting to take *your* car to get herself to school.

Statistically, teen girls are still better drivers than teen boys, although trends show the gap is narrowing. Girls get in fewer accidents, get fewer tickets, and generally are less inclined to show off for their peers or engage in aggressive driving. Girls also tend to be a bit more aware of consequences, though not necessarily of cause and effect—that is, braking suddenly to catch an almost-missed turn could result in a close encounter of the most jarring sort with the car behind.

Oh, Puh-leeze!

It takes more than being tall enough to reach both the pedals and the steering wheel at the same time to be ready for the keys. You'll want to consult with your daughter's doctor if she has any health conditions for which she takes medications, to make sure neither the condition nor the medication puts her at risk when she's driving.

For the record, these are not random observations or gender stereotypes. The insurance industry meticulously studies innumerable facets of the driving experience, including many that most of us would not otherwise think about. (Good that there are others to do this sort of thinking!) The most alarming change is that the accident rate for girls is climbing, while for boys it's holding steady. Why this is the case is anybody's guess; theories abound. It might be that more girls are driving at a younger age, or that teenage girls are driving more often and for longer distances. Whatever the reason, the change tells us we've got to pay attention to the details when we're teaching our girls how to drive.

The Dangers of Distraction

According to Allstate, a 17-year-old on a cell phone has the same reaction time as a 70-year-old. What does this say about driving and talking on the cell phone? In many locations, it's against the law for drivers to be on the phone while the car is moving. Not that this stops the behavior, but it gives more credibility to your warnings. Many states, too, have limited or progressive driver's license requirements that restrict the number and kinds of passengers who can ride in the car with a new driver under the age of 18.

Distractions—not necessarily just being on the phone—are the leading cause of accidents. Changing music selections (switching radio stations, swapping CDs, scrolling options on an iPod), eating and drinking, talking (with others in the car as well as on the cell phone), and looking for something in the car rank at the top of the list. Encourage your daughter, from the beginning of her driving experience, to devote her full attention when she's behind the wheel to *driving*. If she wants to change the music, teach her to do it when she's stopped, or even to pull over. If she's listening to her iPod in the car, make sure she's using an adapter cord to plug it into the car's speakers, not wearing headphones.

You might have to change some of your own driving behaviors—*do what I say, not what I do* is not an especially effective method. Sure, you're an experienced driver, and maybe you can handle multiple tasks simultaneously. But there are lots of drivers out there—like your daughter—who aren't so experienced. At the very least, you've got to be on the alert for them!

We've saved this point for last, and we can't make it strongly enough. Texting should *never* be done behind the driver's wheel of a car. Tell your teen girl that she *must* pull over and stop if she wants to either send or receive text messages when she is the driver. Preliminary studies show that texting while driving leads to accidents. Parents: this goes for *you*, too. No texting while you are driving, *ever*!

Have Car, Will Travel

Your daughter's probably spent the night, weekend, or even longer periods of time away from home—staying with friends, visiting with relatives, going away to camp. When she was younger, it was a pretty safe bet that she'd stay wherever it was that you dropped her off, except maybe to a neighbor of the friend's or with adults to supervise her. You didn't have to worry so much about her and her friends using the drop-off as the launch for another excursion, however brief or local, you knew nothing about.

Ah, those were the days, although you didn't know it then. Trust was simple when there were few options. Now that your daughter's older, has friends who drive, and may herself drive, you have few assurances beyond the ones she gives you that she'll really stay where she says she'll be. Will she? You want to trust this will be so, though it's probably more realistic to recognize that she's going to test her freedom in a lot of ways she's not going to tell you about. After all, part of independence is not having to ask permission.

It's not that she *wants* to lie to you … most of the time. It's just that (choose the excuse that fits) …

- The situation just came up, and before she knew it she was doing it. And by then, what would be the point of calling to ask if it was okay?

- You wouldn't let her do what she's planning to do if you knew what it really was, so she just did it, and it turned out fine so what's the big deal?

- She didn't want to bother you so late at night.

- She knew she'd be right back to where you thought she was, so what would be the point of giving you something more to worry about?

- She's capable of making her own decisions and doesn't understand why you treat her like such a child.

She, like most kids, probably did a bit of this behind-your-back kind of stuff when she was younger—going to the park when she said she'd be at a friend's house, or to a different friend's house. You never found out, nothing bad ever happened (well, except for that time a loose playground dog bit her leg when she was swinging … but she was able to get back to her friend's house before calling you, so in the end even that wasn't really so bad). To her, it makes perfect sense that what you don't find out about maintains the trust that's so important to you.

The thought processes of teenagers continue to mystify parents and other adults. You'd think that, we all having been teenagers once, we could better anticipate some of the illogic—because *that* certainly hasn't changed. But somehow we mostly lose those connections and insights when the door of adolescence closes behind us and we exist fully in adulthood—such that we stand in front of our daughters and listen to the words coming from our own mouths and think, "Oh, my … I sound just like my mother!" (Or father.)

Setting Boundaries

When you're the one driving your daughter around, it's pretty easy to set and enforce the hours of her participation in any kind of event, from hanging out at a friend's house to going to the Friday night football game. She wants a ride; she'll be there when you're supposed to be there to pick her up (and heaven forbid *you're* the one who's running late). It's not so much about respecting the value of your time and effort in chauffeuring her around—and how wonderful, those moments when her peeps thank you for driving—as that she doesn't want to do anything that jeopardizes her transportation. She loves you, but she's got a pragmatic streak.

New freedoms for her and challenges for you come when your daughter's driving herself or riding as a passenger with one of her peeps behind the wheel. She wants to make her own decisions about when to be places and when to come home. You've now got to decide how you're going to deal with her curfew—and we use the term only to mean the time at which you want her home, not in the context of any laws in your community.

Oh, Puh-leeze! _____

In some communities, curfew is less an issue for parents and more a matter of local laws that determine how late minors can be out on their own. Although the intent of curfew laws is to protect young people, the effect can be that they end up in legal trouble. Teens usually know what laws exist in their communities but parents sometimes do not. Make sure you're not first finding out about a curfew law when you have to go pick up your daughter at the police station.

You already know, from the 16 or so years you've lived with your daughter, how she perceives time. She might be the first one at school every morning, or hold the school record for tardiness. She might own five watches and never wear one of them, look obsessively at her watch, or have such an uncanny sense that she always knows what time it is, within a minute, though she seldom looks at a clock. Maybe she's the timekeeper among her peeps, or maybe her friends regularly send her reminders of when and where she's supposed to meet them. Whatever her time issues, you—no doubt better than she—know exactly what to expect from her when it comes to time and timelines.

You have expectations as a parent—you *have* to have expectations as a parent. Your daughter is remarkably quiet when those expectations support what she wants to do. You look at her in equally quiet admiration, thinking, "Wow, my little girl is really growing up." Then she finds herself at odds with your expectations, and instantly she's a screaming and yelling four-year-old. Heavy sigh.

Whichever end she's playing against the middle, you've got to stand your ground. If you've been steady in this all along, it's easier going. If, like most of us, you waver now and again, you can be sure your daughter'll make every attempt to exploit the exceptions. Again, she's not necessarily being malicious (though it might feel that way). She's pushing against her boundaries because they're shifting anyway. She may sound like she wants to set them herself—and in some ways, she does. But mostly she just wants to know where her boundaries are. We're all more comfortable when we know how far we are from the edge.

If pushing the boundaries crosses into flaunting the laws, you've got a bigger issue. It's one thing to come in 12 minutes past curfew, but quite another to bring home a speeding ticket for doing 50 in a 30. These are serious breaches that have real-life consequences. Not only is there the increased risk of being in an accident, but there's the fine, the black mark against her driving record, and quite possibly a hefty increase in your insurance premium. In many states, teens under age 16 automatically lose their driving privileges until they turn 18 for certain kinds of infractions.

 In Her Shoes

Stuff happens. As much as you want your daughter to always be home by her curfew, you know there'll be times when she won't be. Without establishing this as an expectation, do set up the carved-in-stone rule that she always call you when she is going to be late. You can deal with her explanations and other kinds of fallout later; in the moment, you want only to know that she's safe. Part of the learning process is for your daughter to know that although it's not good to blow curfew, it's much worse not to call!

A Car of Her Own

Whether, and how, your daughter gets her first car depends on numerous variables. Many are financial: a car is a significant purchase in itself. Pretty much gone are the days when $500 buys a car you'd trust with your daughter's safety—that amount of money barely buys a set of tires! And then there are the ongoing expenses of gas and maintenance.

Maybe you've been saving for this time in her life, and a new car is her birthday present. Perhaps you've got a car you can hand off to her that she can consider hers. Or maybe there's someone at work or in the neighborhood who's selling a gently used and well-maintained car. Some parents believe their kids should pay for at least part of a car's cost; others are willing to foot all or most of the bill. There are lots of options; the challenge is finding one that works best for you.

Adding another licensed driver to your insurance policy, especially one who's a teen, is certain to cause sticker shock when it comes to looking at the bill.

Bringing another car into your household may have a similar effect. You'll need to check your policy and perhaps talk with a representative from the insurance company to find out what's most advantageous for you. Keep in mind, too, that until your daughter turns 18, she can't legally own anything. Her car is actually your car, and you have legal accountability for how she uses it.

Having a car she considers her own may give your daughter a stronger sense of responsibility about how she drives and takes care of the car. Pride of ownership is a powerful incentive! She's going to be more motivated to learn about things like checking the tire pressure and oil level when it's her car—things she might not feel so inclined to do with your car.

In Her Shoes

To what extent should you expect your daughter to contribute to the expenses of driving? Although this may depend in large part on factors such as whether she has a job, helping to pay for things like gas, oil changes, and windshield washer fluid gives your daughter more of a vested interest in considering just how—and how often—she drives. Driving is one of those things that we so take for granted, we can lose sight of the expenses associated with it.

Riding in Cars with Friends

When she's not driving herself, your daughter's likely to hop in with one of her friends—sometimes not even one of her BFFs, but simply someone who has a car. Especially in the early stages of driving, when some friends are still too young to drive and others have conditional licenses, the allure of someone who can just take you where you want to go is almost irresistible. And it's not like they're going anyplace exotic—mostly places like to the drive-thru to grab something for lunch, or the video store to return the movies that are due back today. The kinds of errands you run all the time that are so mundane you barely think of them as anything but annoying interruptions are grand adventures to new drivers. And sometimes, they don't even really go anywhere but just drive around.

Who are your daughter's friends? Not the ones who hang out in your refrigerator but the ones who hover around the fringes of her friendship circle. The ones who, when she drops their names in casual conversation, you ask, "And who's that? I've never heard you talk about her." *Oh, you know who she is; you just can't remember.* Well, do you? If not, you should at least arrange for a drive-by sighting so you can connect a face and clothing style with the name. Or more pointedly, ask to meet her when your daughter points her out. (Or him.)

You and your daughter may take a significant split when it comes to her riding in cars with friends driving. She sees it first as transportation—a way to get where you aren't so eager to take her. (You're not going to excuse yourself from a meeting to drive her for a burger.) She sees it as a benefit for you, actually, because now she's not asking you to take her somewhere. And she also sees it as a matter of how much trust you have in her.

There's no straightforward answer to this situation—unless the law in your state restricts young drivers from having passengers in the car. Otherwise, you've got to ask yourself: How much do I trust her friends who drive? Where are they likely to go when they're in the car together? Do I trust them to make safe and logical decisions? Maybe you're comfortable with one of your daughter's friends as a driver but not so much the others.

The more effectively you can frame your responses so it's clear to your daughter that your only interests are her safety and well-being, the higher the likelihood she'll comply with your decision. As much as we'd all like to say that as parents we can issue directives ("You will *not* get in the car with her!"), we all know it doesn't always work that way. We've raised our daughters to think for themselves … and sometimes, much to our consternation, that's exactly what they do!

Alternative Transport

If she can't drive and you can't or won't drive her, she's got to find another way to get where she wants to go. For short distances in good weather, she might be willing to just hoof it, or even ride her bike. Longer distances, however, require more thought and planning. Much depends on where you live and what distance of travel is necessary for her to get to where she needs or wants to go. Often the option of choice is to catch ride with one of her peeps who does have the car for the evening. This might not really be what you had in mind. You've got to establish and monitor ground rules for such decisions.

So what about the bus or other form of public transit? It's good for your daughter to learn how to navigate around her community in different ways. Though not quite as liberating as a driver's license, a bus pass at least lets her make her own choices about where she's going without needing so much to consider your availability and willingness to take her.

The Least You Need to Know

◆ Age is only one factor when considering whether your daughter is ready to drive.

◆ Your daughter's growing freedoms and independence still require accountability and responsibility.

◆ Though teenage girls are still safer drivers, statistically, than teenage boys, the trend is shifting and risks are increasing for girls.

◆ Whether to let your daughter ride as a passenger when a teenage friend is driving is as important a decision as letting your daughter drive.

Chapter 17

Reading, Music, TV, and Texting

In This Chapter

- It's a digital world
- C u l8tr g2g
- Will you friend me?
- Safe travel in cyberspace
- Private, public, what's the difference?

Your daughter sits at the computer in the living room, two instant messaging and five browser windows open, as well as Microsoft Word. The TV's turned on, though muted, and she's listening to her iPod. She's got running IM discussions going with her friends about the homework assignment she's working on, the upcoming school dance, and the day's gossip. She turns from the computer every now and then to respond to the text messages coming in on her cell phone.

She's supposed to be writing a current events paper about the most significant advance that's occurred during her lifetime. But she's struggling to decide what that might be. Excuse us, but could it be any more obvious?

This (Un)Wired Generation

Looking for your girl? Send her a text message. No matter where she is or what she's doing, she's got her cell phone with her. She's connected, 24/7, to anyone who calls or texts her. Her cell phone rings when she has appointments—customized ringtones so she doesn't even have to look to see what the appointment is (or who's calling). She uses her cell phone as an alarm clock to get her up in the morning, a calculator to make sure she has enough money to cover the tax on her purchase, and a camera.

And her cell phone's only one of the many ways your daughter connects with her friends and her interests. She's got 5,000 songs loaded on her iPod. She uses the Internet to do her homework, check her bank account balances, see what's playing at the movies this weekend, and buy the latest novel in whatever series she's reading right now. Her MySpace or Facebook page lets all her friends see pics of her trip to Canada, sample her favorite songs, and leave their comments about anything. Welcome to the great digital divide!

Can You Hear Me Now?

From a parent's perspective a cell phone is a safety line; from a daughter's perspective it's freedom. She can call to tell you where she is, when she'll be home, and what she wants you to pick up for her when you go to the grocery store. And you can call her for the same reasons!

LOL

More than half of American teens have cell phones or smart phones (iPhone, Blackberry), according to industry statistics, and their numbers keep going up.

Today's teens don't know life *without* the cell phone. (Though teachers wish they did, at least for the six hours or so that they're in school every day.) And no sooner does she have cell phone in hand than new models—with catchy names, expanded features, and more colors than Crayola (even pink)—hit the market. The cell phone isn't only a device, also it's a status statement.

Text Me!

Even with her cell phone in her pocket, keypad unseen, she's texting her peeps. How is that even possible?! Text messaging has morphed from a sideshow to the main event among teens. Gifted with the ability to handle the unwieldy with amazing efficiency when it suits their needs, teens can work around the awkwardness of the cell phone's keypad to type their text messages faster, often, than we could enter a phone number to call. If you're not texting, you're *way* behind the curve! And if you are texting, bravo!

Texting has its downside, on two counts. One is its emphasis on brevity (the typical message can be only 160 characters … a bit shorter than the two sentences that open this chapter), which has spawned a creative shorthand vocabulary. Spelling, sentence structure, grammar, punctuation—all out the window. Even when kids write out full words and complete sentences for assignments, they tend to craft expressions of thoughts in short forms more like sound bites than thoughtful paragraphs. Further, they expect to read in the same way.

The second downside, particularly as far as teachers are concerned, is that text messaging has revolutionized cheating on tests and exams (although some kids might think of this as an upside). In the most unsophisticated, and common, version of this, kids simply send messages back and forth, often with those who took the same test from the same teacher in a different class period. In this form, texting replaces the age-old sneak-peak at answers penned on a body part.

In more sophisticated cheating schemes a cell phone can store formulas and other data, and text messages might come from sources even outside the school. And teachers have busted cheating rings where a student in an early class period takes photos of the test pages with the cell phone's camera, then sends those to students taking the test in later class periods.

Checking In Even When She Checks Out

It's a great thing to be able to call or text your daughter, just to check in with her about where she is and what she's doing. But she doesn't have to answer to know that it's you. Custom ringtones mean she doesn't even have to look at her phone. If she's not interested in talking to you, she won't.

In Her Shoes

No answer when you call your daughter's cell phone? Send a text message instead. Text messages require a lower signal strength and often go through when a call won't. And on many family plans, your phone lets you know when the phone you're sending to receives your text message.

Mostly she can get away with this because she knows you don't know whether she's in an area with poor reception (wouldn't we all love to have that Verizon team following us around in real life?). She may turn off her phone, even, to bolster her argument. Then she'll listen to your voice mail message, and call you when she can tell you what she knows you want to hear. It's not always something nefarious; she might simply be emphasizing her independence from you and your direct oversight of her activities.

A Picture's Worth ...

When every phone's a camera, what's the etiquette around snapping pictures? On the plus side, the quick click catches everything from newsworthy events as they unfold to comparisons for shopping decisions. In less than the time it would take for your daughter to describe a dress she's contemplating for the spring dance, she can snap a picture and send it to you—and you can snap back a response that says, "Is that a dress or a shirt?"

Within their circles of friends, teen girls have kind of a code of honor around when they take pictures of each other and who sees the pictures they take. Often, the images end up on their MySpace pages, where everyone who's okay to see them can and others have no access. Like other tangibles, though, pictures can be used to cause embarrassment and hurt.

There does seem to be a growing attitude of "everything's fair game" when it comes to capturing gaffes and foibles and putting them out there for the world to see—and not only among teens. Culturally we've always enjoyed a laugh at the expense of someone else—even television has greatly capitalized on this, as the long-running success of shows from *Candid Camera* to *America's Funniest Home Videos* attests. And let's not overlook the rampant popularity of YouTube and its clones.

You've Got Mail ... and More Mail ... and Still More Mail

Whatever communication doesn't take place via text-messaging rolls over to the next best thing: e-mail. Girls can set up free e-mail accounts at any number of domains, from Yahoo! and Hotmail to accounts available through magazines and websites they visit. The typical teen may have as many as a dozen e-mail accounts. Not that they get all that many messages, beyond spam, but simply because they can have all those accounts.

The service providers love that teens spread themselves out on the Internet in this way; it's a great mine for data. Advertisers glean astonishingly detailed information by tracking e-mail addresses. While schools typically block access to web-based e-mail as an effort to regulate the kind of content that can slip onto servers, Internet cafés and free Wi-Fi sites are seemingly everywhere to give access to e-mail and other Internet activities.

LOL

Because instant messaging and text-messaging take place in real time, girls often prefer them to using e-mail. E-mail is taking on more the context of what letter-writing used to be, stepping up when longer or more permanent communication is the goal.

Virtual Reality, Virtual Friends

Community is all about belonging, exchanging ideas, hanging with friends, and meeting new people. The communities your daughter belongs to come and go with the click of a switch—the power switch on her computer. She creates these communities on MySpace, Facebook, and other social-networking websites. It's like a live-action version of the vastly popular computer game *The Sims*, except the players are real people. Most of them, anyway.

It makes sense that teens would flock to virtual communities. Finally, a place where they belong and where they can be who they want to be! Even among her peeps who know her in the real world of school and such, a girl can develop her desired persona and presence on her MySpace page and feel safe from criticism and ridicule. It's a sheltered environment of her own creation, and she determines who she invites to share it. And that's the true beauty of MySpace, the most popular of the social networking sites among American teens: they choose who can visit, from just about everyone who asks to only a select few friends.

MySpace friends for many girls are simply extensions of the circles of friends they have out there in the real world. They view MySpace as just another place to hang out together—only no one has find a ride to get there, or ask a parent's permission, or wait until morning. This community, this interaction, functions 24/7. When it works right, it's great. Girls can share photos, poetry, music, comments—just like they were all sitting together in the same room.

LOL

MySpace (www.myspace.com) and Facebook (www.facebook. com) are the two largest and most popular social-networking websites. Both require users to establish profiles—individual web pages. Profiles may be public—anyone can view them—or private—available only to those on the friend list. Though the sites are free, advertisements bombard the pages.

When it backfires, though, the consequences can be painful and even catastrophic. The flipside of virtual friendships is that the power of acceptance or rejection can be just as intense as it is in the school cafeteria. A single keystroke can wipe a friend from the list, banishing her to the same oblivion she might experience in the school cafeteria or on the bus when others won't let her sit with them or give her the invisible treatment.

Some psychologists worry that the power to instantly vanquish someone comes dangerously close to viewing real-life friendships as virtual
creations, like *The Sims* characters. This depersonalization, psychologists fear, enables teens to escape the sometimes painful but necessary
processes of negotiating disagreements within friendships and other
relationships. If you can just vaporize someone who makes you mad,
why not do it? The person causes you hurt—click! She's gone. At least
from your virtual life. Problem is, of course, it doesn't work that way in
the real world.

And on the flipside, how do you deal with your daughter's anguish
when she's the one who gets erased from the friends list? Sure, she
could take it up with the friend in a real-life encounter. And she will,
if it's a friendship that really matters to her. But the real point isn't so
much whatever is the underlying issue, as it is to reinforce the message that belonging is a fragile privilege. Your daughter's been playing
on this field since preschool; all kids do. But now the whole world can
watch. Invisible would be a blessing.

The Privacy Paradox

"It's okay, Mom. My MySpace profile is private. No one can see it
unless I let them be on my friends list." She says this with the confidence and patience you had with her when assuring her, at five years
old, that there really were no monsters under her bed. Huh. Well,
an interesting perspective about a venue that's so vastly public! Is she
deluded, or are we?

In a certain way, her perspective is not much different from that of
two people who stand in a roomful of people at a party and carry on a
deeply personal conversation. They act as if they're the only ones in the
room, and oddly enough nearly everyone else ignores them as if that
were true. The shared delusion doesn't keep others from eavesdrop-
ping, of course. But even when they overhear conversation, most people
keep it to themselves—until and unless there's an advantage to taking it
public (like being able to be the first one to break some sort of news or
worthy gossip).

So when does your daughter's "private" information take on public
interest? Just like anything else, when there's someone (a disgruntled

former friend, perhaps) who senses an opportunity to make her look bad. Most of what girls put on their MySpace pages tends to be the same kinds of things they'd talk about and otherwise share in the setting of, say, a slumber party.

But pictures might be especially silly (read: embarrassing) when viewed without their context, or even intimate. (Ew! Who needs to see *that*?) Dialogue, via IM and comments, often becomes deeply personal very quickly, partly because emotions are intense but just beneath the surface and partly because the Internet fosters a sense of anonymity, even when communicating with people you know.

Add to the mix that you truly can make anonymous comments—you can say anything to anyone without revealing who you are. This cloaks what common decency would otherwise block—few people would actually say to someone in person, "Your hair looks like you cut it yourself in your sleep and your clothes look like you're wearing them backward." (Well, mean girls might say such things, especially with a big enough audience.) An already hurtful comment becomes all the more damaging when a girl has no idea who left it; now she has to question *all* of her friendships.

Everybody Googles

For many girls, MySpace does feel more like a computer game than anything tangible. But the Internet truly is a vast web—pun intended—that captures and holds information for much longer than the instant-access aspect of it would lead us to believe. As these technologies are becoming staples in our culture, they're acquiring mainstream uses.

College and employment recruiters routinely Google names to see what comes up. What's in a person's MySpace profile—whether the profile itself pops up or information copied from it appears elsewhere—can influence decisions in ways girls can't anticipate from where they are in their lives right now. One filter for considering what's appropriate might be this: is this something you can explain away when it's what stands between you and a scholarship or a job?

Who *Are* You, Really?

There's something about the World Wide Web that allows, and even encourages, people to feel anonymous in their interactions in cyberspace. People who are otherwise straight-up honest may craft entertaining but entirely (and sometimes intentionally deceitful) false identities for themselves in chat rooms and on social-networking sites. Even your daughter and her friends.

Why? The reasons are as varied as the people who do it. Most of the time, teens just think it's funny. Sometimes, there's the intent to pretend to be someone else to trick others into revealing potentially embarrassing information—like what they really think of this girl or that guy. Such a trap is usually good for a week or two of laughs at her expense.

But perhaps more often, it's simply that the Internet provides the opportunity to be anyone or anything, without others knowing whether your presentation is true or false. Most of the time, a teen's friends all know the profile is fake (even, often enough, when the fake post is someone outside the regular circle). The girls say, "We just know" and they're often right.

It's the times when they're wrong that scare the holiness out of parents.

Oh, Puh-leeze!

An acronym every parent should know is PII: personally identifiable information. This is the data a website collects when your daughter fills out forms or creates a user profile. Websites are supposed to post their PII policies so you know how they use this information. It's valuable to know for the websites your daughter uses, and to teach her how to find this important little detail.

Safety in Cyberspace

Teen girls tend to believe adults exaggerate to make a risk or threat appear even more serious than it already is, driven by the underlying principle that to scare someone really bad is more effective than to scare her just a little. This is the fear factor that works so effectively in urban legends that have bad guys lurking beneath cars in the parking lot at the mall or in the woods where teens drive in their cars to make out.

Oh, Puh-leeze!

Do you know what your daughter's downloading? Check those music files to be sure they're from legitimate sources. If she's downloading pirated songs, you could end up on the legal hook for fines and other penalties.

So when coupled with the teen tendency to believe nothing they hear or read about is ever going to happen to them anyway, the result can be a casual attitude that does in fact increase the hazards they face. It never hurts to reiterate safe Internet practices, just as you continuously reinforce no drinking, no drugs, no boys in her bedroom.

Cyber-Stalking

Teenage girls tend to downplay, or simply don't get, the risks of cyber-stalking, even though they all know girls who are the targets of unwanted e-mail messages and other digital contacts. They've probably been targets themselves. But they shrug it off, thinking it's not very important—after all, who's going to come all the way to wherever they live just to do them harm? Most of the time, they're right—which is both the good news and the bad news. Because the problem is, of course, that there's no way to know who's truly crazy enough to be the one who is dangerous.

Teens tend to be casual about what adults would perceive as harassment and stalking kinds of behaviors. Sadly, it's such a part of their world that they are fairly inured to it. However, it's good to have frequent discussions with your daughter about what's in bad taste though likely unharmful, and what's potentially dangerous to her or her friends. Most often it's someone she knows who's behaving in this way, and even as the behavior distresses her she doesn't want to get the person in trouble.

Check in on what your daughter's doing online. Know, as best you can, who she e-mails and texts. Have her give you a list of her passwords. Sure, you won't get them all and she'll probably change them over time, but it gives you that much more information. Who are her MySpace or Facebook friends? If she suddenly changes her digital identities and environments, ask her what's going on. Have her show you messages and other contacts that annoy or trouble her. Learn how to display full headers on e-mail messages to reveal the identities of senders.

If you know or suspect someone is cyber-stalking or harassing your daughter, contact your local police immediately. Don't delete any messages—print them, so you have written records of them. The police can investigate, offer advice about what to do, and otherwise become involved to the extent the law permits. Cyber-stalking may cross the line on what's legal, especially when your daughter is a minor (under age 18). You don't know, any more than your daughter does, who might be just nutty and who might be a risk. But you do know enough to recognize dangers that she does not.

In Her Shoes

As girls get older, they tend to spend less time in front of the TV but increase their screen time overall. They spend a lot of time online—doing research for school assignments, messaging and e-mailing their friends, and playing video games. It's important to help them balance these virtual activities with experiences in the real world.

Cyber-Bullying

The Internet has become a vast new playground for the school bully. The technology—IM, MySpace, e-mail—makes it easy to spread a lot of damage really fast. A girl might walk into first-period class and find that everyone's seen the pictures of her in her underwear that she foolishly let one of her peeps take at Friday night's slumber party.

Bullies use cyberspace to extend their reach for spreading rumors and attacking reputations. The consequences can be far-reaching—once something's out there in cyberspace, it's nearly impossible to call it back. Years from now those underwear pictures may show up when someone does a search for the girl's name.

Cyberspace bullying is still uncharted territory in many respects. The police may be able to step in when messages are threatening. However, there is a fine legal line around the right to freedom of expression. You're not the only one who finds this troubling; legal experts continue to debate the issue. Websites may legally have their own rules of conduct, and often contacting the webmaster can at least get an offensive posting pulled if it violates the site's policies.

Often, the same tactics you might use with direct bullying work with virtual bullying: contact parents and teachers. Print the offensive postings so you have a record of them. Your best shot at enlisting the aid of school authorities comes when school computers or other resources were used to create or post the offensive messages, or when kids are using school resources (including class time) to view such messages.

Most important, encourage your daughter to consider the potential ways in which what happens initially in fun can become embarrassing and hurtful. Sadly, in many respects, our daughters (and all of us, really) must always believe someone is watching and possibly taking pictures or video. Encourage your daughter, too, to tell you or a teacher when someone does cyber-bully her or post offensive messages about her.

No Secrets

Her MySpace profile is private, so confidently she loads it up with her most personal information. Much of this information, fortunately, is important only to her, like the pics of her dog and her with some of her friends. Other information is not stuff you'd put out there about yourself, and you'd be startled to discover your daughter doesn't share your concern about it—things like her address, height and body type, and birth date. She knows of friends who've been hacked, but she's certain her carefully selected password is so good, hacking'll never happen to her.

We hope so—but good luck with that. Computer experts would say, almost in unison, that it's only a matter of time before hacking touches her life directly. Any personal information her profile contains is vulnerable to misappropriation—at the very least, put out there in a public context for everyone to see. The embarrassment factor is itself reason to prevent this. And as we parents

Girl Pearls

In some ways the Web is the most important book in the world.

—Jeff Bezos, CEO, Amazon.com

know, other risks exist. Encourage your daughter to limit the personal information she posts on her profiles, and to not only change her password frequently but also to hold it as her most closely guarded secret.

Literacy in a Digital World

The digital explosion has changed our whole notion of literacy, Kathy observes, creating a sea change in how we approach information as well as how schools teach fundamentals like reading and writing. Where once reading meant sitting down with a novel and physically turning its pages, now reading is screen time. Traditional reading—that novel, or even the print newspaper—is becoming more of a challenge because everything in a teen's life today centers around instant access. The blurb matters more than the story—and, as a result, the stories get shorter.

While the Internet vastly expands the availability and range of news and information, the typical Web surfer encounters little in-depth analysis of, say, the world economy, civil strife in Africa, or natural disasters in Southeast Asia. In short, there's breadth—a lot of information – but not always depth. The entire story's often in the headline and the summary blurb—which feels perfectly natural and adequate to a generation whose primary form of communication is text messaging. On the flipside, news can be updated almost as it's happening—and anyone with a cell phone can be the one to first file the story. Blogs and podcasts further extend the reach of both reporting and analysis. How quaint that we used to diss those folks who got their news from the TV instead of the newspaper!

With little extra effort, a dozen or more articles from news sources around the world can be right at your daughter's fingertips. And today's teens have instant access to even the most obscure research data on just about any subject, file-sharing for group projects, additional notes and guidance from teachers, and 24/7 access to class schedules and missed assignments. Does your daughter need a quote from *Beowulf* to give that final touch of authenticity to the paper she's finishing up at two in the morning? Never fear … it's online.

The Least You Need to Know

◆ Multitasking is no buzzword in your daughter's life—it's the way she lives.

◆ Virtual communities like MySpace and Facebook enable girls to blur the line between reality and fiction in ways that are often difficult to detect.

◆ Teenage girls tend to trust in their ability to detect what's false and harmful, and to believe that whatever potential danger there is in cyberspace won't touch them.

◆ Cell phones, text messaging, e-mail, and the Internet have fundamentally changed the way young people communicate and view the world at large.

Chapter 18

Always Look Under the Bed

In This Chapter

- This time around, it might be you who worries about the monsters
- Talk is good; listening is even better
- Alcohol, cigarettes, drugs, and sex: just another day in the life of your teenage daughter
- What do you mean, you have a *date?*
- The flipside of the statistics

Your daughter's nearly an adult now, increasingly independent in her daily life. You have real adult conversations with her every day. You enjoy spending time with her, and you're able to use your understanding of each other more often in acts of kindness than in moments of anger. When you know she's not looking your way you steal sideways glances at her, proud and amazed.

Then one morning after she's left for school you step into her bedroom to look for the cat, who has a vet appointment at

10 A.M. and must know it because there he goes, under her bed. You reach after him—gotcha! But, say ... what's *this?*

Wake-Up Call

Many parents are stunned when they discover their daughters are smoking, drinking, having sex, using drugs, sneaking out at night, taking the car without permission, having their boyfriends over while we're at work, or whatever other behaviors we catch them in. We don't want to believe our little girls have made such choices—or that they've so flagrantly betrayed our trust. But the reality is that 80 percent of them will try alcohol, 1 in 8 will smoke cigarettes, and by age 17, 6 in 10 are sexually active.

Sometimes we can look back and see signs we chose at the time to ignore, now waving wildly as if to shout, "We're here! Why didn't you see us?" But we've got pretty good selective vision when it comes to our daughters and risky behaviors. According to one recent study, while 30 percent of girls ages 16 to 18 drink alcohol, only 9 percent of moms of girls this age believe their daughters drink. That's a considerable gap, although in a way an understandable one. We all want to believe the best about our daughters, to believe that they take to heart all the advice we give them and use it to make wise decisions. But what seems wise to them often isn't quite what we have in mind.

The Need to Belong

Teenage girls, too, have selective vision but through a different lens. They see pressure to fit in with their peers, and they see giving in to that pressure as the only way to deal with it. If your daughter's peeps sneak "alcopops" into the football games, you can be fairly sure your daughter's at least done some taste-testing. Across the board, teenage girls cite pressure from friends and their fears of being left out as the leading reasons they drink, smoke, have sex, and use drugs.

Knowledge Empowers

The more girls know, the better able they are to make decisions. They may still make some poor choices, but they're also likely to make quite

a few good ones. When your dialogue with your daughter is open
and flowing, you might even hear
about those decisions; your daughter will be more willing to say to
you, "There was drinking at the
party last night but I just had a
soda and made it look like a drink."

In telling you this, she's risking
that you'll say "no more parties!"
but trusting you'll instead recognize that when she found herself

Oh, Puh-leeze!
Teen girls feel a
lot of stress in their
daily lives, and it pushes
many of them into clinical
depression. Girls are 10
times more likely than boys to
experience depression; drinking, drug use, and sexual
activity further compound the
difficulties.

in a difficult situation, she made a fairly adult decision about how to
handle herself. And in telling you about it, she opens the way for you
to talk with her about other choices she could've made, too, and to hear
why she chose the one she did. These kinds of conversations, setting
aside for the moment that this is your *underage* daughter, give you great
insight into how she thinks and how she relates with her peers.

There's Nothing Cheap About Talk

Experts say we should start talking with our daughters about drinking,
drugs, smoking, sex, and other risky behaviors when they're 11 or 12
years old. Seems too young to be dealing with such adult issues. Even
they might think the conversation is unnecessary. Although if you catch
a particularly candid moment, your daughter probably will acknowledge
she does know of at least one kid in her grade who drinks or smokes.

One value of starting so early is that it lays out your expectations as
a foundation you can build on as your daughter gets older and faces
increasingly challenging situations. Your daughter gets the same message from you, over and over, over time. Exactly the same message.
It's a bit like brainwashing, only for the good—*her* good, particularly.
So when she's at a dance or a party and someone offers a plastic cup
of murky-looking spiked punch and says, "Hey, want to try some?"
some little switch flips in her brain and all she hears is your message:
No drinking, drugs, smoking, or sex. It might not happen this way *all* the
time, but at least you're planting the seed. And someday you'll be surprised, when you're two adults sitting together over lunch and she spills

all the secrets she kept from you when she was growing up, to hear the number of times your voice in her head actually did stop her from doing something she shouldn't.

This kind of regular interaction about important topics like drinking gives your daughter the sense that she can talk to you about them. She may come at her questions sideways—the "what would happen if" approach. She may want to talk about a girl in her school who is involved in some of these risky behaviors. No matter her reason, she's feeling you out about how true to your words you really are. Listen to what she says and respond to the questions she asks (don't read into them). Then again reinforce your message: *No drinking, drugs, smoking, or sex.*

And expand on the message, as your daughter gets older and can understand more complexity around concepts. Engage her in dialogue about why these behaviors are harmful, from the pragmatic (for her), "You'll be grounded for life" to the nightmare of every parent, "Some of these things can kill you." Not to venture too far into melodrama, but it's a good thing for your daughter to understand there are potentially very serious consequences to risky behaviors, those consequences scare you because you love her and want the best for her now and in the future, and those consequences should scare her.

In Her Shoes

In surveys, girls say they're more worried that their parents will find out they're having sex than that they use marijuana, drink alcohol, or smoke cigarettes.

Friend or Parent?

You genuinely enjoy sharing time and common interests with your daughter, and that's a very good thing. You might even feel you're more like friends, and you like that. But that's not always such a good thing for your daughter, especially at this stage of her life. She's making a lot of choices that have the potential to affect her life well past the next swim meet or her SATs—but she can't see that.

You can, though. You're her parent, and you're responsible for guiding her to make the best decisions for now and for the future. Sometimes you've got to step back and take an unpopular stand. Someday, she'll thank you for it. Really, she will

Minor Details

Ah, those pesky laws. They regulate drinking, smoking, and sex—and of course, drugs. Even we adults sometimes forget the details of this. But a girl's weekend adventures can take on an entirely different slant when she comes home in a police car with a minor-in-possession citation.

More high school girls than boys now drink and smoke. Even as the balance is tipping on the gender scale, however, overall fewer girls are drinking and smoking, so there's some progress. More good news is that girls worry about the consequences of drinking and driving, so they're less inclined to get behind the wheel when they've been drinking or to get in a car with a driver who's been drinking.

Truth and Consequences

What happens when you find out your daughter's drinking, smoking, using drugs, or having sex? If you've put forth clear expectations around these behaviors, you must follow through with consequences. Some parents establish the consequence for breaking the rule at the same time they establish the rule; for example, losing driving privileges if she's caught drinking. Other parents leave the consequence end of things open, preferring to evaluate the situation when it arises. And of course, there may be legal consequences, depending on how she gets caught in whatever she's doing.

Regardless of any punishment you choose to impose, it's important that you also establish some sort of process for monitoring future behavior and helping your daughter to stay on track. Part of the issue, after all, is that by engaging in these activities, your daughter's betrayed your trust, and you need to set up ways for her to regain your faith in her ability to make appropriate decisions. Don't shy away from the tough talk—she needs to know you're upset and disappointed, and why. More of what you say will reach her than she'll let on.

This is one of those things that sounds so straightforward in a book but in reality is like trying to hold Jell-O in your hands! As you grapple with how to best deal with the situation, frame your thoughts around your daughter's safety, health, and well-being. You want to give her the confidence and skills to make the *right* choices. After all, she's not so far now from the age at which she'll be legally empowered to make these decisions anyway. (Now that's a sobering thought, isn't it?)

Depending on the situation, you might need to seek help from professionals such as doctors, therapists, or substance abuse specialists. As hard as this might be, it's in your daughter's best interest. No daughter, no matter the quality of her relationship with her parents, is immune from the peer pressure and the tantalizing idea of doing something that's forbidden. You do the best you can do to be proactive and give her the skills and support she needs, but she is her own person and she makes her own choices. It's definitely one of the tougher challenges of parenting.

I'll Have One of Those ...

When it comes to substances of abuse, the first one most teens reach for is something many get right from the cupboard or fridge at home: alcohol. Surveys suggest that 4 in 10 American teens do that reaching at least once a month. Think it's mostly the guys who tip back the bottle? Think again. In high school, more girls than boys drink alcohol. They drink in a different way, too. While boys tend to drink (mostly for the buzz) and then look for a group that drinks, girls tend to drink to be part of the group they're with. Girls drink to belong. Girls also drink as a way to relax and cope with stress and pressure.

What happens to girls when they drink is also often very different than what happens to boys. Girls tend to get drunk faster and on less alcohol, have more severe hangovers, and are more significantly impaired for their level of intoxication. While boys might get drowsy and relaxed as they drink, girls tend to become less inhibited. It is, predictably, a recipe for disaster for many girls.

The most effective way for parents to know whether their daughters are drinking is to be up and awake when they come home from parties, dances, dates, and school events. Engage your daughter in conversation about how things went wherever she was, and talk with her about the friends she was with. You'll know, most of the time, just from her demeanor whether she's had a few beverages she's not really interested in telling you about. You also might smell alcohol on her breath, even if she chewed gum or ate breath mints on the way home.

Parents often wonder how their girls manage to get alcohol. Mostly, from you! It's a good idea to check your supplies, even if you don't have much. Other sources are older friends and siblings who are of legal age to buy alcohol. Teens seem to have built-in GPS for finding merchants that'll sell to minors—which are alarmingly abundant.

Oh, Puh-leeze!

Although girls tend not to care much for the taste of beer and hard liquor, there's an entire market of sweet alcoholic drinks—"alcopops"—that go down like the lemonade or fruit punch they emulate but with quite the intoxication factor. The sweetness of these drinks also masks the smell of the alcohol they contain, making it easy to smuggle them into parties and events.

Got a Light?

We have to say it, though you already know it and probably say it yourself to your daughter: there are no benefits to smoking. Smoking damages health, costs money, and stinks (literally). Although teen smoking overall is slowly declining, in 2004 girls passed the dubious marker of smoking more than boys. The trend seems to be continuing, with statistics telling us that one in eight teenage girls smokes.

Girls are most likely to start smoking when …

◆ A parent or other member of the household smokes

◆ Their friends smoke

◆ They're dieting

Girls are more likely than boys to be secret smokers, regular smokers, and long-term smokers once they start smoking. Researchers suspect this is because so many girls take up smoking because they mistakenly believe smoking helps them lose weight and keep weight off. (For the record, and to be clear, it doesn't do either.)

So girls will smoke even when no one sees them. For girls smoking is more about maintaining body image over the long term than presenting a particular image (although sometimes that's a factor, too, especially when a girl wants to appear older than she is). Boys, however, tend to be more concerned with their image in the moment and primarily smoke only when they're with others.

Parents may not suspect their daughters are smoking until they find cigarette butts, packages, and other evidence. However, your sense of smell is your big tip-off that your daughter's smoking. Even if there's no smoke swirling around her when she comes in the house, you'll probably smell smoke in her hair and her clothes. She might tell you she was someplace where other people were smoking—maybe so. But if it becomes a regular line, then it's time for your regular response to be that it's just as unhealthy for her to be where other people are smoking.

Drugs

Teen girls try drugs for the same reasons they drink and smoke. Because drug use is so open in their environments, they often don't perceive it as much different than drinking or smoking. Again, girls are stretching ahead of boys when it comes to the numbers—although overall fewer teens (girls or boys) use drugs than drink or smoke.

Marijuana is the drug of choice among teen girls, and you're deluding yourself if you think your daughter would have to rendezvous with some unsavory character in a back alley to have access to it. Weed is everywhere, and if your daughter's smoking it, she gets it from her peeps—maybe at parties, maybe at school events like football games, maybe even during school. One other difference from when you might've traveled this same road when you were younger: today's marijuana is significantly more potent.

Hard drugs—club drugs like ecstasy, meth, speed, cocaine, heroin, and such—are not very common among high school girls. However, prescription drug abuse is. One of ten high school girls has used a prescription drug (usually someone else's) to get high.

Sex

Sex is a beautiful thing, a wondrous expression of passion and intimacy between consenting adults. And here we go again with the adult thing: sex is for adults. Sex changes everything, and not always in ways girls expect. We don't need Freud to explain why we talk about "losing" our virginity. Sex marks the end of innocence, no matter how joyous the experience. And for most teenage girls, those first experiences are more confusing than enjoyable. For teens—and even for adults—sex is a minefield.

Most of the reasons teens have sex are the same as they've always been: hormones, curiosity, and wanting to be needed and loved. Overlaying these factors for today's teens is their widespread perception that sex is just something they do because now they can, not much different than going to the movies. Girls today feel enormous pressure to have sex, both from the guys they date and from their girlfriends—those who've had sex as well as those who haven't.

The strongest message we can give our daughters is this: it's *your* body. Don't let anybody, *anybody*, push you into decisions and actions that are not what you want. You control who touches your body, and how. You set the boundaries—not your boyfriend, not your girlfriends, not the unspoken "rules of engagement" for what teens do on dates or when they're going together. There's no expiration date on sex—you can, and should, wait as long as you want.

What if you find under her bed a box of condoms and a packet of birth control pills? You probably won't know whether to breathe a sigh of relief or burst into tears—you might do both. Pregnancy and STDs are, of course, the main practical worries about teens having sex. You'll probably want to schedule her an appointment with a gynecologist, just to ease your own mind. These decisions are hers and hers alone, but at least you'll know that she's had an exam and talked with a women's health care provider, and that whatever birth control pills she's taking have actually been prescribed for her.

In Her Shoes

Tell your daughter not to take birth control pills prescribed for her BFF or anyone else! A surprising number of girls do this. Although in a roomful of girls on the pill, two thirds of them may take the same one, there are medical reasons for prescribing different products. A girl who wants to be on the pill needs her own prescription, which she can get from her regular doctor or a clinic such as Planned Parenthood.

How Did *That* Happen?

Pregnancy always comes as a shock to a teen girl. Maybe she thought she was taking all the right precautions, or maybe she didn't believe, somehow, that this could happen to her—it was her first time, it wasn't the "right" time of the month, he said he pulled out in time, he used a condom. But there it is: a big plus sign on the pee stick. Could be flashing neon; the whole world must be able to see it. Now what? Most girls are terrified to tell their parents—and terrified not to.

Each year in the United States about 900,000 teenage girls get pregnant. Two thirds of them carry the pregnancy to term and either raise the baby (alone or with help from their families) or place it for adoption; one third choose to abort the pregnancy. The decision is deeply personal and carries lifelong ramifications, no matter what it is. In the time since *Roe v. Wade*, women, and men, too, have held passionate views championing both pro-choice and pro-life positions. The debate continues today. We do not presume to counsel parents and girls on this issue.

Whatever course your daughter chooses, let her know you're right there with her—even if you disapprove of her decision. Now more than any time in her life, most likely, she needs your support as she makes her way through her decision-making process and its consequences. If she chooses to continue the pregnancy, help her find good prenatal care and begin planning for birth—whether she's intending to keep the baby or place the baby for adoption.

LOL

The 2007 movie, *Juno,* with Ellen Page in the title role, takes a quirky, honest look at teen pregnancy. Screenwriter Diablo Cody won an Oscar for the edgy script.

Chlamydia, Herpes, Gonorrhea ... Oh, My!

Sexually transmitted diseases (STDs) are a significant risk among sexually active teens, although many of them don't know the symptoms and signs of common STDs or don't believe their boyfriend/girlfriend could've given them one (or several). Guys tend to know pretty quickly; their signs are right out there for them to see and feel. Girls may not know, however—chancres and sores may form in the vagina where they're not so apparent. And girls often have vaginal discharge, so it might take a while for a girl to realize there's something different about the one she's now having.

Most STDs are treatable, though some, like genital herpes, are not curable. Prompt medical attention is crucial—the longer she waits, the higher the risk for the infection to cause significant or permanent damage to her fertility and sometimes other body systems (like with hepatitis). Plus, if she's sexually active, she's spreading the infection.

Most communities have some sort of free public health services for STDs and other infectious diseases. Make sure your daughter knows about these services, whether or not you suspect she's sexually active. Schools, libraries, youth/ teen centers, community centers, and other public venues often have information available. Your daughter may be uncomfortable coming to you for help, but she should feel she can go to a health clinic. Doctors recommend that sexually active girls have a health exam twice a year to check for STDs and other health concerns.

Oh, Puh-leeze!

The only 100 percent defense against STD infection is complete abstinence—that means vaginal sex, anal sex, and oral sex. Latex condoms are the next best thing. Birth control pills do not protect against STDs, which a lot of girls fail to realize.

Not Until You're Married!

Some teens are entering into abstinence pacts or "purity pledges," promising to abstain from sexual activity until they marry. Such promises can be powerful statements about personal and family values, and can help girls stand firm when others pressure them. What happens, though, when girls slip and break their pacts? They can feel tremendous guilt, psychologists say, such that it unleashes a backlash of promiscuous behavior. The girl feels like, "Oh well, what does it matter now?"

It's tough to hold to absolutes, especially when "everyone" around you is doing what you've pledged not to do. There are no easy answers for such complex issues. Personal and family values vary widely across the spectrum of communities, cultures, and peer groups. Again, we come back to our guiding mantra: keep talking with your daughter. The more dialogue you have, the better you understand her pressures and she understands your concerns.

If It's Not Intercourse, Is It Still Sex?

We'd like to say, *duh!* And perhaps that's the most appropriate response, because that's likely the response we'd get from either parents or teens—though with opposite meaning. For most parents, the answer is a resounding, "Of course, and you better not be doing it!" For most teens, however, the answer is likely to be, "No way!" Unfortunately teens have some compelling and high-profile precedents to support this position, but we won't go there.

Oral sex has become the preferred sexual activity among teens who believe it's not really sex. Teenage girls in particular often believe oral sex is okay because they can engage in oral sex yet still remain virgins. The point balances on a technicality, perhaps. What's more important than splitting technicalities, though, is for parents to recognize that their daughters likely define "having sex" as vaginal intercourse and believe other sexual activity is not actually sex.

Part of what's behind this belief is the perception that oral sex is safe. Not exactly, although it's safer than intercourse from the perspective that oral sex won't result in pregnancy. But most of the other risks—namely, STDs and emotional ramifications—of sex remain, which many girls (and guys) don't realize. Your ongoing dialogue with your daughter about sex needs to be broad enough to include the full spectrum of sexual activity as her generation—her peer group—defines it.

This isn't to say you must abandon your values around the sanctity of sexual expression just so you can encourage your daughter to take appropriate precautions in her sexual explorations (although certainly if she is exploring her sexuality, you want her to do so as safely as possible). The framework for your dialogue *should* be your values around relationships, behavior, sex—it's a very big picture. Research supports the premise that girls who have a comprehensive sense of all these factors are more confident about their ability to make decisions rather than finding themselves pulled into situations.

> **Oh, Puh-leeze!**
>
> Vaccines are now available that can reduce the risk for some STDs caused by viruses, notably HPV (human papillomavirus) and hepatitis B. Health experts herald the HPV vaccine as a breakthrough because certain strains of HPV are responsible for most types of cervical cancer. The HPV vaccine thus gives dual protection from the STD genital warts and cervical cancer.

The Dating Game

By the time they're juniors and seniors in high school, most girls are dating for real (contrasted to the "going together" of middle school and early high school). They may have boyfriends and consider themselves in relationships.

This is good, for the most part. Girls need these kinds of experiences to help prepare them for adult life and the real mating ritual of courtship and marriage (if they go that path). Dating relationships are normal and healthy, most of the time. Sometimes, however, problems crop up that we wish our daughters would never have to deal with at all, let alone in high school: pressure to have sex, jealousy, possessiveness, and the possibility of date violence (including date rape).

We go back to the intense desire girls have to belong and fit in. By the time girls are in high school, they're interested in boys beyond casual friendship. They're curious how it happens that the dork who's lived next door since kindergarten is now the hunk they—and every other girl in school—can't take their eyes off. Something's changed but they're not quite sure what it means. Convention, however, says it means dating. Some girls are ready for adult-type one-to-one relationships when this pressure strikes; others are not.

The pressure to date stresses both girls and boys, who may not quite know how to conduct themselves in such adult relationships. Both find themselves in situations where they often have little supervision or guidance; long gone are the days of chaperones. When it comes to managing their feelings, the responses of both boys and girls may range from immature to dysfunctional. Girls may give in to all kinds of things, from pulling back in their girl friendships to engaging in activities they otherwise wouldn't, including sexual.

A boy may become unexpectedly demanding and even aggressive, which is confusing to a girl when it's not the kind of behavior that attracted her to him in the first place. Some girls have the maturity and self-confidence to walk away from such situations, while others don't know what to do or are so uncertain within themselves that they feel trapped even though they know the relationship isn't right.

As always, the best way to keep your finger on the pulse of your daughter's dating experiences is to talk with her—often and frankly. Be open about the pressures she feels, and let her express to you what that means in her daily life. It's especially hard to refrain from telling her what to do when you can see it so clearly, but you must—unless she is at risk for emotional or physical abuse. Girls are good at hiding such risks, but your intuition is probably just as good at ferreting them out. Don't be shy about it; in such situations your intervention could save her life.

> **In Her Shoes**
>
> High school—the later teen years—is when girls might question their sexual orientation and explore same-sex relationships. Girls are often more open about such exploration than are boys, and in some settings may encounter more openness about their relationships.

Statistics Don't Show Everything

It's not easy to be a girl in high school these days, clearly. The challenges can be overwhelming. Mentors and strong role models are especially important to help girls recognize their abilities and the resources that are available to support them. With the amount of opportunities out there for girls today, it can be a surprise for parents just to recognize what their daughters are interested in from a positive perspective.

But even those girls who struggle are often able to right themselves, with strong support from their parents and other adults who matter in their lives and who can help—aunts, grandparents, and older sisters as well as school counselors, therapists, doctors, and other professionals. And in the midst of all our worry about the problems our daughters face, it's worthwhile to remember that a substantial number of girls are able to sidestep the potential traps—they don't smoke, drink, use drugs, or have sex. If 4 in 10 teenage girls drink, well, then there are 6 in 10 who do not.

The Least You Need to Know

- ◆ The overwhelming pressures to fit in and belong that teen girls face are key in their decisions to drink, smoke, use drugs, and have sex.

- ◆ More high school girls than boys drink alcohol and smoke.

- ◆ Teen girls who smoke often do so because they believe it will help them lose weight, which it will not.

- ◆ Oral sex is increasingly common among teens because they do not view it as "real" sex.

- ◆ By mid to late high school, most girls are involved in true dating, moving away from the "going together" adventures onto the turf of adult relationships.

- ◆ The flipside of the statistics about teen girls is that more of them do *not* drink, smoke, use drugs, or have sex than do.

Chapter 19

School for Girlz

In This Chapter

- ◆ So many choices, so many pressures
- ◆ Making sure she makes the score
- ◆ Thinking outside the box
- ◆ The benefits of job shadowing
- ◆ Working through college

When your daughter was five years old, asking her the question, "What do you want to be when you grow up?" no doubt unleashed a shower of desires. She might've wanted to be anything from a ballerina to a firefighter to a poet to a "zoo-ologist"—and likely all at the same time!

By middle school or early high school the responses get more narrow and specific: forensic pathologist, teacher, investigative reporter, illustrator, landscaper, dental hygienist, transit driver. Or the answer might be a frantic and somewhat despondent, "I don't *kno-o-o-ow!*"

Expanding Her View, Growing Her Options

It's okay for girls to be anywhere along this spectrum as they're approaching the end of their high school years; few people know at 17 what they want to do for the rest of their lives. But they do know what interests them, and that's the best place to start.

And this is the age where we can most effectively help our daughters sharpen their interests and focus on what appeals to them for how they want to be in the adult world. After all, they're soon to launch into that world, and it expects them to earn their way!

When she's young, you take your daughter to museums, libraries, zoos, political events, the theater (not only for movies), and expose her to all kinds of experiences to help broaden her vision of her community and even the world. You encourage her to play sports, a musical instrument, and games that stretch her vocabulary, math skills, and logical thinking. As a family you go on picnics, bicycle rides, and vacations to exotic destinations like Disneyland (well, exotic from a seven-year-old's perspective) and not-so-exotic locations like Larry's Lizardland (from your perspective). You look for opportunities to include her in conversations among adults so she develops strong communication skills and a sense of value around her viewpoints and opinions.

Maybe she's traveled across the country or even to other countries, experiencing firsthand how other families and cultures live. These kinds of adventures form great foundations for piquing her interest in all sorts of things. Maybe she puts those years of piano lessons to use playing keyboard in a rock band in the eighth grade or serves on the library's teen advisory board in high school.

The great thing about providing such a broad base for her is that even you can't foresee how she will use her experiences to coalesce her own interests and ideas into activities and pursuits. Something as apparently ordinary as watching the fireworks on the Fourth of July or watching seedpods pop from a scotch broom plant might spark an extraordinary intrigue that leads to a career path.

In Her Shoes _____

SATs, ACTs, GRAs ... these are all the scores that matter when it comes to looking at the college application process. Most high schools are on top of the scheduling and testing procedures for the SAT and the ACT, though it's a good idea for parents to talk with a guidance counselor about what their daughter needs and by when.

Shaping and Refining Her Interests

School helps your daughter to put context and structure around her interests. It might appear that all she's doing is taking classes, but in which classes does she excel? Which classes make her groan? Although much of her education—especially up to about her junior year in high school—fulfills mandated requirements, she gains increasing freedom to sculpt her curriculum to suit her interests as she gets older. All those basic classes suddenly make sense when she gets into the more advanced courses.

Some girls do well with maintaining academic focus in high school. They've got good study habits and need little prodding to stay on track with homework and other class assignments. This is good; such study habits will serve them well in college, too. If your daughter has sketchy habits around her schoolwork, her final years in high school offer good opportunities to strengthen them. Though your daughter needs to be increasingly independent, she also still needs for you to ask her about school—every day.

Campus Field Trips

Has your daughter been on a college campus yet? If not, take her to one! It doesn't matter so much which college as that she begins to associate in her mind what a college is—and the earlier, the better. We know what college is, but she has no clue. It'll be an eye-opening experience for both of you, especially if you're able to take her to your alma mater.

How easy this is depends on where you live, of course. If you live in an urban area where there are lots of colleges, just drop by a campus and stroll around. Often you can find someone in the admissions office to answer questions and even give an impromptu tour, show you a dorm, or let you sit in on a class.

As your daughter gets further into high school, encourage her to go to prospective-student events at as many colleges as possible. Include public and private colleges and universities, even if the possibility of her attending an expensive school seems remote right now. With so many financial aid and scholarship programs available, just about anything is possible for those who're determined to achieve it.

And include two-year colleges, technical colleges, and maybe even a trade school or apprenticeship program if that opportunity exists. The more you expose your daughter to the possibilities, the more clearly she'll begin to see where she fits. Many communities have college fairs or trade fairs, with display booths and school representatives. Look for those that are specifically promoting their opportunities for girls.

Testing, Testing

Many high schools work with students and parents to schedule necessary tests for college admission—namely, the SAT and the ACT. Whether your daughter needs to take one, the other, or both depends on what colleges she's considering. She can take the test her junior or senior year in high school, and can take it more than once if she's unhappy with her scores. Girls often feel a lot of anxiety about taking these tests, worrying that they have to achieve certain scores to make it into college. While colleges do, of course, want good scores, they also look at other factors.

Girl Pearls

I don't think of myself as a poor, deprived ghetto girl who made good. I think of myself as somebody who from an early age knew I was responsible for myself, and I had to make good.

—Oprah Winfrey, talk-show host, publisher, and philanthropist

High schools may also coordinate the college application process on behalf of high school seniors, collecting paperwork and application fees, then preparing submission packets. Your daughter's guidance counselor should be in touch with you about this in your daughter's junior year. Although college application materials and procedures are posted online, the application process itself is still one of paper and snail mail.

College Bound

The emphasis—and expectation—for this generation of girls is to go to college. From middle school on, teachers and guidance counselors encourage girls to take the courses that will prepare them for college so that college will prepare them for the careers they want. As a result of this effort, two thirds of high school grads now do go on to some type of further education: two-year college, four-year college, technical college, or apprenticeship program.

College might be where your daughter learns what she needs to know to have the career she wants, hones her focus to prepare for a career, or where she continues to expand her horizons so she can choose a career. As your conversations with your daughter about college become more frequent and purposeful, you get a clearer picture about why *she* wants to go to college and what she expects.

The intense focus in high school on preparing for college often emphasizes career paths and job opportunities, and certainly this is valid. College is a significant investment of both money (yours) and time (hers). But a lot of girls don't know for sure what they want to do in the way of a part-time job, let alone for a career. They feel pressured to make these kinds of decisions while they're choosing colleges. They worry that they'll get to college and not like the choices they've made but be stuck with them. Girls in high school believe college is like high school only bigger and with no parents hanging around. And in high school, they often *are* stuck with choices and decisions—high school curricula are far less flexible.

Certainly if your daughter knows she wants to be an engineer, she needs to be considering colleges that have strong engineering programs. However, it's easy to overlook one of the most significant reasons to go to college: to continue learning. Of course we want the college experience to have lifelong value for our daughters—especially if

 In Her Shoes

It's important for parents to recognize that girls make decisions based on their experiences, so anything parents can do to give them more rounded experiences expands their sense of choice. Often, too, girls choose career paths because other family members do.

we're footing the bill. But no matter what your daughter studies, simply the fact that she earns a college degree improves her earning potential when she enters the workforce.

The Friend Factor

Girls often consider factors that confound their parents when it comes to deciding where to go to college, from if there's a shopping mall nearby to whether any of their friends are planning to go to the same school. The "friend factor" again plays out as part and parcel of the need to fit in and the fear of being rejected or left out. Starting college is, in her mind, like starting high school all over again. (Of course, you know it's nothing like high school, but she has no framework for understanding that.) These are her peeps, and she's invested a lot in her relationships with them. Of course she wants to take them with her!

Having a friend or two go to the same college also extends a sense of comfort around one of the most significant turning points in your daughter's life: leaving home. Sure, she'll be back. You know that, even if she doesn't. Nonetheless, it's a major step to live away from the family and routines she's known all her life. Even if she doesn't actually move away but instead commutes to college, she's making a big shift. And a lot of the time, your daughter and at least one of her friends might end up going to the same college.

Boyfriends can become a strong influence, too. Girls are more likely than boys to choose a school option—where to go to college, or even the option *not* to go to college or to delay the start of college—on the basis of what their boyfriends think or are planning for themselves. Here's where strong and consistent encouragement for your daughter to feel confident in following her own path is crucial, though not foolproof.

Money, Money, Money

Many girls worry about—or at least think about—how they'll pay for college. *You* worry about how you'll pay for college! Even if you have a college fund, odds are it won't cover everything. So you've got to sit down with your daughter to figure out a realistic plan. What scholarships might she qualify for? Should she apply for student loans? Should she get a job—and if so, does the job follow her school or does she schedule school around the job?

Even if you have a solid plan in place, or at least in your head, to pay for your daughter's college, involve her in discussions about it. Some parents want to tie a free ride to college to attending a particular college. Sometimes this opens the door to an opportunity your daughter might not have considered, although more often she might feel you're trying to extend your control over her life. She's not entirely wrong; you want the best for her and you're trying to make that happen. This approach is especially risky if your intent is for her to go to the college you attended. She may have strong (and valid) feelings about going there—or not. After all, this is about *her*.

Sometimes tuition costs and other expenses limit the college choices available for your daughter, even after considering financial aid and scholarship opportunities. Be clear and upfront with your daughter about this; don't let her make plans knowing they'll be difficult or impossible for her to fulfill. Instead, work together to find schools that interest her and are within her (your) financial scope. Maybe starting at a two-year college is a more practical and affordable approach than launching into a four-year college.

> **Girl Pearls**
>
> I totally felt a waste of space. I was lousy. Yeah, I did, yeah. And now I feel that, it turns out there was one thing I was good at, and I'd always expected I could tell a story ....
>
> —J.K. Rowling, author of the *Harry Potter* series

Let Her Passion Lead Her Way

There's never been a time when it was so *absolutely* true that a girl can become *anything* she wants. She had a list as long as your arm when she was five but what interests her now? Maybe she's narrowed her interests to a specific career, or a career field. Sometimes the narrowing part is the challenge ... there are too many choices! And some girls have strong interests in areas like art, history, drama, or music but don't know quite how to view them as possible careers, or how to combine those interests with other areas where they have abilities and skills.

As parents we sometimes influence—and even try to push—our daughters to follow passions that aren't theirs. (We do! We may not see it that way or want to admit it, but we do.) Maybe they're our passions, unfulfilled because the opportunities may not have been available for us, or readily so, when we were her age. Or maybe they're interests teachers or guidance counselors suggest because they perceive an aptitude in those areas based on test scores or other observations about your daughter's performance in school.

> **Girl Pearls**
>
> No one gets an iron-clad guarantee of success. Certainly, factors like opportunity, luck, and timing are important. But the backbone of success is usually found in old-fashioned, basic concepts like hard work, determination, good planning, and perseverance.
>
> —Mia Hamm, American soccer star

We mean well; we only want the best for our daughters. Sometimes, though, we're not always aware this is what we're doing, especially if the "dialogue" around college has been fairly one-sided—we talk, she listens. A girl may feel she has little choice but to follow a career path someone else has chosen for her—with the best intent but perhaps not what she wants, in her heart of hearts, to do. It's certainly worthy to consider and discuss a range of ideas and perceptions, but in a low-key, nonpressured way.

Butcher, Baker, Candlestick Maker ... No, Make That Welder

A mother of four sons and one daughter jokes that while she always thought it would be handy to have a plumber in the family, she didn't expect it would be her daughter! The trades—skilled building occupations like plumbing, welding, electrical, carpentry, and such—can't get enough women into their apprenticeship programs.

Yet for many parents, hearing their daughters say, "I want to be a welder" or "I want to be a heavy equipment operator" is so far out of the box that their stunned response might be, "Why would you want to do *that?*" Well, for the same reasons a boy would want to do it: it interests her, she has some aptitude for it, and jobs pay well with good job security. From your daughter's perspective, what more is there to want? Unconventional? Not so much, anymore.

Trade organizations hold informational fairs to introduce high school girls to these occupations. Some even have hands-on demonstrations to give girls a real sense for what the occupation involves. Like college, most apprenticeship programs typically take four to five years to complete. Unlike college, however, they've got the job end of things covered: apprenticeship programs offer a combination of classroom and on-the-job learning.

Shadow for a Day

The mentors in your daughter's life can provide additional perspective and guidance, particularly those who work in career fields that interest your daughter. (Chapter 9 talks about mentors.) Can your daughter job-shadow any of them? This is a great way for her to get a realistic picture of what the career or job really involves. Most career fields present some opportunity for job-shadowing for girls who are in their junior and senior years of high school, because by this age they're mature enough to follow any rules and procedures within the workplace.

Job-shadowing should be more than just a tour of an office or work site. Your daughter should be able to spend a half to a full day with her mentor, observing the mentor at work. Job-shadowing is always an eye-opening experience for the shadow and often for the mentor as well. We all tend to lose perspective about just what it takes for us to perform our jobs well! A mentor is often as enthused after a day with a shadow as is the girl.

Some high schools require seniors to complete special projects that combine their academic studies with activities that relate to their career interests. These kinds of projects help girls to expand their perspective from narrowly focusing on assignments and test scores to practical applications of the subjects. What does chemistry have to do with real life? An interesting question for a nutritionist, a physician, a chemical engineer, a landscaper, or a photographer.

When girls connect with multiple mentors in the community, they can explore multiple dimensions of their interests and gain better understanding of how those interests might become job opportunities. And on the flipside, learn how those interests might not work out so well if they become what you do day in and day out. Maybe her interest in drama is something she pursues through community theater, while taking a study track in college to pursue a career in something like nursing or mechanical engineering. The great thing about girls at this stage of their lives is that even as their interests are narrowing and deepening, they still have lots of them.

In Her Shoes

Girls who show particular aptitude in fields still more traditionally male—math, physics, technology—may attract attention from prospective employers who are willing to offer scholarships and other assistance in exchange for future (or even current) employment.

To Work or Not to Work

Should your daughter work her way through college? Any more, it's difficult not to do this! It's a personal call, of course. But most girls find that working while they're in college brings a sense of balance to their lives—no longer is the entire focus of everything they do on classes and studying. And from a parent's perspective, it's good for a girl to have a real-life sense of what it takes to put the money in the bank that covers all those checks you write on her behalf.

Working to contribute to her education also helps a girl feel a sense of value around her efforts and studies. It's a rare parent who doesn't wonder, at some point during her daughter's college career, whether the college experience is more about learning or having fun. Ideally, it should be both.

It's a definite asset for your daughter to land a part-time job that lets her either test her interest in a career or gain experience working in that career. Competition for jobs across the career spectrum is increasingly tight, and the more well-rounded your daughter's overall resumé (school and work achievements), the greater appeal she has to employers who are all too tired of bringing people on only to have them leave within months because the job or field isn't what they expected.

That said, her education is still top priority. Though many girls successfully work their way through college holding down a full-time job and a full slate of classes, it's a tough challenge.

On Her Own at Last!

No surprise: your daughter's looking forward to college as much because she'll finally be on her own as for any other reason. (She might be surprised to learn that you, too, are looking forward to this.) She's already no doubt making plans for what her living arrangements might be—sharing an apartment or a house with some of her peeps, moving into the dorms, perhaps even getting an apartment on her own. While you're checking into curricula, professor credentials, and campus safety, she's scoping out the housing possibilities. Whether she's planning to go some distance away to go to college or stay fairly close to home, the experience of independent living in what will still be somewhat of a controlled situation is healthy and enjoyable for both you and your daughter.

The Least You Need to Know

- ◆ The more experiences you offer your daughter, the broader her base for making college and career decisions.

- ◆ With two thirds of high school graduates going on to college, high schools are increasingly involved in the college application process.

- ◆ Women are in high demand in career areas traditionally male, from science and technology to the trades.

- ◆ Job-shadowing can offer in-depth insight into jobs and careers that interest your daughter.

- ◆ Working while she's going to college gives your daughter the ability, if only in a small way, to contribute to her education.

Chapter 20

Maidenhood, Marriage, and Mom

In This Chapter

- The joy of just being friends
- Roommates ... not quite like TV
- Life balance
- Not so much about biology

Even as teens in high school, girls today worry most about acquiring the knowledge and skills they need to take care of themselves when they're adults. Though they may consider the possibility of someday getting married, they don't view marriage as a replacement for being able to live independently.

And when they do think about whether they want to have children, girls come back to this same foundational concern: can they take care of themselves and a baby? The idea that someone else will take care of them both doesn't enter into their thought processes. Our girls intend to be independent and self-sufficient in all that they do.

I Am Woman!

For today's girls, becoming a woman means being able to take care of yourself. And today's young women expect to be able to do, and be, what interests them without artificial or imposed barriers that block their efforts. Our daughters are not thinking in terms of limitations or excuses or even frustrations. They see the world as wide open, offering all kinds of opportunities. They want only to take part, in whatever ways they can.

Growing Up, Not Apart

It's a milestone in your daughter's life when she turns 18. She's been waiting for this day for longer than you know—although if you search your own memories from your high school years, you'll remember how important it was for you, too. This is the age of legal freedom; she's accountable for herself, and her actions separate from you now. She's an adult!

The shift in your relationship with your daughter as she moves into this new era of her life is likely to be palpable. Even though you might still have the "my house, my rules" caveat in place, your daughter now tells you where she's going (sort of), when she'll be back (more or less), and who'll she be with (sometimes). You both know you, as parent, can't really *make* her do anything any more. Her choices and decisions are hers and hers alone to make. Until she needs your guidance or wants your input—a moment that comes much quicker than either of you anticipate.

Oh, Puh-leeze!

We don't know whether anybody really believes you can have everything, that a woman today can "have it all," whatever "all" means to her. Our daughters watch our struggles to balance our interests and lives, and they learn from what they see.

This transition is sure to be mostly enjoyable and smooth for both of you when your relationship all along has been one of mutual negotiation and dialogue. You delight in seeing her step out as a woman, confident and happy. She feels strong and capable. She knows you're right there behind her, but excited to be skipping ahead on her own. Sort of like the first time she walked to school by herself … she knew you were walking a half-block behind but felt gloriously independent heading off on her own. This time the path leads into a future neither of you can see but both anticipate with great excitement and promise.

Staying Parent, Becoming Friend

All along, it's been a sometimes difficult line to walk between fulfilling your responsibilities as parent and enjoying your daughter as a friend. Now that she's an adult herself, that line's not quite so important, at least not in the same ways. You can be her friend and her confidante. You can go shopping, to the movies, or out for lunch.

It's fun to discover that you have more in common with each other than either of you realized. It's hard to appreciate your daughter's quick wit when you're worried whether she's studied enough for her history final or if she's driving while she's talking to you on her cell phone. And for her to likewise appreciate your dry humor in your observations about situations that perplex her. She's more mature and you're more relaxed, and it can be a delightful intersection for the both of you.

Yet she still turns to you, in a heartbeat, when she needs help, advice, or some extra cash. She'll call you at two in the morning and express surprise that she woke you up. She'll arrive on your doorstep with her dog in one hand and a bouquet of flowers in the other, giving you a quick kiss as she says, "Thanks! I'll pick up Buster on Tuesday!"

In Her Shoes

An unexpected benefit for you of your daughter becoming an adult is that now you can turn to her, too. You might need for her to take care of your cats while you go on vacation or drive you to pick up your car at the shop. And who knows, maybe you'll even show up on her doorstep one day to say, "Can I crash on your couch?"

Didn't She Just Leave?

Adult daughters come back home again … again … and again. They come between semesters at school, between boyfriends, between jobs, between apartments. They might drop by on weekends to do their laundry, stop in for dinner several times during the week, or just show up with all their stuff, asking, "Are there clean sheets on my bed?" She may want to stay for a weekend, a week, or until she gets on her feet (whatever that means).

For as hard as that day was when she walked out the door, suitcase in hand and Bowboo her favorite stuffed dog tucked under her arm, to head off to college or her first apartment, it's sometimes even harder to have her come back home—even for a short time. You've established new routines and probably rearranged rooms and furnishings.

As much as you love her, and she loves you, you each have your own way of dealing with *everything* from your routine when you get up in the morning to how you sort laundry and when and where you eat meals. When you were teaching your daughter the fine points of house-work, it was somewhat amusing to watch her find her own way to do things—now it's downright annoying that she does things differently. After all, this is your house, your kitchen, your bathroom—yet there's all her stuff alongside all your rearranged stuff.

The challenge for both of you when the visit turns into a living arrangement is deciding when the situation no longer benefits either of you. You may tire of it before she does; she's got it pretty good. Maybe you negotiate an arrangement under which she stays for a certain length of time or until she reaches a specific goal or objective.

There aren't really any right or wrong answers when it comes to your daughter's forays back to mom and dad; it's important only for you to remember that she's an adult now, so living with you (if that's what it becomes) is a matter of mutual agreement, not a single-sided obligation. And in truth, she genuinely wants to be on her own. She just might not know quite how to make it happen. The Real World, as you've no doubt told her all along (or at least once in exasperation), is not always a friendly, inviting place.

Woman, on Her Own

Once your daughter's out on her own, she's certain to find that life as an independent young woman is in many ways quite exciting. There's no one to tell her what to do or when to do it. She can sleep all day on Saturday, if she wants, or get up at the first light of dawn to head off on a grand adventure somewhere. She can let the dishes pile up in the sink or wash plates and utensils as she uses them. How she keeps house is entirely up to her—much to her delight most of the time, and much to her dismay at other times.

Playing House for Real

Girls love to help out with all kinds of tasks around the house when they're young. Even when your daughter was only three or four, she probably loved helping you fold towels or get things ready for dinner. As she's grown, she's had progressively more responsible chores, from making her bed and keeping her room picked up, to clearing dishes from the table and loading them into the dishwasher, feeding the dog or cat, vacuuming, and perhaps even doing her own laundry. She's likely had outdoor chores, too—weeding the garden, mowing the lawn, washing the car, or raking leaves.

The more tasks she has, the less enchanting she finds them, of course. Such is the nature of chores! But household chores are important for your daughter to learn, not because housework is woman's work but because keeping house is something we all must do (even men!). Maybe for your grandmother it was "going housekeeping" … for your mother, "keeping house" … and for you, "I don't do housework." But over the generations, we've seen the distinct province of "women's work" shift. Cleaning and cooking are the abilities and skills we all need—women and men alike—to live independently. Whether your daughter marries and starts a family, cohabitates with roommates or a boyfriend, or lives on her own, someone's got to clean those toilets! There's nothing sexist or demeaning about teaching your daughter (or your son, if you also have one) these tasks.

Not that your daughter should become the family's housekeeper, but she should be able, by the time she's in high school certainly, to see what needs to be done around the house and help do it. If she has younger siblings, maybe she helps supervise them in doing their chores. If she has siblings within a few years of her age, perhaps they're able to negotiate and share chores. Not always, but we live in hope.

In Her Shoes

Has your daughter moved in with her boyfriend? Don't presume this is a prelude to marriage! Although some couples do decide to move in together as a "test marriage" of sorts, many view living together as no more permanent or binding than were they moving in with a friend without any romantic connection.

So now that she's on her own, she knows what it takes and what to do to maintain her own household. She can do the grocery shopping and fix her meals. She knows to change the vacuum cleaner bag when the vacuum starts spitting out more than it sucks up, keep the fridge relatively free from biology experiments, and turn off the oven after she's baked a pizza.

Roommates and Other Complications

Some girls ache for the solitude of living alone, while others yearn for the sense of family that comes with a houseful of people. Often the driver is economics: it's hard to make it all by yourself when you're young. First jobs, even for college grads, often don't cover the lifestyle a girl wants to enjoy. Adding one or a few roommates eases the living expenses.

She might invite friends she already knows, which is the option that's least anxiety-producing for you as her parent. She might find roommates through word-of-mouth (people who know other young people who are looking for roommates) or might respond to a house-sharing ad in the newspaper. This can be a process of anxiety for parents; we of course worry about all kinds of things that she doesn't yet realize are dangers out there in the Real World. (Though truly, she's much more savvy than you give her credit for … in large part thanks to you teaching her.)

If your daughter grew up with siblings, she's got an edge when it comes to dealing with roommates. And so do you, when it comes to dealing with the issues she might bring to you, like she did with grievances about her siblings. Many roommate situations work out great—the girls all get along well with one another and are able to work through problems and issues that arise. Sometimes things don't go so smoothly, and your daughter will turn to you for advice.

The most effective role you can play most of the time is simply to listen. Part of her final maturing process is to deal with adult challenges in adult ways. You can no doubt see the reasons for the problems and the likely solutions. In conversations with your daughter, you might be able to guide her toward recognizing them herself. Of course, if there are personal safety issues, you have the responsibility to point them out.

And you might have particular insights that are appropriate for you to share, as you might with any friend. However, it's important for her to figure out for herself how to deal with roommate issues, because, in the end, you really can't deal with them for her now. It's never easy for parents to watch their daughters struggle, but she knows you're there to support her and that's a great gift.

Motherhood's Changing Landscape

We (collectively, as a society) don't put a lot of emphasis on marriage and motherhood for today's girls. While once these were pretty much the only choices a girl had—and was expected to make—today they're almost afterthoughts for many girls. High school focuses on academics and preparation for college, with the underlying expectation being that after college comes a career. Not at very many critical junctions in their lives do we stop to ask our daughters: where do you see family in your vision of the future?

Most girls do want to be in stable, long-term romantic relationships. Within those relationships, they may choose to live with a partner or to maintain independent households. Most girls just coming out of high school and many coming out of college consider themselves too young to embark on the commitment of marriage. They're focused on their careers and establishing themselves in the world. As young women venturing out on their own after knowing only boundaries defined by others (parents, school), they're also eager to explore the opportunities newly unfolding before them.

Some girls may want more than anything to have children of their own and can't wait to become mothers, yet may feel uncomfortable or reluctant to express this desire. Maybe none of their friends share this desire, or they feel it's not right to want to get married, stay home, and have babies instead of pursuing a career working outside the home. Indeed, it's a difficult challenge to raise a family on a single income, so often even women who want to make this choice find they still need an outside job to make ends meet.

And it's a desire that, ironically, runs counter to current cultural expectations. We're not so eager, as a society, to see our girls come out of high school at age 18 and go right into being mothers, if for no other reason than we know all too well the challenges of parenting. As much as we want raising children to be an option for our girls, we also know that it's an intense commitment that precludes, or at least makes much more difficult, other options that also might interest them.

Other girls may think they don't want to have children at all, for various reasons. Maybe they feel there are already enough people on the planet, or believe they can make more of a difference in the world by dedicating themselves to the careers they've chosen. And still other girls—probably more than we know—aren't even thinking about the future at all, including whether or not to have children, but are instead caught up in the intensity and details of their day-to-day lives.

> **In Her Shoes**
>
> The median age at which American women have their first babies has increased by nearly five years from 1970 to 2000, from just over age 22 to about age 27.

So Long, Supermom

The supermom model seems to be no longer the model mom, as best we can tell. Gone is the expectation that women can work 60-plus hours a week in the office, maintain an impeccable house, attend soccer games and swim matches, read to the kids every evening after dinner (dinner that she cooks and serves, by the way), and work out in the gym five days a week. To this we have to say, woo-hoo! We're shedding no tears. We tried it and we didn't like it; it didn't work very well for us or for our families.

The shift to a more balanced approach looks to be a very good thing for our daughters, giving them the freedom to figure out what works best for them in their lives and how they can best prioritize their interests and needs—career, family, and "me time" to relax and enjoy life. Balance is still sometimes more about juggling—that will probably never change—but at least we recognize and accept that no one can do everything.

Young women contemplating the blend of career and family are making careful choices on each front. Employers as well are mindful of this; in general, the workforce is fairly supportive of such balance. Efforts to make this balance possible end up supporting multiple purposes— job-sharing and telecommuting are great ways to structure time outside the conventions of "regular" work hours and also help employers meet needs for easing commute issues (which may, depending on the size and nature of the employer, be mandates of local government). The changing dynamic of the workplace, in which technology offers new ways to do just about everything, encourages women and men alike to look for nontraditional ways to apply their talents and interests, too.

The Boundaries of Biology

First comes love, then comes marriage, then comes Janie pushing a baby carriage. The ageless playground chant defines a longstanding perspective of motherhood. But according to the CDC's National Center for Health Statistics, nearly half of all babies born today are to single mothers—many of them single mothers *by choice*. This is an enormous cultural shift in our society. Women may decide they've reached the point in their lives where they want children but not necessarily to be married (or stay married). Though debates around family values rage over such matters, these options are nonetheless part of the landscape our daughters inhabit.

Girl Pearls

The women I know who have children and have careers, they seem to be very happy. They love their children and they love their jobs. But happiness comes out of being willing to do your work in your twenties to find out who you are, what you love. There are lots of studies out there about women who leave their work and it turns out that they didn't like their jobs. We need to encourage young women to find what they love to do. That is a very valuable pursuit—more so than the pursuit of a boyfriend. When you have that core, you bring that core to every aspect of your life.

—Candace Bushnell, American author of *Sex and the City* and *Lipstick Jungle*

Thirty years ago a lot of women put off marriage and/or the decision to have babies to build careers. But when they reached their thirties and forties and had achieved their career goals and decided they now were ready to be mothers, they found themselves often blocked by biology. Their bodies weren't so interested in cooperating with their interests. It was not an expected outcome of the "we can do anything" movement.

Though the biology of a woman's fertility remains pretty much unchanged from what it's always been—about 20 years of optimal, natural fertility—the options for addressing the desire to have a baby are vastly different than they were 30 years ago. Technologies like in-vitro fertilization make pregnancy possible for women who are in their late forties and even early fifties. Adoption, once done only in secret, also is widely accepted. So waiting to start a family, though fraught with its own challenges, is no longer a gamble with biology.

Women and men who wait until later in their lives to become parents often feel more relaxed and capable. They've got a lot of life experience by this stage in their lives, they've satisfied their career ambitions, and they're ready to give a child their full and undivided attention in ways they couldn't when they were younger. Often parents can alternate years in the workforce so that there is always one parent at home.

A girl who is reaching the age of womanhood today may truly plan her child-raising years in the same way she might plan her career advancement—and likely with more control. A challenge, of course, is that it truly does take a village to raise a child—or at least a mix of immediate family, extended family, and an expansive network of friends.

In Her Shoes

Many people say that when they become grandparents, it's like they get the chance to put to use all they now know that they wish they'd known when they were raising their own kids. As grandparents they can feel more relaxed because they know the baby can eat a Cheerio she finds under the rug on the kitchen floor and she'll be just fine!

Hey, Gram and Gramps!

Did you ever think those words would identify you? Your daughter's decision to become a mother changes your status, too: now you're a grandparent. It's a different and exciting role. You can enjoy your grandchild with a sense of carefree delight because you're not the one responsible for all those details of parenting. Whew! Finally, you can step back and relax. A little.

The Least You Need to Know

- As our daughters become young women, they want to be independent in their lifestyles from what they do to how and where they live.

- Today's girls view marriage and motherhood as separate, and not necessarily related, options.

- A girl who wants to become a mother instead of establishing herself in a career outside the home may feel uncomfortable about expressing her desires because it's outside the framework for what we expect of girls today.

- Young women want first to establish themselves as independent and self-sufficient; then they'll consider whether they want to marry or have children.

Chapter 21

It's a Girl's World

In This Chapter

◆ New skills, new opportunities

◆ Challenges and pressures

◆ Staying centered and balanced

◆ Looking at the bigger picture

Every generation likes to—and to some extent can—make the claim that it's different, even unique, from the generation before it. But this generation of girls truly does stand out from any other because they're the first generation for which it's no longer groundbreaking to be a woman and do something. Even the offices of the president or vice-president of the United States are no longer hypothetical I-wish-I-may-I-wish-I-might goals for girls, when in the 2008 election women from both political parties made serious bids to serve in these jobs. Women lead corporations and countries. Women fly jets and space shuttles. Women are scientists, poets, and, (sometimes) priests. Women.

Generations of women, each standing on the shoulders of the one before it, crafted these inroads and made these achievements possible. Our daughters are now traveling them. What a very different focus! Our daughters are *learning forward*, with the freedom to craft the future as they go, rather than looking back at what's come before. Yet none of our girls will be able to rest on their laurels in the future. The pressure on them is to take this gift they've been given and push on: to keep learning and exploring, to push for progress and improvement. It's exciting and daunting for our girls at the same time—and for us, too, as we watch them go into the world.

A Revolutionary World View

Everything is everywhere, and girls have instant access to it. There are, literally, no borders when it comes to information these days. When your daughter carries a smart phone, she carries the Internet. The whole world is right there in her hand. A fingertip connects her to all kinds of experiences and information, from chatting with her BFF to finding directions to the nearest Starbucks when she's away from home to getting news reports about events across the country or halfway around the globe.

This is virgin territory. Our girls are, in a profound way, on their own as they forge into their futures. The past exists in pieces without direct lines to anything in the present … or the future. The old rules don't apply, and they're making up the new rules as they go. And while this is vastly freeing and presents amazing opportunities, it's also a bit unsettling. What's familiar to our daughters that they're bringing into the workplace and into their lives in general is new and mostly unknown to us who are the generation preceding them.

The New Landscape: Technology

One of the most profound, interesting, and challenging differences for this generation of girls is to deal with the ever-increasing supply of information and technology in our culture. Girls today need to be fully literate in this technology—to be able to interpret, evaluate, organize, and use information to solve problems we aren't even aware of yet. To do this, girls need to possess the skills to …

◆ Read and interpret complex texts for work as well as in other contexts

- ◆ Write clearly and with authority in a variety of modes and genres

- ❤ Navigate new forms of technology that don't even yet exist in the dreams of their inventors

Girls are no less fully literate in these skills than boys, although their ability to relate to technology might be different. In some ways, although boys may be "hardwired" more efficiently to deal with the technology itself, girls are better able to manipulate the information that the technology enhances.

This generation of girls has a unique opportunity to change the world through the increased community and communication provided by technology. They see this opportunity and they're ready to go for it. Because girls—our lucky girls—no longer have to fight for the most basic rights to pursue their passions, and because they *know* they can do anything they set their desire and abilities to, they're free to develop a broad vision and act upon it.

Today's girls, too, want to change the system from *within*. If any generation of girls can make equal pay for equal work a reality, it is this one.

Save the rain forest? Bring it on! Improve human rights in Darfur, China, or Nepal? Let them at it! Educators like Kathy know that today's girls are smart, motivated, and independent. They're ready to tackle bigger and different issues than we can even imagine, bringing fresh perspective and renewed tenacity to their efforts.

> **In Her Shoes**
>
> Want to know why teachers encourage girls to take math, physics, chemistry, engineering, and technology classes? When economic forecasters look into their crystal balls and data reports, these are the areas of widest career opportunity in the foreseeable future. Women hold fewer than 10 percent of engineering jobs today, yet the most explosive growth is in technology fields.

Breaking from Tradition

As our daughters hit the workplace, they bring with them the attitude that if what they want doesn't exist, they can just create it. It's an approach that's resulting in new and exciting ways to turn personal interests into job and career opportunities. Sometimes this means they collect experience that may not pay especially well or might even be a work-for-trade sort of arrangement where she provides skills she already has (like accounting or writing, perhaps) to learn the new skills she wants to acquire.

In the end, she pulls together a range of expertise that otherwise wouldn't happen. It may seem a bit free form within the conventional get-a-job framework, but remember, this is your daughter's world, not yours. You've got to come around and look through her window to make sense of it.

There's a growing niche of jobs that defy traditional classification, too. Employers, especially those in entrepreneurial fields, are always looking beyond the basics to find people who can grow with their companies to meet changing and expanding needs.

Workin' for the (Wo)Man

Odds are about even that as your daughter enters the workforce, her boss will be a woman. In 2008, just about half of managers in the U.S. job market were women, a trend employment analysts expect to continue, such that women soon will surpass men in management positions. It's time to let money talk, though: women still earn less than men for comparable work.

Tomorrow's women—today's girls—are the ones who will push this envelope as they surge into the workplace with their abilities and sensibilities. Why *wouldn't* they earn the same pay as men? It simply doesn't fit with their concepts of who they are and what they can do!

To Thine Own Health Be True

A more challenging characterization of this generation of girls is the incredible amount of stress, physical and emotional, that they encounter in their daily lives. They must deal with this stress on multiple levels, which takes a toll on their physical and emotional health that we're only just beginning to understand. Physicians like Gary increasingly see the detrimental health effects of this stress as girls struggle to achieve balance around what they want to achieve—or feel pressured to achieve.

The Cutting Edge of Competition

Girls are increasingly competitive in sports, which is on the one hand a hallmark of the great strides we've made in establishing opportunities for girls to participate in sports. In the decades since the president of the United States signed into law Title IX of the Education Amendments in June 1972, colleges increasingly offer scholarships for a wide range of women athletes, which further expands these opportunities—yet at the same time increases the pressure on athletically gifted girls to push themselves. As has always been the case for boys, athletic scholarship opportunities for girls can make an otherwise unobtainable college experience possible.

> **Girl Pearls**
>
> Some people say I have attitude—maybe I do ... but I think you have to. You have to believe in yourself when no one else does—that makes you a winner right there.
>
> —Venus Williams, American pro tennis player

On the other hand, however, as more girls seize these opportunities, the competition for them gets stiffer. It becomes a spiral of intensifying pressures, just as it's been for boys. Even as young as middle school, girls are experiencing overuse injuries more commonly seen in college-level or professional athletes! And more commonly seen in boys ... leveling the playing field in this way has its downside, and the health consequences of over-competition rank high on that list.

Excelling in sports can be more than a ticket to college for girls now, too. There's a wide range of professional athlete possibilities for young women who truly are at the top of their games, from tennis and golf to soccer and basketball. The incentives, as for male athletes, can be quite lucrative both as competitive athlete and through endorsement contracts. It might seem a far stretch, but as in all career areas, there are the few who so stand out that these opportunities are very real for them.

You Look Great ... Really!

Body image issues remain significant health factors as well. Though as they leave high school and enter either college or the workplace girls tend to center within themselves rather than being quite so caught up in peer pressure, there's still a lot of influence from outside sources about how a girl should look.

Still, young women remain sensitive to perceptions about their appearance. A comment from a roommate or a boyfriend about how a particular outfit looks may trigger a spurt of dieting or other efforts to lose weight—even if the comment was intended as a compliment. Self-confidence and self-esteem can be more fragile than we would expect, looking at a young woman's accomplishments and apparent zeal for life.

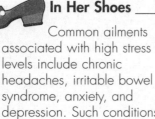

In Her Shoes

Common ailments associated with high stress levels include chronic headaches, irritable bowel syndrome, anxiety, and depression. Such conditions often respond best to a combination of medical treatment and methods to reduce and manage stress.

Problems with eating disorders like anorexia nervosa and bulimia tend to peak in the early years of college.

As young women get out more on their own and see a bigger view of the world, they're able to develop a broader sense of reality about what's healthy and what's not. We can continue to encourage them to look inward to define who they are and what they want to do with their lives, and to feel confident and strong in themselves.

Blue Is the New Pink

School. Work. Friends. Roommates. Boyfriends/significant others. Expenses and bills. Laundry. Tests and grades. Parents (yes, even parents). These are but a few of the stresses girls face as they head out into the world on their own, whether to college or to work or both, and they underlie much depression, anxiety, and social dysfunction. Girls are far more susceptible than boys to these conditions. Some health experts believe there is a hormonal influence at play; others believe it's more a reflection of the added pressures girls feel to please others.

It's hard, sometimes, for us as parents to understand these pressures and how they affect our daughters. We look at their lives and think: what's with the blues here? Look what opportunities they have … would that we'd had even a fraction of them! They've got no reason to be depressed! But those opportunities are themselves highly stressful as girls try to figure out which of them they want to pursue, how to meet their demands, and how to negotiate differences between what they want for themselves and what others (like parents) want for them.

How do we help relieve the pressure our daughters feel? We can start by helping them to look more realistically at what they want in their lives and how to reasonably go after it. The challenge sometimes, when they feel everything is just there for them take advantage of, is that they've got to take it all, right now, before it disappears. The opportunities that await our daughters aren't going anywhere, and neither we nor they need worry in such of a way. If anything, the changes we've experienced in our lifetimes are all the evidence we need of this! Our American society, with luck, only creates *more* opportunities for its citizens, women *and* men, and not less!

It's important to encourage your daughter, as always, to follow her passion—to keep what *she* loves first and foremost in her sights. If you're putting pressure on her for other reasons, take a few steps back and a couple deep breaths yourself. Of course you want the best for your daughter. But you've done your part to get her this far; now it's your role to support her in whatever choices she makes about how to use and enjoy her talents and skills.

> **Oh, Puh-leeze!**
>
> Health experts estimate that one in two young women between 18 and 25 suffers from clinical depression serious enough to need medical attention. Yet many girls—and their parents—brush off symptoms as just moodiness.

For the Greater Good

Girls today have a significant sense of social conscience, which is especially strong when they've grown up participating in volunteer efforts in their local communities as many of our daughters have. They care about the world beyond their classrooms and their jobs, and desire to make positive differences in the lives of others. People used to talk about how television brought the Vietnam War into living rooms and changed Americans' perceptions about that war. For this generation, events around the globe are accessible and unfolding around them, analyzed and evaluated in real time by bloggers. Our girls may choose to contribute their talents to organizations and agencies in service to needs around the country and the world, like Habitat for Humanity, the Peace Corps, and other programs. Certainly, they will see the world through a new lens as global consciousness becomes more than just a concept; it, too, enters real time.

Others may look to work for corporations and organizations that express commitment to improving circumstances for those less fortunate. These might be small businesses that actively support local and regional community efforts, or large companies that have organized philanthropic programs. By virtue of being plugged in, via technology, to a larger picture, our daughters can see ways to nourish and satisfy their own passions while also working to make the world a better place for their (future) daughters.

Well, now we've got to bring this wonderful book to a close: gtg, right? And after all, these are *your journeys* with your girls, on paths as unique and beautiful as each of you are as individuals, and also as loving families. For your daughters, who are no doubt your most dearest BFFs, we offer one last hearty cheer from the sidelines. We'll all be watching for great things in times to come. Anything *is* possible. And, for our daughters, *how cool is that?!!* Love your girls, enjoy your girls, and learn from them, too. *You go, grrls!*

The Least You Need to Know

- ◆ As today's girls become young women, they bring to the workplace and their communities a collective mindset that they can accomplish *anything*.

- ◆ Technology will continue to drive the direction and character of the experiences our daughters have through their lifetimes.

- ◆ The increasing pressure girls feel to meet expectations and to succeed are resulting in physical and emotional health problems.

- ◆ Our daughters have a strong sense of social conscience and the desire to make the world a better place—and the skills to allow that to happen.

Resources

Here are some books and websites to take you further on your quest for information about raising daughters.

Books

Buchanan, Andrea, and Miriam Peskowitz. *The Daring Book for Girls*. New York: HarperCollins, 2007.

Cohen-Sandler, Roni, Ph.D. *Trust Me, Mom—Everyone Else Is Going! The New Rules for Mothering Adolescent Girls*. New York: Penguin Group, 2003.

———. *Stressed-Out Girls: Helping Them Thrive in the Age of Pressure*. New York: Penguin Group, 2005.

Cohen-Sandler, Roni, Ph.D., and Michelle Silver. *I'm Not Mad, I Just Hate You!: A New Understanding of Mother-Daughter Conflict*. New York: Penguin Group, 2000.

Copeland, Cynthia L. *The 312 Best Things About Being a Stepmom*. New York: Workman Publishing Company, 2006.

Cosby, Bill. *Fatherhood*. New York: Penguin Group, 1987.

Deak, JoAnn, Ph.D., with Teresa Barker. *Girls Will Be Girls: Raising Confident and Courageous Daughters*. New York: Hyperion, 2003.

Hamkins, SuEllen, M.D., and Renee Schutz. *The Mother-Daughter Project: How Mothers and Daughters Can Band Together, Beat the Odds, and Thrive Through Adolescence*. New York: Penguin Group, 2008.

Hartley-Brewer, Elizabeth. *Raising Confident Girls: 100 Tips for Parents and Teachers*. Cambridge, Massachusetts: Fisher Books, 2001.

Keyers, Janis, M.A. *Becoming the Parent You Want to Be*. New York: Broadway Books, 1997.

Kindlon, Dan, Ph.D. *Alpha Girls: Understanding the New American Girl and How She Is Changing the World*. New York: Rodale Press, 2007.

Lamb, Sharon, Ed.D., and Lyn Mikel Brown. *Packaging Girlhood: Rescuing Our Daughters from Marketers' Schemes*. New York: St. Martin's Griffin, 2007.

Lutz, Ericka. *The Complete Idiot's Guide to Stepparenting*. Indianapolis: Alpha Books, 1998.

Meeker, Meg, M.D. *Strong Fathers, Strong Daughters: 10 Secrets Every Father Should Know*. Washington, D.C.: Regnery Publishing, Inc., 2006.

Nevius, C.W. *Crouching Father, Hidden Toddler: A Zen Guide for New Dads*. San Francisco: Chronicle Books, 2006.

Norwood, Perdita Kirkness, with Teri Wingender. *Stepmother: Revolutionizing the Role*. New York: Avon Books, 1999.

Rimm, Sylvia, Ph.D., with Sara Rimm-Kaufman and Ilonna Rimm. *See Jane Win: The Rimm Report on How 1,000 Girls Became Successful Women*. New York: Three Rivers Press, 1999.

Rosen, Rosanne. *The Complete Idiot's Guide to Mothers and Daughters.* Indianapolis: Alpha Books, 2001.

Sax, Leonard, M.D. *Why Gender Matters: What Parents and Teachers Need to Know about the Emerging Science of Sex Differences.* New York: Broadway Books, 2006.

Seinfield, Jessica. *Deceptively Delicious: Simple Secrets to Get Your Kids Eating Good Food.* New York: HarperCollins, 2007.

Shearin-Karres, Erika V., Ed.D. *The Everything Parent's Guide to Raising Girls.* Avon, Massachusetts: Adams Media, 2007.

Simmons, Rachel. *Odd Girl Out: The Hidden Culture of Aggression in Girls.* New York: Harcourt, 2003.

Spencer, Paula. *Momfidence! An Oreo Never Killed Anybody and Other Secrets of Happier Parenting.* New York: Crown Publishing Group, 2006.

Swedan, Nadya, M.D. *The Active Woman's Health and Fitness Handbook.* New York: Penguin Group, 2003.

Wardley, Bridget, and Judy More. *The Big Book of Recipes for Babies, Toddlers, and Children: 365 Quick, Easy, and Healthy Dishes.* London: Duncan Baird Publishers Ltd., 2004.

Wiseman, Rosalind. *Queen Bees & Wannabes: Helping Your Daughter Survive Cliques, Gossip, Boyfriends, & Other Realities of Adolescence.* New York: Three Rivers Press, 2003.

Witmer, Denise D. *The Everything Parent's Guide to Raising a Successful Child.* Avon, Massachusetts: Adams Media, 2004.

Ziegahn, Suzen J., Ph.D. *7 Steps to Bonding with Your Stepchild.* New York: St. Martin's Press, 2001.

Websites

http://familydoctor.org   Health and parenting information from the American Academy of Family Practitioners. Articles are parent-friendly yet comprehensive.

http://kidshealth.org   Health, family, and parenting information from The Nemours Foundation's Center for Children's Health Media. Three sections tailor content for parents, young kids, and teens. Really!

www.familyeducation.com   A broad collection of content and resources about parenting, school matters, and child growth and development. This website is the parenting channel of the Family Education Network. Other channels are www.TeacherVision.com, for teachers; and www.FEkids.com and www.funbrain.com, for kids.

www.parenting.com   A commercial website from Parenting and BabyTalk magazines that offers articles, quizzes, recipes, and stories about kids and parenting. Frequent subscription-offer pop-up windows can be distracting but go away with a quick click.

www.pbs.org/parents   A website from the Public Broadcasting System, your favorite educational TV folks, that provides educational content for young kids. And, of course, about PBS television programming.

www.sallyridescience.com   The website of former astronaut and first American woman in space, Sally Ride. The site provides sections for educators, parents, and girls. Content features information and activities to encourage girls to study and explore careers in science.

www.stepfamilies.info   The website of the Stepfamily Association of America, serving as a clearinghouse of information and resources for stepparents. Content includes educational, legal, and statistical information.

Index

D

N

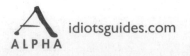